TWO PLAYS OF ANCIENT INDIA

Prepared for the Columbia College Program of Translations from the Oriental Classics
Wm. Theodore de Bary, Editor

TWO PLAYS OF ANCIENT INDIA

THE LITTLE CLAY CART

THE MINISTER'S SEAL

Translated from Sanskrit and Prakrit, with an introduction by
J. A. B. van Buitenen

Columbia University Press   New York and London 1968

J. A. B. van Buitenen is Professor of Sanskrit and Indic Studies at the University of Chicago.

Library of Congress Catalog Card Number: 67-25441

Printed in the United States of America

FOREWORD

TWO PLAYS OF ANCIENT INDIA is one of a group of translations sponsored by the Committee on Oriental Studies at Columbia University. The Committee's intention is to provide scholarly, readable translations of representative works of the great Asian civilizations, and this purpose has been admirably fulfilled in Professor van Buitenen's rendering of two Sanskrit plays of great literary merit.

While India's religious and philosophical tradition has received intensive study in the West, her dramatic literature is less well known. The two plays Professor van Buitenen has chosen to present suggest the richness and variety of classical Indian culture as well as providing insights into its social structure. *The Little Clay Cart* is an elaborate and ingeniously constructed work of art that could only be the product of a highly evolved dramatic tradition. *The Minister's Seal*, aside from its literary values, has a special interest in being one of the few surviving Indian literary works that have a definite historical theme.

Professor van Buitenen has added to the value of his translations by including an introduction to the theory and practice of Sanskrit drama that will add much to the reader's understanding of the plays. We are confident that students in courses in comparative literature and Asian studies, as well as the general reader, will find in these pages a unique introduction to the intellectual and artistic achievements of one of the world's greatest civilizations.

AINSLIE T. EMBREE
Committee on Oriental Studies
Columbia University

PREFACE

THE HEARTENING success of an earlier collection of translations, *Tales of Ancient India* (University of Chicago Press, 1959; Bantam Books, 1961), encouraged me to try my hand at two ancient Indian plays. Expectedly, it turned out a far more difficult undertaking, as an Indian play is written in a variety of languages, and in prose as well as verse. While the differences in language are inimitable in English, the alternation of poetry and prose is so characteristic that it demands to be retained in translation; though by no means always, in the majority of cases I have attempted to render verse by verse.

The choice of the plays came out of two considerations, one of them negative. The more usual kind of play is based on the Indian epic, and reading it requires a vast knowledge of mythology and a comfortable accommodation to the supernatural that does not come naturally to the Western reader away from his own classics. While this consideration made me exclude plays that are among the finest of Sanskrit literature, the two plays chosen have each a uniqueness that hardly makes them a second choice.

The Little Clay Cart is a rambunctious comedy of manners that is unequaled in Sanskrit; *The Minister's Seal* is a taut political drama that draws on history rather than myth for its subject matter. Both plays are set in real life, even though romanticized, and the supernatural and spiritual have no role in them. They present the familiar values of power, wealth, and love in an Indian treatment; and these values deserve our attention as much as those of Indian religion and philosophy.

A special word of thanks is due Mrs. Bonnie Crown, the tireless and spirited director of the Asian Literature Program of the Asia Society of New York. Her enthusiasm and help encouraged me to take the plays out of the classroom and have them published. I am grateful to Ainslie T. Embree for his help in bringing the translation to the attention of Columbia University Press.

Helen Singer was kind enough to read the plays, and made many suggestions that improved the translations; while Professor V. Raghavan, when visiting Chicago in 1965, took out precious hours to go through them, and offered valuable criticisms.

The ambition of giving a versified rendering of classical drama exacts some sacrifice of the literal meaning of the text. But I believe that the liberties I have taken have remained minor and that the translation has remained what it should be, an honest rendering of the originals.

Chicago, 1966

J. A. B. VAN BUITENEN

CONTENTS

INTRODUCTION

INTRODUCTION

THEATRE AND WORLD VIEW

In the cultural history of classical India the theatre had a unique place.[1] Simultaneously it straddled several language barriers in northern India with an ease which seems to deny that they *were* barriers, and yet became the most lofty expression of a typically Sanskritic literature. It provided a spectacle for all classes of the population, yet at the same time it was mainly directed to the most highly educated among the audience. It drew on epical and folk lore which was the common heritage of all, yet presented the well-known stories with a subtlety that could be savored only by the connoisseur. At once accessible to all and impervious but to the few, the theatre was the image of civilization itself.

Its origins are dark. Fragments survive that go back to the first century A.D., which show that the principal conventions were already established: multiplicity of languages reflecting a diversity of characters; a high moral tone; alternation of prose and verse; division into a number of separate acts; a happy outcome of the plot. There has been much controversy about specific origins, but this need not concern us now. What does concern us is that by the fourth century the genre of plays had developed completely into the form that it would retain for the next millennium.

The simplest way to define the classical play is as a story told in dialogue. In this the play was in many respects the much refined successor of the great epic which essentially presents itself as being recited by professional bards. A short example shows the continuity. In the romantic epic of Vālmīki, the *Rāmāyaṇa*, King Rāma, after recovering his wife Sītā who had been abducted, finally is compelled by public opinion to reject her, since doubts had been cast on her chastity. She is accepted by Vālmīki into his hermitage and bears Rāma two sons,

Kuśa and Lava, who are brought up as bards. And there can be little doubt that the names of Rāma's sons are formed from the word *kuśīlava*, which means "actor."

More substantially, the continuity between epic and play is shown by the heavy dependence of the playwrights on the stories of the epic. If Aeschylus called his tragedies the crumbs from Homer's table, the Indian plays with equal right may be styled the crumbs from Vyāsa's[2] millennial banquet. And just as their reliance on Homeric materials in no way limited the originality of the Greek playwrights, their predilection for epical themes put no restraint on the imagination of the Indian authors.

If one then may venture to see the Indian play as arising from the bardic tradition, as a well-known story first recited by a troupe of bards taking different parts of the narrative, or taking on the speaking parts of the different characters figuring in the narrative, this by no means sums up the origin of the classical theatre. For to it was wedded another performing art, in which the story was not so much *told* as enacted, the mime; the play is a *show*. Again, the history of the mime is obscure, but it seems clear enough that it was the refinement of dances in which a story was told by leap and gesture, dances that at one time might well have come to accompany the recitations of the bards. Dance in the form of mime will remain inseparable from the theatre.

These antique and no doubt rustic performances to which we are groping back were not just the incidental recreations that the populace found at country fairs. They were rooted in religious pageantry. The staging of an old myth where the good triumphs over the evil, where near tragedy is averted and resolved in final felicity and harmony, could have a fine propriety at festivals in the annual cycle which sought to secure the fertility of the fields, the promptness of the monsoon, the well-being of a king on whom the prosperity of a country depended, the birth of a prince which secured the survival of a dynasty.[3] The traditional play begins and ends with a benediction, and however sophisticated the later plays will become, in many the quality of prayer persists. This, along with the dance that contributed to it, gives the performance a style of rite, of this world no doubt but also out of this world, both in its subject matter and in its style.

Realism, as we understand it today, was *not* sought in the traditional epical play. But a measure of verisimilitude inevitably crept in, in costuming and even in character, especially that of the lower classes.[4] And here still another art form contributed to the evolution of the theatre: the farce. Enough examples, some quite coarse, remain to show that the wildly rambunctious slapstick of the farce was a genre by itself. But the traditional epical play adopted, and only partly refined, the popular farce within its own context. It added to its list of characters that of the Buffoon, who at times comes to play a very considerable part, and of the worldly-wise Libertine.

It is this complex of influences, that of the stylized recitation, the almost ritual mime which accompanies the words (and the music surely brought along with the dance), and the vulgar farce, which makes the traditional play the fascinating experience which it is. And in its variety it contained enough seeds to make for a rich development.

What I have called the traditional epical play is known to the Sanskrit critics as the *nāṭaka* (heroic drama). The word is interesting by itself because it is closely related to the words for dance.[5] It is in this genre that some of the finest plays have been written: Kālidāsa's *Śakuntalā* and *Urvaśī Won by Might*, Bhavabhūti's two Rāma plays, the *Geste of the Hero* and *Latter Days of Rāma*, to name the greatest. While the *nāṭaka* deals exclusively with the "imitation of the deeds of the great kings and sages of the past," it helped develop a more strictly secular play, which drew not on the epic for its plot, but on the author's own inventiveness. In effect, many of these "original" plays, *prakaraṇas*, owe almost as great a debt to the narrative literature as do the others to the epic. Once more the play is a story told in dialogue, but for the epical saga the narrative tale is substituted. Otherwise there are hardly any formal distinctions.

The plays selected here present the two genres, *The Little Clay Cart* being a *prakaraṇa*, while *The Minister's Seal* is a *nāṭaka*. This latter qualification shows how loosely the terms really were used. The *Seal* is a *nāṭaka* because all history is styled "epic" and because one of the protagonists is a king. Together, the plays illustrate many of the possible choices open to the Sanskrit theatre.

A century ago attempts were made to show the influence of Hellenism on the development of the Indian theatre. In principle, the possibility cannot be rejected out of hand: the history of Indian art shows sufficiently the influence that the Hellenistic art of Gāndhāra (200 B.C.) has had on India. Similarly, much of Indian astronomy is of Hellenistic origin. However, the attempts to show a similar development in the theatre were abortive and the notion has now been abandoned. But there survives a tendency to consider the Greek theatre and the Indian stage as at least comparable. Such comparison can be misleading. The most obvious distinction of the Greek theatre, between tragedy and comedy, for example, has no relevance whatever in the Indian context.

This "absence of tragedy" is sometimes pointed to with a mildly accusing finger, as though any theatre worth the name should have it. Apologists then point out that India was "prevented" from developing true tragedy by the underlying climate of its thought. This argument takes for granted that tragedy is an almost natural expression of any culture. But why not argue that Greek tragedy constitutes the exception, not the rule, and that it presupposes a very specific notion of *moira* (fate) that was peculiarly Greek? The hero who demanded more than his share became the victim of the fates who had set for him this much and no more, and exacted excessive repayment if he overreached. The guilt thus incurred, or incurred by heinous crimes that flaunted human and divine law, could be visited on later generations, until an entire great dynasty was brought to doom. The hero or heroine might achieve a brief grandeur, defying what was ordained by the fates, but in the end he—or she—would be brought down by those guardians of the impossible.

In comparison with this Promethean view of the human condition, Indian thought might well be said to have forfeited *any* view. The doctrine of transmigration that governs it—the concept that the actions of one life predetermine the circumstances of an automatically occurring next life—makes any single life an episode in a far longer chain. No single life makes ultimate sense in itself; the chain of life does. And the chain itself does so only in contrast with the higher condition of Release outside it.

Yet, it is doubtful whether the nontragical character of the Indian play is in the first place to be explained from a world view that considers life so insignificant that it could not possibly rise to the level of high tragedy. Both in thought and in practice the Indian has always been capable of making clear distinctions between the needs of this life and the blessings of eventual release from a chain of lives; between a present governed by dharma and a future that demands full renunciation. Dharma describes the entire complex of law and custom, all the rules and regulations set for man according to his station and his age, while renunciation demands complete withdrawal from one's social and domestic roles. Although instances of this renunciation are not lacking in Indian drama, especially in secondary characters, the theatre as a whole is concerned with the realm of this dharma and this world.

This world is seen as a hierarchically ordered society, in which individuals have their being. In the dharmic view, these individuals are not regarded as unique, self-identical, irreplaceable human beings, of one time and of one place, but as incumbents of positions which survive them. The textbooks on Law, the *Dharmaśāstras*, work with a simple model of "class" and "stage of life." There are four such classes: the Brahmin—teacher, ritual specialist, arbiter of good conduct; the Baron—protector of the oppressed and avenger of the injured; the Artisan—maker of vessels and tiller of the soil; and the Servant—hewer of wood and carrier of water. The first three of these "classes" or "colors" are the twiceborn who live in a ritual communion from which the servant or Śūdra is sharply excluded. These twiceborn are supposed to go through four stages of life: the first is that of student of the Veda, which marks their second birth; the second is that of householder and family man when he is productive in society; the third is that intriguing one of semiretirement from his social duty and withdrawal outside the village to a hermitage in the woods; beyond that there is the ultimate state of complete renunciation of family, society, and world. The dharma books lay down specific tasks for each of these classes and stages of life.

These models are taken over by the theatre, and the stereotypes of the plays seem, to me at least, first of all to be dharmic stereotypes. Every theatre produces it own types; but the Indian theatre seems to have started from a set of types that was provided by the official theory of society, and then to have expanded them. The king is at all times king, with both the dharmic and with the folkloristic character that kings have: they are noble, protective, impetuous, and just; they also like women, horses, and hunts. Just so, a forest recluse is an aged man with a white beard and a braided knot, bent on profound thoughts while he tends the ancient fires with his fellow recluses; he is also likely to succumb to the wiles of loose women. Housewives are faithful, self-effacing, honoring their husbands even under the most tragic circumstances, and also likely to be beguiled by parasitical priests, monks, and soothsayers. Courtesans, on the other hand, are faithless, greedy, sophisticated, and artistic, but sometimes irresistibly carried away by a love they may not own.

The theatre, then, has not created its stereotypes out of the inexhaustible supply of human individuals, but out of the hieratic roles of the dharmic society. True, the strong conviction that the hieratic role exists *before* its human incumbent is correlated with the doctrine of transmigration: no conception of divine justice can explain the inequality of human beings, and their present estate can only be the end result of the sum total of acts they did or failed to do in a previous existence. Man finding himself in the world has already created the conditions of his life. But they are of his own making, and to the extent that he abides by the law in the exercise of his own free will he can improve his station in his next life.

In this view his existential effort should be toward harmony. Basically, the society which is laid down by the dharma books and in the end rests on the Veda is the *good* society. It is not the invention of a God or the creation of man; it is given with the world itself. A Prometheus is impossible in it; a hubris which defies it is inconceivable: it is as though one were to protest the law of gravity. The happy outcome of the Indian play therefore is not an escapist solution; given the fact that society is good, conflict demands resolution in a reconciliation so that in the end harmony is restored.

Tragedy is what is tragedy *in the end*. And the Indian world view (at least as its most official spokesmen, the lawgivers, have it) is that, in the final analysis, this is a good world. Whatever is bad in it for any given individual is ultimately his own fault. He cannot improve the world, but he can improve himself.

Of course it is always dangerous to see in any art form too precise a reflection of the world view of a culture. But the Indian play comes out of the Sanskritic tradition where nothing counts as much as to abide by the rules. Just as the paradigms of the Sanskrit grammar are given, so are given the paradigms of the grammar of dharma. But fortunately, this is not only the world of Sanskrit and Sanskritic dharma. No doubt in the end they dominate it, but they are not always in full control.

The first thing any translation of an Indian play must sacrifice is one of its most fascinating peculiarities, the different languages and dialects that are spoken. The Indian theatre may hardly seem unique in this, as the theatre elsewhere quite often differentiates in the use of language, whether for formal reasons as in the Greek tragedies, or to indicate region and status of the character as in, for instance, Shaw's plays. But to me there would seem to be a difference in quality in the linguistic diversity of the Indian play. The difference might be described by a comparison: suppose we had a thriving theatre in medieval Europe where one character would exclusively speak Ciceronian Latin, another one French, a third one Provençal, a fourth Spanish, a fifth Italian, without being in the least discomfited by language barriers?

Though the comparison exaggerates, there is a measure of truth in it. The first major division in our example would be between Ciceronian Latin and the other languages, as on the Indian scene between Sanskrit and Prakrit. There is, as it were, a division between one culture and another.

Sanskrit is one of the few languages of the world with a name that does not derive from either a region or an ethnic group. Its name is not so much a sign as a program: it is "the tongue perfected." One may define the language as that language which is spoken and written in complete conformity with the grammar laid down by Pāṇini in the fourth century B.C. This definition implies that Sanskrit is an artificial language, as opposed to a natural language; if the latter is defined as the "mother tongue," this is correct. Were such a usage possible in our experience, we could say that all Indians had a mother tongue, but that a few also acquired a father's tongue.

Sanskrit belongs to the Indo-Iranian branch of the Indo-European family of languages from which English, French, German, Greek, Latin, and Russian in various degrees descend. The first representative of the Indo-Iranian group in India is the language of the Ṛgveda, probably from about 1400 B.C.; this language begins the heritage of Indo-Āryan.[5] In the form in which this language survives, it is by no means a colloquial tongue, but already a highly refined literary language based on Northwest Indian speech with dialectical variations. This language is commonly called Vedic.

Vedic continued from 1000 to 500 B.C. in the liturgical literature that terminates with the Upaniṣads. Liturgy, the central concern of the texts that have survived, produced a number of auxiliary branches of learning. Among them was grammar, or, as the technical term has it more precisely, *vyākaraṇa* (analysis and derivation). There is some dispute about the exact identity of the language thus analyzed and derived; in any case it is likely that it was that of the late Vedic expository texts.

In a process that culminates in the Grammar of Pāṇini, *vyākaraṇa* ordered the language, which, as it were, was taken apart, its building elements calibrated and numbered, and then was put together again. The use of language henceforth was not with the almost unconscious ease with which we employ it, but with a highly conscious deliberation and erudition. The resulting language, used strictly according to fixed rules, is Sanskrit.

To give an example of this analysis and derivation. "He would have liked to know" may be translated into Sanskrit as *ajijñāsiṣyat*. This form can be taken apart bit by bit, but before one can do this he must know the language sufficiently well so that he sees at once the regular application of the morphological devices that are combined in this form. At one time, one may presume, a speaker might have used this word almost unconsciously, because he happened to be a native speaker of the language and learned it the way language is learned in childhood. He would with equal assurance say *aditsiṣyat* if he meant to say "he should have liked to give," but probably would be incapable of explaining why the forms are so different. And at times he might well find himself in the dark about what form to construct.

Sanskrit grammatical science undertakes to take all the guesswork out of the language, and builds up a science from the basic phonemes to the most complicated formation of verbal forms and nouns in a system of ordered rules, until the student is instantly able to see through *ajijñāsiṣyat* as *a-ji-jñā-s-i-sy-a-t*. Conversely, he is able to create out of the raw material of some 1,800 basic roots the precise expression of his intentions. Language has, once and for all, been made predictable, and equally predictable is the speaker's perfect intelligibility to anyone who has similarly studied the language.

Since no language is as regular as all that, it is clear that the grammarians on occasions had to impose order where none existed. Some Vedic formations were discarded, others normalized; the end result is the refined and perfected language, Sanskrit. The use of the language was self-conscious to an extreme degree; the speaker was at all times recreating what he firmly believed to be the original language in its purest form as it was spoken by the ancient seers. In this respect it was a sacred language; but it became more than that. It became the language of culture. For being always a second language, an ancestral tongue, its acquisition demanded a formidable education, first in the language itself, then in those provinces of culture of which Sanskrit was accepted as the only proper expression. The whole range of cultural experience was received through Sanskrit and conceptualized through Sanskrit. Those experiences might to some extent be capable of paraphrasis in the vernacular, but their true and precise expression was Sanskrit. Thus, to speak Sanskrit was the sign of a civilized man, for only through that language did he have access to the culture of the past and could he transmit his culture to the future. It spelt literacy, an expertise in a variety of scholarly and literary disciplines, a ready framework in which to experience the world, a facility to converse with fellow literati across the boundaries of languages, regions, and centuries. In a vast country with highly diverse ethnic groups and many languages from different families, the possession of Sanskrit was possession of the foremost instrument of civilization. It was the incredibly meticulous analysis and inventory of the grammarians which had created this instrument.

But meanwhile people went on speaking without benefit of grammarians. The languages they spoke are known as Prakrits, from *prākṛta* in the sense either of "derivative, namely from Sanskrit" or "natural." Among the oldest of such languages is the Pāli of the Buddhist canon; for Buddha reportedly told his pupils to address the people in their own tongue. The great emperor Aśoka wrote his edicts in a variety of Prakrits in the third century B.C. The changes are those of the inevitable attrition of time. Some vowels disappear, the three *s*'s of Sanskrit collapse to one. Of a number of aspirated consonants only the aspiration survives. Consonant clusters are reduced. Just as Latin *septem* produces Italian *sette*, so Sanskrit *sapta* (seven) produces Prakrit *satta*. This natural process of change continues through several layers of Prakrit, to the point that it would be folly to maintain that the languages were mutually intelligible. Prakrit (*prākṛta*) is pronounced Pāio. And finally we arrive at the ancestors of the modern North Indian languages. But during all this time the cultivation of Sanskrit went on.

In its linguistic differentiation the Indian play presents another instance of the hierarchic view of life which above I related to dharma. There is, as it were, a pyramid of languages at the top of which stands Sanskrit. When Sanskrit is spoken it reflects status, or education, or wisdom. Status entitles King and Brahmin to speak Sanskrit. But as Sanskrit comes naturally to no one, it bespeaks not only status but also a rigorous education. The child of one who speaks Sanskrit will not yet be able to speak it and speaks in his mother's tongue. The mother may be of royal or brahminic descent, but she does not speak Sanskrit. Among women only female ascetics—in principle no longer women—and on occasion courtesans—who often were better educated than the most regal matron—are found to speak Sanskrit.

The Prakrits, too, reflect social differentiation. Saurasenī, the more Western one, is nicer than the eastern Māgadhī, which is spoken by undesirables. More lowly characters, like executioners, speak a language that can only be described as "corrupt" (*apabhraṣṭa*).

The ability to speak Sanskrit, though often bespeaking status and always bespeaking education, does not necessarily bespeak high moral character. Even the dharmic society allows, however reluctantly, voice to its demimonde of urbanites; and it is here that the neat hierarchy is broken down. There are those Brahmins who have fallen on hard times by gambling away their patrimony, or have been lured into a burglar's career by their expensive love for a courtesan. Yet, education will tell: the burglar will have developed his thiefcraft into a science, accompanying his dastardly acts with a running commentary on his dexterity and proper quotations from the correct authors. The gambler, while roaming around in rags, will burst into Sanskrit verse on the inconstancy of luck. They appear in the plays without the tidy background of family and moral upbringing which alone show status. They are on their own, living by their wits and exploiting their education.

On the other hand, so exalted a personage as the brother-in-law of the king may be found to speak a despicable dialect when his utter worthlessness is to be demonstrated, and likewise the buffoon, often an oafish Brahmin, will not speak Sanskrit.

The theatrical convention is that these languages are all mutually intelligible. One may well doubt that this was the case. But in this convention the theatre reflects at least this reality of Indian life that, until today, different languages lived more or less peacefully together and that bilingualism in some measure was always assumed.

The variety brought to the Indian play by the constant shifts between languages and dialects is further elaborated by a variety of styles. The most striking is the alternation between prose and poetry.

The history of prose in Indian literature is very intriguing. Our oldest documents, the Ṛgveda and Atharvaveda, are in verse. But these early compilations are succeeded by a titanic liturgical literature, spanning half a millennium, which is almost entirely in prose. The Upaniṣads, the last phase of this "Vedic literature," mark a shift back to verse: some of the later ones are composed in meter. But from the same period begins to emerge the colossal text of the great epic, the *Mahābhārata* (eight times the length of the *Iliad* and *Odyssey* combined), and the shorter but still sizable *Rāmāyaṇa*, both of which are in verse. Then from about the beginning of the Christian era a scientific, largely commentatorial literature begins which, like the earlier liturgical texts, once more resorts to prose. But by no means always. Until quite late, expository tracts on the most abstruse subjects may equally well be composed in meter, and prose expositions may have metrical portions scattered through them.

The distinction, then, between prose and verse in the ancient literature is far less sharp than it is in modern Western literary history. Indeed, writers on poetics hardly make a difference between literary prose and poetry. Prose is poetry without benefit of meter. In non-Sanskrit literatures the matter is somewhat different. The canons of the Buddhists and Jains are largely in prose; in the Prakrit narrative literature, what little survives of it, the tendency also is toward prose.

In a literature where the transition from prose to poetry is such an easy one, we may expect that verse is resorted to for more topics than we would consider poetic. The Indian play illustrates this quite nicely. There is first the character who uses no verse at all. In *The Little Clay Cart* this is Maitreya, the Brahmin friend of Cārudatta, who plays both the buffoon and the ever-ready confidant of the hero. Although he has a large part and quite a number of occasions to burst into verse—especially his visit to the establishment of the courtesan and his description of its marvels—he sticks to prose (with one exception which illustrates my point: "This poor little mother is a bum, / It's the brandy plagues her and the rum! / If she dies, the poor little mum, / /She will last a thousand jackals some!"). This is no doubt deliberate on the part of the author. Maitreya is painted as the determined lowbrow who has no truck whatever with the refinements of life, who comes away disgusted from a concert, and, except for his friend, is mainly interested in food. He has no pretense whatever. In contrast, in the same play Cārudatta's antagonist, Saṃsthānaka or Śakāra, who speaks a most atrocious dialect, is all pretense and at the least pretext bursts into song. Like all he says and does, his verse is coarse:

Where are you going, running, rushing, tripping?
Stop, little morsel, please, you are not dying!
Oh, my poor heart ablaze with love, and dripping
Like a fat chunk of meat the cooks are frying!

When he makes his entrance in the last act to see Cārudatta executed, his entrance line is typical:

I dined at home on tamarind sauce,
On first-class rice and extra dishes
Of meat and pea soup and stewed greens
And candy cakes and two small fishes.

Thus verse may be used to bring out the vulgarity of a character. If Maitreya had been allowed to use verse freely it no doubt would have sounded vulgar, too. But the author likes Maitreya and does not permit him to make too much of a fool of himself.

Quite a bit of the verse in the *Cart* is intended to be humorous, especially when spoken by the lower characters who to the cultured city man are almost by definition funny. It can also be a means to sharp satire. A hard-up masseur decides to become a Buddhist monk and gives voice to his decision in this piece of doggerel:

Now I have done with gambling
Which everybody hates
And baldly I'll be rambling
With all the highway greats.

Bald highway greats is hardly a flattering description of pious Buddhist mendicants who have given up home and family; but to the author they must have been a ragtag lot, right company for a masseur who is down on his luck.

Satirical verse eases into gnomic verse that takes a jaundiced view of the world and its follies. This is a genre that is extraordinarily popular in Sanskrit literature, and the plays are full of it. From the *Cart*, on women:

They laugh, they cry, but gain they must,
They make you trust them, but never trust.
If you're born high and aim still higher,
Shun them like flowers by a burning pyre!

On gambling:

The gambler never counts defeat,
His revenues keep flowing in,
And all he has goes waste.
But future bills he's sure to meet—
As to a king come bowing in
The wealthy making haste.

On poverty:

And poverty reduces one to shame,
And a shamed man will lose his dignity;
Without his dignity he is despised,
And once he is despised he must despair.
Disconsolate, he falls a prey to grief,
His grievances will rob him of his mind,
And out of mind, he is completely lost:
The lack of money brings all evils on.

On a secret agent, from the *Seal*:

If you have sold your soul to a rich man
And traded family and decency
And reputation and your self respect
For a too quickly disappearing sum,
The question does not rise whether the job
You have been told to do is good or bad.
You are beyond that stage. The only thing
Remaining for you is to wonder *what*.

Quite distinct from the use of verse to show up a character, to parodize, or to comment sadly on the world is the use of verse as lyric. It is here that the intention of the verse becomes poetic. The occasion may be anything from the large repertory of topics, of which Daniel

H. H. Ingalls recently has given us a brilliant exposition and translation in *An Anthology of Sanskrit Court Poetry*[6] and nothing need be added here but the role of the lyric in the play. As the lyric is very often descriptive, it can in a few lines paint a scene which is directly significant to the action. In the *Seal*, the minister Rākṣasa, whose king and family have perished, finds himself in a dilapidated garden, which for him becomes the image of his condition:

The white pavilion, carefully laid out,
Has like a clan of noble deeds collapsed.
The pond is dry, dry as a good man's heart,
Whose friends have one by one been lost to death.
The trees bear no more fruit than policies
That were frustrated by a bitter fate.
And like the mind of a misguided sage
The ground is covered with some futile straws.

When his antagonist Cāṇakya stages a mock quarrel with his own king, the description of the burning-field where the defeated dynasty has been cremated warns of the fierce consequences of his quarrel:

The fires that burnt their corpses blaze today
And cast upon the sky, where patient vultures
Circle about on wide unhurried wings,
A cloud of smoke that obfuscates the sun,
And with their tempting smell of dripping marrow
Gladden the beasts that haunt the burning-grounds.

Or when a prince's cortège is ordered to stop:

Some chieftains check their steeds so forcefully
Their stalwart withers crouch before the reins
That sharply bridle them and their fast hoofs
Paw wild before them in the empty air.
And others on their splendid elephants
Have stopped so quickly that the collar bells
Are stricken dumb: like ocean tides, my Lord,
They halt before the flood line of your word!

But often in an exaggerated fashion, as in the fifth act of the *Cart*, lyrical verses are introduced for the good reason that the author feels inspired to them, and they remind us that the Indian drama is not *just* a story told in dialogue, where every word should contribute to the action, but is also a feast for the ear. After all, a story does not have to be told rapidly; frequently the verses provide a point of rest, as in act three of the *Seal*:

The autumn sky flows like a river, slowly,
And pure, with here and there a late white cloud
Emerging like a sand bank—all around
The skies are noisy with the gabbling cries
Of cranes, and when night falls clusters of stars
Dot the heavenly lake with lotuses.

Finally, we may distinguish a use of verse which is narrative. In the *Seal* the king finds that a festival he ordered is not being held:

No courtesans do grace with lazy steps,
Slowed by the burden of their hips, the streets
In the gay company of libertines,
Bandying jokes and witty compliments.
Nor do the wealthy rival one another
With mansions festively displayed nor shed
Their wonted caution to indulge the whims
This feast brings thought of with their womenfolk.

Or the exchange between two police officers in the *Cart*:

Come here, it's safe here, but be quick, work hard,
Work fast so that the fortune of our king
May not desert his line! Search everyone,
In gambling dens and gardens, on the road,
In town, among the markets, in the fields,
Wherever your suspicions may arise!
Vīraka, why are you beckoning me?
Who broke his chains? Trust me and tell me all!
Who freed Prince Āryaka? At whose foul birth
Stood Sol in the eighth house, Moon in the fourth,
And Venus in the sixth? And who has Mars
In his fifth house, Jupiter in the sixth,
And Saturn in the ninth? What ill-starred man
Dares free the prince while Candana is alive?

Vīraka replies:

I swear it, Candana, upon your heart
That someone has abducted him at dawn,
The sun had not yet risen half when he
Up and released Prince Āryaka from jail.

The examples that have been given above may also illustrate the variety of styles in the verses themselves. What they have in common is what they have in common with all Sanskrit poetry, namely, that their basic unit is one stanza. Even when a number of stanzas follow one another, the subject and often the meter will differ. But every glittering little piece in the end forms part of the mosaic in which the action as it unrolls is depicted. The prose that connects them often does no more than provide the adhesive for the variously colored chips.

On other occasions, however, we may have large stretches of prose, as, for instance, in the beginning acts of the *Seal*. This prose is direct, fast, and often quite strong. Practically speaking, the prose of the plays is the oldest literary prose, dating well before the prose novels of Bāṇa and Daṇḍin. But as it is relieved by verse, it avoids the trap of overornamentation that in the end became the bane of Sanskrit prose.

18

STRUCTURE, CHARACTER, AND MOOD

Indian poetics enumerates three basic components which together make up a play: substance (or plot), the hero, and the mood. As we are dealing with an Indian phenomenon, it may be worthwhile to follow the Indian classifications; at the same time we should not forget that the dramatic theory was developed after the flourishing of the theatre itself and is less a theory than an abstraction from available plays, so that we should not expect concrete plays to conform too strictly to the abstract model. I follow here the outlines of Dhanaṃjaya's tenth-century compendium, the *Daśarūpa* (Ten kinds of show).[7]

PLOT

Dhanaṃjaya laconically defines a play as "the imitation of a situation." This "imitation" has both a *principal* plot and an *incidental* one. The principal plot leads the hero to the acquisition of the result of this plot, while the incidental plot serves the interest of another character but at the same time contributes to the interests of the hero. In the *Cart* this incidental plot, or subplot, is the rebellion of Prince Āryaka which in the end will lead to his succession to the throne; but this succession in turn contributes to the restoration of Cārudatta's fortunes. In the case of this particular subplot we have a continuous series of events which at regular intervals intersects with the events of the main plot; this is one kind of "episode," but there may also be incidental episodes.

The *object* of this plot is the fulfillment of one or several of the Three Human Pursuits into which Indian tradition divides all human activity: the Pursuit of Virtue, the Pursuit of Success, and the Pursuit of Pleasure. The *Seal* is typically the plotted Pursuit of Success, with no admixture of virtue or pleasure; the *Cart* is basically the Pursuit of Pleasure, but at the same time Cārudatta regains his former importance, and attains Success.

The "objective to be achieved" grows out of the *seed*, an event that seems at first of small importance but develops in all kinds of ways. In the *Cart*, the seed seems to be the encounter of Cārudatta and Vasantasenā in the courtyard of the temple of the God of Love, which ramifies in their falling in love, the hostility of the king's brother-in-law, and the consequent murder attempt on Vasantasenā, Cārudatta's indictment, etc. In the *Seal*, the seed is a letter that the hero has copied by a scribe who is the friend of his rival. The development of the plot is picturesquely described as the *spreading drop*; the original seed begins to spread out as a drop of oil spreads over the surface of a pond.

Thus there are five elements in any plot: the seed, the spreading drop, the subplot, the incidental episode, and the final object to be achieved, which is the *dénouement*.

The action proceeds in five stages and starts appropriately with the *undertaking*. In the *Seal*, Prime Minister Cāṇakya undertakes to win the minister of a rival prince for his own king. This initial undertaking prompts the hero to energetic *enterprise*: Cāṇakya at once starts rolling up the allies of his rival, arranging for faked defections and the dispatch of unwitting double agents. All this enterprise prompts a *hope for success*, which thereupon turns into *assured success* and finally to complete *attainment* of the objective.

While these are the principal moments of the play, they have to be linked together by *junctures*. Once more there are five of them, each preceding a principal moment: the *opening*, which establishes the seed; the *progression*, or development of the seed, which is intermittently observable; the *gestation* in which the seed is searched out; the pause for *reflection*; and finally the *conclusion*. Our text analyses a great number of subdivisions of each of these junctures which need not concern us here.

There is another overriding distinction to be made in the entire substance of the play which is of considerable importance: the distinction between situations and events that are actually shown and discussed on the stage and those that are only intimated. Factors in the plot which do not contribute to the prevailing mood of the play should not be portrayed, nor should events that are unseemly; portrayable are only pleasing and noble moods and emotions. Not ancillary to the mood or not seemly are a "long journey, an assassination, a battle, the ruin of a kingdom, a country, and the like, a siege, meals, baths, sexual intercourse, massage, dressing and undressing." Nor should the death of the hero be either portrayed or intimated.

This distinction between the direct and the indirect is formalized into a distinction between *acts* and *entr'actes*; the latter, usually very short and enacted by low-class persons, describe what has gone on behind the scenes, including war, assassination, etc.—all the events that should not directly be portrayed.

The act itself is defined as a direct presentation of the hero; it should have a unitary subject matter and represent the action of one day, with the hero present and engaged with three or four other characters. At the end of an act all the characters leave the stage. (In practice, however, the hero does not invariably enter every act of the play.) In their speaking parts the actors may employ several devices. The normal way is "aloud," but the character may also address *himself* for the benefit of the audience alone. If he wants to speak to another character without being overheard by others, he raises his hand with three fingers up and addresses him *privately*. If a secret or a confidence is to be imparted the speaker turns around to the character addressed.

CHARACTER: THE HERO AND THE HEROINE

"The Hero is courteous, kindly, generous, competent, gentle-spoken, popular, pure, eloquent, well-descended, stable, young, intelligent, energetic, with a fine memory, insightful, artistic, self-respecting, courageous, consistent, vigorous, learned in the sciences, and observant of the Dharma." He may be any one of four types, "playful," "serene," "exalted," or "violent"; but he is under all circumstances steadfast. As he is more often than not involved in amorous intrigue, his behavior once more calls for classification: he is "dexterous" when he remains kind-hearted to his old love, "deceitful" when he conceals his new love, and "reckless" when he shows signs that he has been making love to another. Finally, he may also be "agreeable" when he remains faithful to his love.

He has a little court, which is made up of the main characters of the subplot, a Libertine and Buffoon. If he has an adversary, the antagonist is of the violent type, greedy, arrogant, criminal, and full of vice.

Apart from the above qualities, there are in particular eight virtues which adorn the hero's character: he has *splendor*, or compassion for the humble, competitiveness with the great, courage, and competence. He has *grace*—a firm step, a straight glance, a smiling voice. He has *resilience*—even great disturbances hardly change his even tenor. He is *imperturbable*—one sees no change in him. He is *purposeful*—no number of obstructions will make him stray from his set course. He has *self-respect* and suffers no insult even if his life is at stake. He has *charm*—an innate sweetness of bearing and behavior that inspires love. And finally he is *generous*, giving gifts throughout his life, always with a kind word, and conciliatory towards the more virtuous.

This paragon of virtue will play opposite no less capable a heroine, of whom there are three main types: she may be his own woman, someone else's woman, or a public woman. His own woman, who is always proper in her conduct and upright, may be naïve, moderately experienced, or fully experienced. To each degree of experience answers a mode of responding to the hero's love; a fully experienced wife, for example, is "blinded by her youth, maddened by passion, dissolving as it were in her lover's body from sheer ecstasy, and no sooner is love play started than she goes out of her mind." Quite another story is the courtesan: "She makes love, as though she were in love with them, to men with dark desires, hedonists, fools, martinets, egotists, and the impotent, provided they are rich; when they are mulcted she has her mother throw them out." But male indignation wins out: "Except in a farce, she should actually be in love with the Hero."

Since the heroine is of importance only in relation to the hero, the author meticulously traces eight models. Surprisingly, the first is that of the wife of a henpecked husband: he sits happily at her side, forever dependable. The type "always eager to dress up" prettifies herself when her lover is about to come. She "who yearns in separation" is upset the moment her lover is late, even without his fault. The "insulted" woman tenses with jealousy when she finds out that love play with another woman has changed her lover. The "one withdrawn in a pique" quickly repents that she has indignantly rejected her man. The "cheated" woman is highly offended when her lover fails to turn up at the promised date. Or the woman may simply "have her lover abroad" if he is out of the country on business. Of great frequency is the *abhisārikā*, the "rushing" woman, who, sick with desire, runs off to her lover or awaits his coming. While the first two types are "playful, radiant, and overjoyed," the other six "worry, sigh, despair, weep, weaken, and take off their ornaments."

The learned author also catalogues the qualities that grace the heroine: she has exactly twenty graces. Three are physical: sentiment, whimsy, passionateness. Seven more are "spontaneous": beauty, radiance in being loved, charm, a higher degree of radiance, imperturbability, dignity, poise. Rooted in character are the other ten: playfulness, coquetry, taste, nervousness, hysteria, intenseness, coyness, standoffishness, elegance, and modesty.

Fortunately the best plays were already written before the virtues of heroes and heroines had been so painstakingly catalogued. Particularly the types of women seem to have been abstracted more from erotic poetry than from the dramatic literature. But the system of classification brings out the concern of the author with what he considers the principal *moods* that a play should convey, the heroic mood and the erotic mood. Thus the hero is depicted as valiant, energetic, imperturbable, and resilient, a man of action; and the heroine as responding almost passively to the changeable amours of her man.

MOOD

Dhanaṃjaya, whom we are still following, first described the structure of a play almost in the terms of an objective ritual that starts with the "undertaking" as a ceremony starts with an "intention," and, like the ceremony, culminates in the "objective to be achieved." Then he turned his attention to the character of the hero, who is the one to be "qualified" for the act of the play, as a sacrificer is "qualified" for his rite. But after all, the play remains a play, an "imitation," and a "show," and it is now necessary to turn to what the performance does to the audience who watches it.

Although in principle a play was accessible to anyone, even if he did not have the culture and education to enjoy its subtleties (there was always the colorful spectacle mostly based on familiar stories and enacted in mime), it is to the cultivated and artistic that a playwright addressed himself. The ideal spectator is a *sahṛdaya*, a man "whose heart is at one with the author's." The playwright, according to Indian dramatic theory, wants to create a specific mood in the audience which is sustained and reinforced as the play goes on. Thus the spectator does not enjoy the play directly—for if the play has to portray violence and loathsomeness, could he enjoy that?—but indirectly through the mood that the play through its scenes creates in him.

This theory of mood, or *rasa*, was built into a complex conception as time went on. The definition in the *Daśarūpa* expresses it as follows: "What is known as *mood* is a stable emotion which is made to become enjoyable through the cooperation of the antecedents, the consequents, the natural expressions, and the transient feelings."

The aestheticians identify nine emotions that are stable in the sense that they are not emotional reactions of a moment, but can be sustained over a longish period of time; and it is only through enduring emotions that a mood can be built up during the time that it takes to witness a play. These nine *emotions* are: love, energy, disgust, fury, merriment, wonderment, fear, and grief, with, as the ninth, introspective tranquillity. In so far as this last mood, tranquillity, cannot be dramatized, it is further left out of consideration. These emotions may produce a *mood* through the receptive spectator's own capacity of enjoying them; it does not derive directly from the actions of a hero, for he should *not* identify with the hero.

To each of the stable emotions, then, corresponds a mood that can be enjoyed by a sensitive person. To love corresponds an erotic mood, to energy a heroic one, to disgust a mood of hatred, to fury a mood of anger, to merriment a mood of good humor, to wonderment a mood of astonishment, to fear a mood of terror, to grief a mood of compassion.

The stable emotion that in the end produces the mood must itself be excited. There are a number of *antecedent* factors which determine the emotion. The most fundamental of all are, of course, the characters themselves; but then there are outside factors which through their very assocations make a person receptive to an emotion, put him, so to say, in the mood. For instance, there is an ancient association, persisting until today, of the coming of the rainy season with love; thus in the *Cart*, the duet between Vasantasenā and the Libertine depicting lightning, thunder, cloud, and rain is the elaboration of one antecedent of the emotion of love. When the antecedent factor has excited the emotion, it produces through the emotion itself the *consequent* feeling of being in love.

However, in the excitation of the emotions other factors contribute. First of all, the natural expressions. Depending on our receptiveness, the hero's trembling on seeing his beloved may make us tremble, the heroine's fainting may make us feel faint. And again, there are a number of fleeting sentiments that accompany any stable emotion "which emerge from it and submerge in it as waves in an ocean." When anger is displayed, it may excite such fleeting feelings as apprehension, anxiety, indignation, fright, agitation, depression. Through the interplay of all these factors the emotion is excited, corroborated, and sustained; and when the spectator begins to be more and more aware of his enjoyment of this emotion, he has the *rasa*, he has the *mood*.

Among the moods the erotic and the heroic are the most highly honored. We shall discuss them briefly to show the manner in which the Indian theoreticians treat them. The erotic mood is of three kinds:

love forbidden, love in separation, and love in union. Love forbidden is the love of a couple that is prevented from being consummated because their guardians will not permit it or because of the interference of fate. Quite reminiscent of the Arabic text quoted by Stendhal in *De l'amour*, this deprived love may evolve through ten stages, from yearning, worrying, musing, and dwelling on the beloved's virtues, to anxiety, raving, madness, fever, coma, and death.

Love in separation, perhaps the most popular theme of Sanskrit erotic poetry, may have two main causes: absence abroad or pique; this pique itself might be the pique of a lovers' quarrel, when two lovers have made up their minds to be angry, or may be occasioned by the lover's infidelity. In order to resolve the woman's pique, the lover will strategically resort to reconciliation, alienation of the woman from her sympathizing friends, inducement with presents, humbling himself, and, if that is not enough, he will simply ignore the woman, or create a distraction—make her laugh, in spite of herself, for example.

Love in union is just that: the lovers cherish each other agreeably, playfully watching out for each other and finding joy in each other's touch. The lover courts the woman with little love words, with artistic diversions, games, and the like, but he should never do anything boorish, nor anything that interferes with her pleasure.

The heroic mood rests on the emotion of energy, which is excited by such antecedents as majesty, good breeding, resoluteness, courage, delusion, refusal to despair, firm policy, surprise, and valor. The consequence of this emotion may be benevolence, war, or munificence. Contributing sentiments are self-assurance, pride, poise, and joy.

Thus, in brief, a summing up of the traditional way in which the Indian theoreticians looked at the plays. It is both an abstraction and an inventory of the substance of the great classical plays, and it contents itself with a general analysis rather than with close criticism of any one author's plays. The text of the *Daśarūpa* is fairly recent, but it summarizes much of what is already in the earlier *Nāṭyaśāstra* of Bharata. It cautions us that, even though all the conventions certainly were not yet formulated, there did exist a canon of sorts which the playwright recognized, if not meticulously observed. The wonder, therefore, is that among the classical plays at least there is such a fascinating variety. These generalities may guide us in some measure when we consider the individual plays.

THE STYLE OF THE PERFORMANCE

There must have been a great variety in the ways in which an Indian play was performed. Our oldest source of dramatic theory, the famous *Nāṭyaśāstra* of Bharata,[7] mentions four regional styles, a Southern one and three of the North: Western, Central, and Eastern. The author exhorts the producer to take these regional usages in account when staging a play. Similarly there must have been different kinds of playhouses. While the *Nāṭyaśāstra*, which will be followed hereunder, has considerable detail about the construction of a playhouse, it is doubtful whether these models were universal. As the Indian theatre disdains the use of props, staging a play was a simple affair; all that was needed was a raised platform surmounted by a canopy and closed off by a curtain at the back. Since Indians prefer to sit on the floor, no benches were needed. All the actors had to do was unpack their costumes, jewelry, and greasepaint.

Where playhouses were constructed they were of small size. Bharata cautions the builder not to make the structure longer than about a hundred feet; the width was usually fifty feet, and half of the comparatively modest area was set aside for the stage and the backstage. This playhouse would not easily accommodate more than four or five hundred spectators, even as Indians sit. Bharata's reasons are excellent: from a greater distance the facial expressions, the gestures, and the words become indistinct, and, as he rightly remarks, the success of the play depends on them. An Indian play with its peculiar style could not have succeeded in the gigantic theatres of the Greeks and Romans. Though we occasionally find theatres in palaces, and, more frequently, playhalls about the larger temples, it is safe to assume that the play was normally performed in the open air, in a partly enclosed area.

Bharata notes that marriage, the birth of a son, the visit of a son-in-law, festivals, and the celebration of one's prosperity make fine occasions to stage a play. We hear of no admission prices, and undoubtedly entrance was free, the cost being underwritten by a local patron, a learned assembly, or a guild. In a number of plays there is evidence that they were performed at auspicious occasions, and Bharata provides for a religious ritual as preliminary to a performance.

Plays were not necessarily performed at night. The Indian's remarkable inventiveness at classification would not allow the custom of just one set time a day; on the contrary, there are morning, afternoon, and evening plays, just as in Indian music there are *rāgas* or melodies suited to the time of day. A play that dealt mainly with virtue was to be performed in the morning; a play of force and energy, accompanied by much music, in the afternoon; and a play of love in the evening. Thus the three Human Pursuits, of Virtue, Success, and Pleasure, are tidily distributed over the waking day. These daylight performances also made for excellent visibility; Indian playwrights did not have to resort to descriptions of facial expressions, as Shakespeare had to do because his playhouses were too murky.

Although the stage itself was a simple platform, to the well-informed it was divided into several zones which indicated distances. By crossing from one zone into the other, the character could telescope the space traversed. By this simple device a character could move quickly over sometimes considerable distances, without wasting the audience's time by a pretended wait. Thus in the *Seal,* Minister Cāṇakya moves from his own house to Candragupta's palace in no time at all, simply by crossing an understood zone on the stage. The device is quite similar to dissolves in modern cinematography.

At the back of the stage hung a curtain through which the characters made their entrances and exits. It was split in the middle, and when a character entered two beautiful girls would hold it open for him. Suddenness, violence, and furtiveness would be illustrated by the sudden appearance of a character through the curtain "without its being opened." The color of the curtain could indicate to the audience the mood of the play.

Behind the curtain was the dressing room, used not only for costuming, but also to provide the source for "backstage sounds," when a person was being called, or a celestial voice spoke.

There was no painted scenery, although the sides of the platform might be permanently painted with auspicious figures and the white stuccoed walls of the playhouse itself decorated with flowering creepers and loving couples. No props were used normally, except perhaps an occasional throne and the like; this would depend on the lavishness of the establishment that sponsored the play. This lack of properties was deliberate, for in very large part the representation of a play depended on mimic suggestion.

Bharata distinguishes four elements in representation, which is
called *abhinaya*: the use of body, voice, costuming, and temperament. With his usual penchant for enumeration and classification he divides physical expressions into two classes, those of the major limbs and those of the minor ones. The latter include eyes, brows, nose, lower lip, and chin. The lower lip can be moved six ways: *curling* to indicate jealousy, pain, contempt, or laughter; *trembling,* from pain, fear, anger, cold, haste, etc.; *pouting,* to indicate a woman's indifference, or simply to apply lipstick; *sucking in,* to suggest that one is trying hard at a difficult task; *biting,* to show anger; and *pursing,* from pity, to kiss, or to greet.

The most important among the hundreds and hundreds of precise gestures are those of the hand. We have met the hand with three fingers upraised as a gesture indicating privacy; but the same gesture will also suggest an invocation, one's family descent, farewell, prohibition, entering, raising one's chin, a bow, comparison or alternatives, placing an auspicious object on the head, putting on a crown, covering mouth and ears—all depending on where the hand is held. All this of course is to be done not with awkward angularity, but with the graceful undulations that are still visible in the classical Indian dance. The same gesture with the fingers pointing down will recall the flight of small birds, a cascading stream, a snake, or a swarm of bees. In the same gesture the ringfinger is used to pink away a tear, to place an auspicious mark between the eyebrows, and to touch one's hair.

The *abhinaya* emerges as a paralanguage which is completely capable of conveying the meaning of the spoken text which it accompanies as a running paraphrasis. There are a number of basic gestures on which variations may be made. One gesture for instance is the *arāla*: the index finger is curved like a bow, the thumb is curved, and the other fingers are spread and turned upwards. Among other meanings this gesture signifies a woman's gathering up her hair or spreading it out. Both hands in this gesture circling each other and the fingers crossing in the auspicious *svastika* sign indicate the preliminaries to marriage when the bride goes around the bridegroom. The same gesture becomes the "pincers" gesture when the index finger and thumb are crossed and the palm is slightly hollowed and will then represent the plucking of flowers and the weaving of them into a garland.

Similar attention is given to the use of the voice. Distinctions are made between the kinds of moods that the plays are to suggest. In plays with an erotic or comic mood, the musical notes, pitch, and intonation are different from those used, for instance, in the heroic mood. The speed of diction in the erotic play is medium, in the compassionate slow, in the heroic fast.

Of special importance is costuming and make-up. Jewelry is considered essential and the various kinds are described with precision; in the end, however, Bharata warns against too heavy golden ornaments since they may hamper the movements and tire the actress. He sensibly suggests light-weight ornaments of lacquer inlaid with a few precious stones. Hairdos should be arranged according to regional fashions, so that a character is readily identified. In fact, every single item of dress and appearance is aimed at recognizability. People belonging to different regions, and even to different castes, should be made up with the appropriate colours. Tamils, for instance should be made up very dark, while Greeks, Scythians, Persians, and Bactrians should appear light-complexioned. It is the same with dress, weapons, and precious stones.

Finally, a good deal of attention is given to temperament, the portrayal of emotions. The character has to live his part and to be able to laugh, cry, have gooseflesh, a twitching eye, a throbbing cheek, bloodshot eyes, as the occasion of the emotion demands.

What emerges from the pages of the *Nāṭyaśāstra* is the existence of a flourishing stagecraft, a highly developed and stylized method of acting, and a remarkably refined pantomime. To the performing arts that contributed to the theatre, song and music should also be added. A number of the verses, particularly love poems, could be sung with the accompaniment of music. The play was at once drama, tableau, declamation, recital, dance, and concert, and it presented in microcosm all the performing arts. Reading a play, therefore, gives us as little immediate contact with its reality as reading a good libretto of an opera. It is not much, but it is all we have.

The actors themselves did not enjoy a high reputation. We have not much evidence, but it seems clear enough that in the acting profession the role of the courtesan was considerable. She is often described as an artiste, and literature records that she gave dance recitals. Then, too, there must have existed traveling troupes, not dissimilar to the yātrā troupes that have continued to travel through Bengal until today.

Since so much in the staging of the play depends on the identity of the character, it is likely that as a rule male roles would have been taken by men and female ones by women. But we read also that sometimes an actor had to play two roles because there were not enough actors available. Bharata, who comments on practically everything else, is strangely silent on the subject of actors. He devotes two verses to the qualities of a good actor: he should be intelligent, strong, handsome, conversant with beat and tempo, proficient in the emotions and moods, have the right age, a sense of the marvelous, an easy knack of memorizing a role, a good singing voice, a talent for dance, and, last but not least, he should be insensitive to stage fright and have a proper enthusiasm for his profession.

A play opens with the appearance of the director, who first intones a benediction. This benediction is normally addressed to Śiva, who has been the patron of the theatre ever since he became famous for his dances: he is the *naṭarāja* (king of actors). The director then briefly introduces the play, by mentioning its title, its type, and its author: no further program notes are provided. Next he will often enact a little skit with an actress which smoothly provides an opening into the main play, where both the director and the actress take on their own parts. The number of acts is not regulated; it ranges from six to ten. This makes the Indian play a rather long one, lengthened no doubt by musical intermezzi.

The audience of such a play might be quite mixed, but for a proper understanding of it a number of accomplishments would be demanded of the spectator. He should have a complete facility, not only in Sanskrit, but also in the other languages that are being spoken; not only that, he should know the theatrical conventions for the use of certain languages by various characters. The aim of creating a mood makes the spectator in many ways a participant in the play. It is the playwright's task to create the conditions for the mood, the actor's to bring it across, but the spectator's to open his artistic sensitivity to it. The efflorescence of the Indian theatre is proof that the playwright's confidence in his audience was not misplaced.

THE LITTLE CLAY CART

THE AUTHOR

An ancient Indian play, it was said, is traditionally signed with the name of its author in the prologue. The director of the play appears before the audience and announces its title and the name of its author, so that no confusion can arise. But as luck will have it, in *The Little Clay Cart* there is considerable confusion.

Scholars have spent considerable effort on identifying the King Śūdraka to whom the play is attributed in the Prologue. But at least part of the Prologue must be by a later hand, since it is said that Śūdraka died at the age of one hundred years and ten days; and however many accomplishments are ascribed to him, he could hardly have written his own obituary. As King Śūdraka was a legendary figure in narrative literature, the probabilities are that a *later* tradition linked him with the author of the play. It has been argued convincingly that such a linkage could have been forged only if the author's name was in fact Śūdraka. The name is not at all uncommon; it means "little Śūdra or servant" and might even have been adopted as a sobriquet or pseudonym.

There is some reason to believe that it might indeed have been a pseudonym. At the beginning of this century manuscripts were discovered which purported to contain the plays of a Bhāsa who had long been known as a playwright, since Kālidāsa mentioned him with respect in the prologue to one of his own plays. Controversy has raged ever since as to whether these are indeed Bhāsa's plays or late fabrications. The question is of interest to us since these Bhāsa plays include a fragmentary play called *Cārudatta.* On perusal this play, of which we have four acts, proves to be the basis of *The Little Clay Cart.*

Although in matters of "borrowing" and plagiarism the criteria of Sanskrit literature are rather more lenient than ours, it is hard to find another example of such complete appropriation—from main plot to characters to lines spoken—as Śūdraka has here perpetrated. This is not borrowing, this is grand larceny. Are we to assume that if the remaining part of Bhāsa's *Cārudatta* were found we would find that the rest of the *Cart* was similarly plagiarized? I am inclined to doubt it. It is worth pointing out that among the surviving plays only the *Cārudatta* is incomplete. It breaks off suddenly after Act IV, when Vasantasenā, the heroine, expresses her intention to visit Cārudatta. Of the eight plays of Bhāsa that are intended either as *nāṭakas* (heroic dramas) or as *prakaraṇas* (phantasies), only the *Cārudatta* lacks the concluding auspicious verse, the *Bhāratavākyam* (epic statement); this again indicates that the *Cārudatta* is incomplete. Also, in the corresponding Act IV, Śūdraka makes an important innovation on Bhāsa, by laying the seed of the subplot of Prince Āryaka and the resulting revolution which restores Cārudatta's fortune.

I should like to submit that Śūdraka himself found Bhāsa's play incomplete, whether the author had left it that way or chance had destroyed the latter part; and that he set out to write the completion of it. The name Śūdraka might then well be a modest gesture showing his indebtedness to Bhāsa from "the little servant." If this conjecture is correct, it also suggests an explanation of the name of the play. Titles of plays ought to show at least the name of one of the heroes, if not both; the other word in the title should indicate a crucial element in the play: *Śakuntalā and the Ring, The Minister's Seal, Yaugandhārayana and His Promise, Vāsavadattā in the Dream,* etc. The little clay cart figuring in the title hardly figures in the play; if it be true that Vasantasenā's jewels contained in the *Cart* seem to indict Cārudatta for her murder, the point is that Cārudatta is not finally executed and that what saves him are Vasantasenā's timely appearance and Āryaka's palace revolution.

But the choice of this title makes nice sense if once more the intention is modest: compared with Bhāsa's chariot, Śūdraka's play is just a fragile little cart of clay.

There are other examples in Sanskrit literature of works completed by others. Bāṇa's prose novel *Kādambarī*, for instance, was completed by his son. If my hypothesis is accepted (and at least it makes sense of the strange evidence), Śūdraka's play is a fascinating *tour de force*, his adoption of Bhāsa's first four acts entirely justified, and his solution brilliant. Considering the spiritedness of the play, its humor and ebullience, I find it hard to believe that it is just a plagiarizing rehash of a play by a widely famous author.

It is generally agreed that the *Cart* is one of the earlier plays of Sanskrit literature, and prior to Kālidāsa. Certain resemblances to *The Minister's Seal*—the dilapidated garden, the execution scene, etc.—make it likely that it is close in time to Viśākhadatta's play (the reign of Candra Gupta II Vikramāditya); one is likely to have borrowed from the other, and, given Śūdraka's more ancient style of Prakrits and far looser adherence to the dramatic conventions, he was the earlier writer and Viśākhadatta was the borrower.

Śūdraka knows his Ujjayinī quite well. The Square of the Provosts means something to him; his park has a specific name, Puṣpakaraṇḍaka; when a character sees the bloated bulk of Vasantasenā's dipsomaniac mother, he exclaims that they must have carried her in before constructing the gateway, just like the Great God whose statue was carried into the temple (no doubt the famous Mahākāla temple of Ujjayinī) before they erected the gates. There is good reason to place him in Ujjayinī, perhaps during the early Guptas.

SYNOPSIS

The hero of the play is Cārudatta who, a merchant in Bhāsa's version, is a Brahmin in Śūdraka's. Cārudatta's governing virtue is generosity: it pervades the entire play and his relations with everyone, except his wife. He had been a rich man, but has now fallen on hard times, because he has doled out all his wealth to hangers-on and solicitors. His constant companion is the buffoon Maitreya, who is, in fact, the only friend that has stayed with him. The play opens with Maitreya bringing Cārudatta a present from a rich acquaintance: a sad reversal of roles for the once-liberal Cārudatta, who describes his poverty as "the deadly sin they forgot to count." It is evening. Suddenly the focus is upon a wild chase which occurs close to Cārudatta's house: the courtesan Vasantasenā is being pursued by Saṃsthānaka the Śakāra, the villainous brother-in-law of the king. Vasantasenā stumbles through a door into safety in Cārudatta's house, and before leaving she deposits a golden box of costume jewelry with Cārudatta for safekeeping.

The second act is a series of sketches, illustrating the lowly but fascinating life which flows around a courtesan's establishment. While Vasantasenā is musing lovingly of Cārudatta, a barber-masseur comes seeking refuge: he has lost ten gold pieces gambling, cannot pay his debt, and is now pursued by the winners—a banker and a gambler—to a temple, and finally to the courtesan's door. This barber-masseur proves to be one of Cārudatta's old retainers; Vasantasenā pays his debt—unheard of generosity in a courtesan, a member of a group proverbial for its greed. In a fit of disgust the barber decides to take the Buddhist cloth, and immediately gets embroiled with an elephant, which he hopes to tame with his monastic serenity, as the Buddha once did. A retainer of Vasantasenā rescues him, in reward for which a stranger throws the rescuer his cloak. The beneficent stranger is Cārudatta.

Act III introduces a learned, Sanskrit-speaking burglar, Śarvilaka, who gives an erudite running commentary on his craft. The burglar enters the house and steals the golden box which Vasantasenā had entrusted to Cārudatta. On waking up, the generous victim is saddened that the thief has had to leave empty-handed, until it dawns on him that the box has been stolen. It was a sacred trust, and he fears that his poverty will immediately make him suspected. In a very touching scene, Cārudatta's wife, the mother of his son, gives the Fool a pearl necklace, her sole remaining property and incomparably more valuable than Vasantasenā's box, to pass on to Cārudatta for Vasantasenā.

The thief, however, is in love with one of Vasantasenā's handmaidens. In Act IV he wants to buy her freedom with his plunder. Though at first she is uncertain as to Cārudatta's safety, Vasantasenā, who, in a favorite dramatic device, has been eavesdropping, learns the truth and generously sets the handmaiden free. With a sudden switch, departing from the play which was his model, Śūdraka now introduces a political plot: Āryaka, a pretender to the throne, has been jailed. The thief suddenly decides to join his party, leaving behind his newly married bride. Meanwhile the Fool arrives with the necklace to replace the box, which Cārudatta pretends he lost at gambling—thereby generously avoiding naming a thief: Vasantasenā accepts, because it gives her a pretext to return to Cārudatta.

Act V finds the Libertine, who has been previously introduced as a companion of Saṃsthānaka, the villain, conducting Vasantasenā to Cārudatta's house; probably he had been sent as an envoy on his master's (the villain's) behalf to request the courtesan's favors. The monsoon is about to break, though untimely (and the coming of the monsoon, when travelers rejoined their wives, was ever the time for love-making), and Libertine and Courtesan engage in a veritable duet of poetry. Finally the courtesan reaches Cārudatta's house, where she spends the night.

The sixth act finds Vasantasenā trying to return the necklace to Cārudatta's wife, who declines. The merchant's little son enters, crying because he has only a little toy clay cart to play with; Vasantasenā stuffs it with pearls, so that he may buy a cart of gold. This little cart—from which the play has its name—thus becomes the sudden symbol of Cārudatta's poverty and of the generosity of both his wife and his mistress (the latter might well have been expected to consider the pearls as payment for services rendered). But, as I have suggested above, it may also betoken the new author's modest imitation of the "golden chariot" of the playwright Bhāsa. Thereupon, confusion at once ensues. The courtesan is to join her lover in a park. Meanwhile the pretender Āryaka has escaped and is abroad. In a traffic jam, Vasantasenā takes the wrong carriage, while the escaping Āryaka leaps into the carriage of Cārudatta, which was to carry Vasantasenā to her tryst. Āryaka is detained shortly, but escapes when one of the constables chooses to defend him against the other and starts a fight.

In the following act (VII) the fugitive meets Cārudatta, who lets him go, himself intent upon finding his mistress. She, meanwhile, is being carried off in a coach on its way to pick up her erstwhile pursuer, the Śakāra. This gentleman we find talking with his Libertine and abusing a Buddhist monk (none other than the barber-masseur whom we noticed taking the Buddhist vows earlier). Saṃsthānaka tries to win Vasantasenā, but she refuses him. He then orders his Libertine and his slave to kill her. They refuse. Feigning calm, he sends them on their way. When they are gone, he begins to beat Vasantasenā, who collapses. He covers her with leaves and departs. The masseur-turned-monk reappears, to hang out his robe which he has been laundering. He finds Vasantasenā, restores her to consciousness, and takes her to his monastery. Basically an act of gratitude, for she had been his benefactress, this act has about it the flavor of satire: the great courtesan being conducted by a lowly friar to a Buddhist cloister.

The satire becomes savage in Act IX, which takes place in a court of justice. The villain accuses Cārudatta of the murder of Vasantasenā (that there is no *body* does not seem to bother anyone). An interesting parade of witnesses now appears, bearing testimony which seems to incriminate Cārudatta. First comes Vasantasenā's mother, an old harlot who has fattened on brandy and rum. Then one of the constables involved in the fracas centering around Āryaka's escape in Cārudatta's coach testifies to the pretender's movements: this reflects badly on Cārudatta. To make matters worse, Cārudatta's friend the Fool, on his way to return to Vasantasenā the pearls which she had given to Cārudatta's son, comes by the court and, in his flustered indignation on hearing the charges, drops the pearls. Further evidence shows that Vasantasenā had spent the night at Cārudatta's house, and that they had had an assignation in the park. All this, plus the powerful presence of the Śakāra, brother-in-law of the king, convinces the judge, who is pictured as a well-intentioned and confused old man, that Cārudatta has murdered and robbed Vasantasenā. He sentences Cārudatta to exile (after all, she was only a prostitute). The king, however, understandably concerned with Cārudatta's apparent role in Āryaka's escape, converts the verdict into a death sentence.

The last act sees Cārudatta being led to his death by two outcastes. The Śakāra's servant, who had witnessed his master's assault on Vasantasenā and had been put in chains, manages to escape and tell his story, but his master discredits him. While the act is melodramatically lengthened in order to increase the suspense, all kinds of things happen at once: the courtesan and the monk appear in time to stave off the execution, and the lovers are reunited; while Āryaka kills the king, succeeds to the throne, and grants Cārudatta a fief. The crowd demands the Śakāra's death—not only did he commit murder, he is no longer the king's brother-in-law—but Cārudatta once more demonstrates his generosity by granting the villain a pardon. All's well that ends well: the lowly monk is appointed by the new king as chief abbot of *all* the kingdom's monasteries, and Vasantasenā is by royal decree elevated from her caste and thereby made an honest woman, so that she can become Cārudatta's legal wife.

It was certainly not Śūdraka's intention to give a completely realistic picture of life in Ujjayinī, nor was it his intention to write a satire on it. Nevertheless, he takes great delight in picturing the life of the demimonde. Thus he can present characters who are not provided for by the tidy classifications of the *Dharmaśāstras*, for it is in the cities that the neat system of four classes and four stages of life most visibly breaks down into a diversity of castes and a multiplicity of types. While Cārudatta and his wife are cast in the mold of Dharma, as is the Judge, the *Cart* presents us with a roll call of characters that is unique in the history of the Indian theatre.

Cārudatta's poverty has dragged him willy-nilly into this untidy world. Had he remained rich he would never have become involved in all these goings-on. Poverty, as he says, is the root of all evil. This poverty is however rather relative. He still has an establishment, even though his roof leaks. His wife has been able to save a pearl necklace from her dowry, "prize of the four oceans." He is still able to feed his Buffoon, and also a male servant who doubles as a driver, and a maid servant; and he is able to muster an elegant bullock-drawn carriage. But obviously he has dissipated the heritage of two generations of great merchants. Had he remained rich, his affair with Vasantasenā would have been decorously conducted; she would have been commensurately recompensed, and that would have been that. In some ways, the hero becomes a touching figure, finding himself suddenly entangled in a series of events which he can face only as the rich man he psychologically still is and with the easy generosity which his erstwhile fortune has made a habit. Shamefacedly he becomes the recipient of other people's generosity: that of Vasantasenā, who freely spends on him her otherwise expensive love; of his house Brahmin, the Fool, who does not desert him in his misfortune; even of his former barber-masseur, who unintentionally does him a good turn; and most of all of his noble and hardly visible wife.

Cārudatta's character is that of the ineffectual rich man's son who was so nice when he was rich, and is now so undeservedly poor, that good sense demands that his fortunes be returned—he himself seems to think so too, for while he bitterly laments his poverty, there are no indications that he intends to do anything about it; he probably has never worked for a living. He is the rich man's son who excels where the rich inevitably fail: in generosity to a fault. In the Indian context, however, generosity can *never* be exercised to a fault; Cārudatta's admiration for the artistry of the burglar, the liberal gestures with which he rewards with his last cloak the man who rescues a friar, and exonerates the villain of the piece, must have been deeply moving to an audience that knew the value of magnanimity.

Vasantasenā becomes less clear to the Western reader. Here we grievously lack the persuasion of actually seeing her on the stage, and of seeing her with Indian eyes: a free woman, walking and dancing with the self-assurance of the courtesan, darling of a sophisticated town, with almost every gesture and word excitingly violating all the proper ways for a matron to behave—a woman watched and admired like sin itself. To the fascination of seeing a courtesan on the stage (and the actress may well have been playing herself), there was the added fascination of seeing a courtesan actually and passionately in love. The Indian gallant, waited on hand and foot by the women of his household, meets on his escapades women who are out solely to exploit him. He must have enjoyed the poetic justice of a woman of that stripe becoming herself enslaved by the passions she so assiduously and lucratively excites in her admirers. The literature is full of stories of passionate men who ruined themselves for a cool courtesan. The balance is now somewhat restored by Vasantasenā, unmistakably in love and most generous with her possessions.

It is in the minor characters that Śūdraka excels. Saṃsthānaka the Śakāra—stockpiece of villainy—is so wicked that he is fun. He has absolutely none of the manly virtues. While Cārudatta's complaints about his poverty were no doubt well received, the Śakāra's bragging about his own wealth is in the worst possible taste. He is incredibly ill-educated, but has a streak of sly cunning. He is the ultimate boor, but a boor of wealth and powerful connections. Willing to corrupt a court of justice, capable of strangling a woman, with not a touch of courtesy or generosity in him, he is the complete opposite of Cārudatta. Conflict between them, however unsought by the noble hero, is inevitable. So is the outcome. In the end we find the villain chastened—"Let him die of gratitude!" orders Cārudatta. But are we quite sure that his single-minded brain will not devise a means to return to his old power?

Another stock figure of the stage, which, like the Buffoon, may well have come from the farce, is the Libertine or Wit. He is a Brahmin, but unaccounted for by the official view of Dharma. In the Libertine the theatre has made a type of the urban sophisticate, the literate sponger and *bon vivant* for whom the *Kāmasūtra* (Textbook on pleasure) was composed. He is equally at home among the staid pillars of society, the addicts of gambling dens, and the refined connoisseurs of the better brothels. He has no trade, perhaps a small patrimony, and his way of life is that of a *nāgarika*, a "city man." Poet and wit, universally informed and always at loose ends, he naturally gravitates to the patronage of an oaf. As Roman nobles would travel with their Greek philosophers as a kind of status symbol, a boor like the Śakāra parades his Libertine, to instruct and to amuse him. In the *Cart* the Libertine is a bit precious, spouting verse and despising his patron, but not without a certain nobility, however ill he can afford it.

Perhaps the most fetching character is that of Maitreya, the Buffoon, a man without pretense but loyal to the end, ready to follow Cārudatta into death. With the exception of the Śakāra, all the low figures are attractive—the Brahmin-thief Śarvilaka, the Brahmin-gambler Dardura, the masseur, the captain of police, the executioners. But their redeeming quality, of course, is that they all strive for some measure of respectability; one cannot help feeling that when the new king Āryaka has made them all respectable Ujjayinī will become a rather more boring town.

THE MINISTER'S SEAL

THE AUTHOR

No more is known of author Viśākhadatta than what he tells us in the Prologue of his play; he was the son of Mahārāja Bhāskara and the grandson of Governor Vaṭeśvaradatta. This lineage and the fact that he is also known as Viśākhadeva, *deva* being a royal appellation, indicates that he must have belonged to the high nobility. His age is, as usual, in dispute. However, there seems to me to be little reason not to accept the name Candragupta in the final benediction of the play and not to take this name to refer to the great king Candra Gupta II Sun of Valor (*c.* 376–415). The name is preserved in the best manuscripts; moreover, the benediction makes a point of associating the king with the Boar Incarnation of Viṣṇu; it is known that the Gupta dynasty actively promoted the cult of this Incarnation. Besides,

Viśākhadatta is known to have written another play, in which the same Candra Gupta II was the hero; regrettably, only fragments of this play have survived. This concern with Candraguptas, even though they belong to different dynasties, must show a close connection with the Gupta dynasty. One may assume that the author was a high courtier at the Gupta court.

SYNOPSIS

The *Seal* is semihistorical in the sense that the king whose throne is at stake in it was a historical person whose authenticity is vouched for by Greek sources; he defeated Alexander's general Seleucus Nicator in 305 B.C. Indian tradition further recounts that this king, Candragupta Maurya, was instated by a Brahmin of the name Kauṭilya, who, in turn, is the reputed author of a celebrated book on statecraft, the *Arthaśāstra* (Science of success). However, the circumstances of the play are, as far as we can see, fictitious, although it is probably true that Candragupta Maurya was a usurper who ended the earlier rule of a dynasty known as the Nine Nandas.

Viśākhadatta himself is rather vague about the Nandas, and it does not become clear whether these Nandas were successive rulers or contemporaneous despots. In any case, they were notorious for the avaricious way in which they exploited the country. Nor does it become fully clear who Candragupta's father was; perhaps the author preferred to gloss the question over, for if the last of the Nandas was his father, the new king might well be considered a parricide, since his own minister had the Nanda ruler assassinated. It is clear enough that his birth was low; his family name Maurya is a metronymic from *murā*, a lowborn woman, possibly a slave woman about the Nanda palace; consequently he had some family standing, but not enough to lay claim to the throne.

The play presents the following background. The Nandas, whose extortions had made the people rebellious, had as their minister and general a Brahmin, named Rākṣasa; as the name means "demon," it is probably a nickname; no other name is recorded. At a public occasion another Brahmin, Kauṭilya, was disgraced, in his own words because "I was dismissed from the first seat of the kingdom"; whether this means that he had held high office under the Nandas does not become clear. The disgrace was enough for him solemnly to vow the destruction of the dynasty which had humiliated him, and he allied himself to the young Maurya. In a further alliance with a northern king Parvataka, the Maurya marches on Pāṭaliputra, the capital of the Nandas, and takes it. Rākṣasa, who had taken a last-ditch stand in the city, takes charge of the last king, Sarvārthasiddhi, and smuggles him out of the city by an underground passageway, and the king retires in self-exile to a hermitage. Rākṣasa continues to harass the victorious Maurya, but his schemes are all deflected by Kauṭilya, or, as he is usually called in the play, Cāṇakya. The Maurya's original ally, Parvataka, had been promised half the kingdom as his price for the alliance. This possible threat to the Maurya's power is neatly eliminated by Cāṇakya: Rākṣasa had sent a poison girl to assassinate the Maurya, but Cāṇakya intercepts her and directs her to Parvataka. In the ensuing panic Parvataka's son Malayaketu is abducted from the city by an agent of Cāṇakya's and gathers his forces at some distance. Rākṣasa, continuing the Nanda's war with the Maurya, joins Malayaketu as his minister.

The basic plot of the play is formed by Cāṇakya's plan to win Rākṣasa over to the Maurya's side. Rākṣasa's loyalty is, to Cāṇakya, his basic strength—but it is also a weakness through which he can be vanquished. Like a master spider Cāṇakya in the first act starts weaving the web that will catch his rival. A spy, seen conferring with the minister, reports on the hostility of a certain Jain monk (in reality Cāṇakya's or

Kauṭilya's agent), of a Scribe, and of a Jeweler. The spy has discovered that the Jeweler's house harbors the wife and son of the fugitive Rākṣasa (the loyal man is a family man); in fact, when the child tried to dart out of the house a woman's hand appeared to pull him back in. From the hand had slipped a man's signet ring, too big for a woman's finger, and the spy had recovered it. It bore Rākṣasa's seal.

To build up a system of mistaken loyalties, Kauṭilya has the Scribe arrested and, when his execution seems imminent, rescued by an agent of his own. This agent, called Siddhārthaka, then flees to Rākṣasa's camp. The Jain monk is also exiled, a feint, and he joins Rākṣasa. The Jeweler is interviewed by Kauṭilya, who admires his loyalty in not betraying Rākṣasa, and jailed. Kauṭilya's pupil (Kauṭilya is a Brahmin, and therefore a teacher of his own Science of Success) reports in consternation the defection of a certain Brahmin courtier named Bhāgurāyaṇa and some ranking officers. This is all at Kauṭilya's instigation. In the meantime, Kauṭilya has used Rākṣasa's seal to seal a letter which he has had copied by the Scribe who is loyal to Rākṣasa.

The self-confidence of Kauṭilya and the success of his schemes is matched in Act II by Rākṣasa's diffidence and the frustration of his plans. His spy, appearing as a snake charmer, reports that all the attempts on the Maurya's life have backfired. The new king had had to pass under a triumphal arch before taking possession of the throne, and the arch was to have collapsed on top of him. Instead, the plot was foiled, and the brother of Parvataka had been killed. Parvataka himself had been killed by the touch of a poison girl, a *femme fatale*, destined by Rākṣasa for the Maurya; and Kauṭilya had engineered the rumor that he himself was responsible, which had caused the flight of Parvataka's son and heir and the subsequent succession of his brother to the allotted half of the realm; the son was in flight, the brother dead, and the Maurya in sole possession of the throne. So too with the other plots: a physician who had prepared a poisoned drink for the Maurya was discovered and forced to drink it himself ("Oh, a great scientist lost!" exclaims Rākṣasa); the double agent, the Jain monk, had supposedly been exiled, the Scribe condemned to death, the Jeweler jailed.

But while gloom reigns, new hope is imparted by the arrival of Kauṭilya's agent Siddhārthaka, who has helped the Scribe escape. As proof of his good faith he returns to Rākṣasa the signet ring he had picked up at the Jeweler's house; he asks to join Rākṣasa, who immediately consents. Rākṣasa's spy reports that the Maurya is beginning to resent his overbearing minister, and Rākṣasa sees his chance. But another thread is being woven by Kauṭilya: a merchant offers Rākṣasa some precious jewelry, which he buys, asking Siddhārthaka to see to the price.

In Act III Kauṭilya starts a diversion. To feed the rumors of the alienation between him and the Maurya, he imperiously cancels a festival that the king had made a point of restoring after years of war. The king pretends anger, and the minister is insolent and threatening. Finally, he resigns in a fury over the king's ingratitude.

In Act IV Kauṭilya's agent Bhāgurāyaṇa lays plans to bring about a *real* alienation between Rākṣasa and his prince. Bhāgurāyaṇa insists that he and other defecting officers deal directly with the prince, since they suspect Rākṣasa of playing a game of his own: to disaffect the Maurya from Kauṭilya, so that he can step into Kauṭilya's place. This is of course precisely Kauṭilya's goal. The prince is confused and suspicious that perhaps this is his own minister's aim and he is confirmed in his growing distrust by overhearing a conversation between Rākṣasa and a runner, reporting the feigned alienation of Kauṭilya and the Maurya: when Rākṣasa congratulates himself that the Maurya has now come to hand, the prince concludes that his minister refers to a covenant by handshake. This distrust prevents the prince from deciding on an offensive. And finally the Jain monk, when pressed for an astrologically suitable date for action, stalls and seems to predict a calamity. It is curious that none of the principal characters speaks outright lies, preferring *double-entendres* from which the other may conclude what he wishes: it is the great art of engineering misunderstandings.

These misunderstandings are brought to a head in Act V. The Jain wants to leave the camp, and Bhāgurāyaṇa is in charge of exit visas. The Jain says that he is afraid of Rākṣasa who used him in arranging for the poison girl that infected Parvataka, the prince's father, and who wants him out of the way, now that he serves the prince himself. The prince, who had been led to believe that Kauṭilya was responsible for his father's death is outraged. Bhāgurāyaṇa counsels patience and a cooler head. Just then the agent of Kauṭilya who had rescued the Scribe returned Rākṣasa's seal, and supervised the purchase of the precious jewelry is apprehended leaving the camp without a visa. He is thrashed and confesses that he is carrying a letter from Rākṣasa to the Maurya; this is the letter which Kauṭilya had had copied by Rākṣasa's loyal friend the Scribe and sealed with Rākṣasa's seal. It describes the intended treachery of the prince's main allies. The king questions Rākṣasa about the arrangements for the march on Pāṭaliputra, and it transpires that these main allies are the ones to be stationed about the prince's person. Rākṣasa is perplexed by the letter; it is in the handwriting of the Scribe, whose loyalty to him personally has been unquestioned, and sealed with his own ring. This evidence practically proves Rākṣasa's duplicity, and Rākṣasa himself is hurt in his most sensitive spot: can the Scribe have betrayed his loyalty? Rākṣasa is wearing a piece of the jewelry which he had purchased earlier, the prince now recognizes it as one of his father's pieces. The case against Rākṣasa is now complete: the jewelry was Rākṣasa's price for betrayal. The prince then orders his supposedly treacherous allies killed, confusion ensues, and Rākṣasa, whose true faith to the prince has been shredded by the prince himself, sets out, disgraced, on a final errand of loyalty: to rescue the Jeweler who was jailed because of his loyalty to Rākṣasa.

In Act VI Rākṣasa has slipped into the Maurya's capital Pāṭaliputra, and has hidden in an abandoned park. There is here a curious and, as noted, not accidental parallelism with the *The Little Clay Cart*, where a scene in a park is similarly followed by a scene on the execution grounds. But what in the *Cart* was pure accident and mistake is here carefully engineered design. Rākṣasa has been followed by one of Kauṭilya's agents, who now prevents his suicide by hanging: Rākṣasa has heard that the Jeweler is about to be executed, and he would rather kill himself than see his friend die. Kauṭilya has left only this course open to Rākṣasa, one of final devotion: he must sacrifice himself for his friend.

In Act VII the Jeweler is being led to his execution, followed by his wife, who does not wish to survive him. And here Rākṣasa gives himself up to Kauṭilya to save his friend. Loyalty has forced him into the precise situation where Kauṭilya wanted him: at his mercy because of Rākṣasa's inability to be disloyal. The master has his condition: he wants Rākṣasa to accept the sword of state and serve the Maurya, while he himself retires. This would resolve all the issues: as minister, Rākṣasa could restore his prince (since taken captive, after his armies mutinied when the allies were killed) to his ancestral lands; and the Jeweler would live. Rākṣasa accepts the condition and pledges his precious loyalty to the Maurya.

CHARACTERS

The ascent of Candragupta the Maurya to the throne of Magadha in Pāṭaliputra marked, according to one tradition, the defeat of the old Kṣatriyas, the barons of the Vedic age, who claimed descent from the great solar and lunar dynasties. This new aristrocracy was not the god-given, or rather dharma-appointed, one of birth, with its dharmic obligation to protect and succor, and its dharmic virtues of courage and strength. It was a manmade aristocracy that could be overthrown by men, and would be, if it were not constantly on the alert. In the *Seal*, the Maurya's kingship is consequently the kingship of diplomacy as well as valor, of administration as well as battles, of hard ministers as well as faithful companions.

In its hero Cāṇakya or Kauṭilya, Viśākhadatta has created a type no less dear to the Indian heart than the serene sage—the powerful man of affairs. He is minister to the Maurya and represented as the principal architect of the great Mauryan empire. Typically—and here the man of affairs brushes the sage—he has no ulterior motives of selfish purpose. And not unlike the sage he is moved by the curse that he has pronounced on the Nanda dynasty. In a way he is the victim of his own curse. The beginning of the play finds him tired: his oath is fulfilled, but Rākṣasa keeps harassing him.

The play is as close to a problem play as the Indian theatre has come. Kauṭilya, whose conception of statecraft is informed by a universal suspicion ministered to by a network of spies and agents, has reached the realization of the paradox of this statecraft: a king must be able to rely absolutely on the honesty and the loyalty of his chief minister. Every human being is corruptible, everyone has his price—but ultimately there must be complete trust in the man who is in charge of this nationwide implementation of suspicion. What commends Rākṣasa is that he has the virtue as well as the *talent* of loyalty.

In the final analysis Kauṭilya himself does not have this loyalty. He has joined the Maurya to fulfill his oath to the world and his promise to himself. He is a man entirely by himself, without wife and children, a practitioner of his own cold brand of statecraft which, according to tradition, he had founded with his textbook, the *Arthaśāstra.* He is the ascetic who is still in this world and whose brilliance cannot prevent him from reaching a pinnacle of power that does not interest him any longer. One may well imagine him after his retirement, perhaps settling down in a hermitage, a cool recluse. A circle of pupils would form around him while he developed his *Arthaśāstra*, holding the world for no better than it is and, in the end, not caring very much for it.

Rākṣasa, on the other hand, is the passionate friend in search of service. He is content that his own well-being is interwoven with and contingent on that of others. Such a man will have a wife who wishes to follow him into death. He will have friends whose loyalty is inspired by his own. He is a delicate poet of the beauties of a world made handsomer by his being of it; and as an early, not religious but complete, model of bhakti (devotion) he is no less an Indian hero than Kauṭilya himself. If a man like Kauṭilya is able to defeat him by the means of his loyalty, it can *only* be for the sake of this loyalty.

The *Seal* is an entirely masculine play; women have no place in it. Nor is there a place for a Buffoon to relieve the mounting tension, for here tension is the entire point. While the *nāṭaka* style of play loves the great epical battles and conflicts, even if it cannot portray them on the stage, in the *Seal* intrigue and counterintrigue take the place of armed conflict, and incidental assassinations of key persons are preferred to massive battles. Thus it is principally a play between two persons; the other characters remain shallow.

King Candragupta himself is a straw man of Kauṭilya, young, obedient, and so conscious of his role of devout disciple that even feigning a quarrel with his minister gives him a headache. He is inexperienced and aware of it. His counterpart, Prince Malayaketu, is equally inexperienced, but at the same time imperious and quickly suspicious of his minister. It is ironic that the king never suspects the essentially unattached Kauṭilya, while the prince is quick to cover the utterly loyal Rākṣasa with the darkest suspicion. But then, may be he was right, his entire entourage was infiltrated by Kauṭilya's agents.

One wonders what kind of statecraft the author Viśākhadatta himself in the end favored. Kauṭilya's brand of suspicion, which terminates in the perfectly controlled police state, or Rākṣasa's brand of compassion and devotion? As he makes Kauṭilya himself responsible for the winning of Rākṣasa in order to succeed him, one tends to think that he prefers the latter. But will Rākṣasa in his old age be looking around for a pupil of Kauṭilya's to succeed him?

THE LITTLE CLAY CART

ascribed to Śūdraka

CAST OF CHARACTERS

CĀRUDATTA, a Brahmin, impoverished heir of a merchant's fortune.
LIBERTINE, wit-in-waiting of Cārudatta's adversary, Saṃsthānaka; may be the same as Vasantasenā's Libertine.
DARDURA, a gambler.
ŚARVILAKA, a Brahmin turned burglar.
ĀRYAKA, son of the late king Gopāla who was the reigning king's brother; pretender to the throne.
JUDGE, presiding at Cārudatta's trial.
(These characters speak Sanskrit.)

VASANTASENĀ, a courtesan in love with Cārudatta.
MAITREYA, a low-grade Brahmin, buffoon and friend of Cārudatta.
SAṂSTHĀNAKA or ŚAKĀRA, brother-in-law to the king, boorish hedonist, suitor of Vasantasenā.
SLAVE, servant of Saṃsthānaka, possibly identical with Sthāvaraka.
STHĀVARAKA, slave and coachman of Saṃsthānaka.
MASSEUR, old retainer of Cārudatta, now down on his luck.
GAMBLER, winner in a game with Masseur.
KARṆAPŪRAKA, a braggart, servant of Vasantasenā.
VARDHAMĀNA, servant and coachman of Cārudatta.
KUMBHĪLAKA, a servant of Vasantasenā.
RADANIKĀ, maid servant of Cārudatta.
MADANIKĀ, maid and lower courtesan in Vasantasenā's house.
BASTARD, a male inmate of Vasantasenā's establishment.
ROHASENA, son of Cārudatta.
WIFE, Cārudatta's Brahmin spouse.
VĪRAKA, captain of the constabulary.
CANDANAKA, captain of the constabulary.
BAWD, mother of Vasantasenā.
BAILIFF.
PROVOST.
SCRIVENER.
FIRST EXECUTIONER.
SECOND EXECUTIONER.
(These characters speak several Prākrits.)

Act One. Scene: Cārudatta's courtyard, and the adjacent alley, of his house on the Square of the Provosts in Ujjayinī. Time: Evening, shortly before the rainy season.

Act Two. Scene: Vasantasenā's establishment and surroundings. Time: the following day in the morning.

Act Three. Scene: Cārudatta's house and surroundings. Time: a week later, in the late evening.

Act Four. Scene: Vasantasenā's establishment. Time: the next morning.

Act Five. Scene: The road to Cārudatta's house, its outer grounds, and its interior. Time: the same evening and night.

Act Six. Scene: Cārudatta's house, and adjacent streets. Time: the next morning.

Act Seven. Scene: The Puṣpakaraṇḍaka park. Time: the same morning.

Act Eight. Scene: The same. Time: noon of the same day.

Act Nine. Scene: The courthouse. Time: the next morning.

Act Ten. Scene: The execution field. Time: later the same day.

PROLOGUE

BENEDICTION

May Śiva's Meditation favor thee,
When doubling up the snake that spans his knees
He folds His legs in the Paryaṅka Seat—
May Śiva's Meditation favor thee,
When He has checked His breath so that all senses
Cease working and His conscience is suspended—
May Śiva's Meditation favor thee,
When with the eye of truth within Himself
He contemplates, free from all acts, the Self—
May Śiva's Meditation gazing down
The Void, sunk in the Brahman, favor thee![1]

And may the throat of the Blue-Throated God,
Dark as a thundercloud upon which flashes
The lightining streak of Gaurī's arm, protect thee![2]

After the Benediction enter the Director.

DIRECTOR: No more of this tiresome waste of time that'll only wear thin our audience's curiosity! I prostrate myself before you gentlemen and beg to announce to you that we have decided to stage a Phantasy for you, which is entitled *The Little Clay Cart.* The poet, of course, was a King whose steps had the poise of an elephant, whose eyes the light of a cakora bird's,[3] whose face the beauty of the full moon, King Śūdraka, stalwart leader of the twiceborn, celebrated poet, profound man of character! Indeed, he was a scholar of the Veda of the Hymns and the Veda of the Chants, mathematician, arbiter of elegances, and trainer of elephants. Darkness was lifted from his eyes by the grace of Śiva; and when he had seen his son established as king and offered with great magnificence a Horse Sacrifice, he entered, at the age of one hundred years and ten days, the sacred fire. Śūdraka was addicted to battle, but without imprudence. He was a paragon of theologians as well as a great ascetic, a king of the world, it has been said, eager to wrestle with enemy elephants.

In this play of his you will meet

One poor young merchant from Ujjayinī,
A Gentleman, whose name is Cārudatta;
And, lovely as the Spring, a Courtesan,
Vasantasenā, who is in love with him:
King Śūdraka has shown here how their love
Provokes against them a conspiracy,
How justice is perverted, and how crooks
Conduct themselves, and Destiny disposes.

(*He walks about the stage and glances around him.*) Why! But our stage is entirely empty! Where could the players have gone? (*He thinks.*) Of course!

Empty the house of a man without a son,
Empty the hours of a man whose friends have gone,
Empty to a fool the road beyond him,
Empty to the poor all the world around him!

And now I am done rehearsing! I have been rehearsing so long that my eyes are popping like dry seeds in the summer sunshine and they are crackling from hunger! So I'll call the woman of the house and ask her if there is any breakfast. Here I go. Hullo! But if I want anything done, and done properly, I'd better change to the vernacular. (*He changes to Prākrit.*) Ah, poor me! Poor me! With all that rehearsing I am so ravenous now that my whole body has withered like a dry bed of lotus stalks. So I'll go home and find out if the wife has cooked anything this morning. (*He walks about the stage and looks around.*) Here I am home now. Let's go inside. (*He enters his house and looks around.*) Well, I never! Why all these unusual arrangements in my house? The drive is one long river of rice-gruel. The floor is covered with round black spots where the iron pots have been turned upside down, pretty as the face of a young girl with beauty spots! I am getting terribly hungry now. Have they uncovered an old hoard? Nothing, of course; I am just so famished that the whole world looks like one big bowl of rice. Nothing to eat for me this morning. I am starving to death! They are making all kinds of special preparations. One of the girls is making ointments, another is stringing garlands. What is going on here? All right, I'll call the wife and find out what the matter is. Madam! Come here!

Enter the Actress.

ACTRESS: Sir, here I am!

DIRECTOR: Well, you are welcome, ma'am!

ACTRESS: Pray, my lord, what orders may I take?

DIRECTOR: Madam, I have been rehearsing so long that I am ravenous and my body is withered like a dry bed of lotus stalks. Is there anything to eat in the house?

ACTRESS: There are all kinds of things, sir.

DIRECTOR: Ha, all kinds of things?

ACTRESS: Yes, rice-gruel, for instance, and ghee, and curds, and boiled rice. You can eat a complete elixir of life!

DIRECTOR: Everything? In our house? Or are you joking with me?

ACTRESS (*to herself*): Of course I am joking! (*Aloud.*) Everything, my lord. In the shops, that is.

DIRECTOR (*angrily*): You whore! May your own hopes be cut as you have cut mine! May you dissolve into nothingness! Like a bundle of hay you have thrown me up in the air only to drop me down again!

ACTRESS: Forgive me, sir, please! I was only joking.

DIRECTOR: What are all these special preparations for? One girl is making ointments, another is stringing garlands, and the floor is made pretty with an offering of flowers in five different colors.

ACTRESS: I am starting a fast.

DIRECTOR: What kind of fast?

ACTRESS: A fast for a good husband.

DIRECTOR: A good husband, ma'am? In this life, or your next?

ACTRESS: My next life, of course.

DIRECTOR (*piqued*): Now look at this, gentlemen! I have to pay for the food so she will find herself a good husband in her next life!

ACTRESS: Please, please, sir! I am fasting so that you will be my husband again in my next life.

DIRECTOR: Who suggested this fast?

ACTRESS: Your own great friend Cūrṇavṛddha.

DIRECTOR (*indignantly to the absent Cūrṇavṛddha*): You son of a whore!

I'll see to it that King Pālaka cuts you up like the sweet-smelling tresses of your new bride!

ACTRESS: Please, be calm now, sir! I am only doing the fast so that you will be my husband in my next life! (*She throws herself at his feet.*)

DIRECTOR: There, there, get up, ma'am. Now tell me, who is going to officiate at your fast?

ACTRESS: We must invite a Brahmin who does not mind serving our kind of people.[4]

DIRECTOR: You go now, madam. I myself shall invite a Brahmin who serves our kind of people.

ACTRESS: As you command, my lord. (*Exit.*)

DIRECTOR (*walking back and forth*): Ujjayinī is so rich! How am I going to find in this town a Brahmin who will serve our kind of people? (*He looks around.*) There is Cārudatta's friend Maitreya coming. All right, I'll ask him. Master Maitreya, will you come and preside at a feast in my house?

VOICE OFFSTAGE: Better ask another Brahmin, fellow. I am busy today.

DIRECTOR: Sir, our food is perfect, absolutely unrivaled! And I'll give you a fee too!

VOICE OFFSTAGE: Now why are you asking me again and again? I refused you already, didn't I?

DIRECTOR: So he refused me. All right, I'll ask another Brahmin. (*Exit.*)

ACT ONE

Enter Maitreya with a cloak over his arm.

MAITREYA: Ask another Brahmin, fellow, I am busy today! Yes, but on the other hand I am going to have to accept the invitations of strangers if I want to eat at all. What a situation! Just make the comparison! First I sat at the gate of a big house, stuffing myself with delicious morsels, with a smell so good you could belch from anticipation, all fresh and carefully prepared, day and night, thanks to Master Cārudatta's great wealth. Like a painter amidst his color bowls I was surrounded by hundreds of little dishes which I picked and picked and discarded with fond fingers, and when I was full, I ruminated leisurely like the bull of the town square. And now Cārudatta is poor, and I am obliged to wander about, and if I come back to his house, it is as a homing pigeon, because I have to have a place to sleep. . . . This cloak, which is positively reeking with jasmine scent, is a present for Cārudatta from his good friend Cūrṇavṛddha. He told me to give it to him when Master Cārudatta had finished worshiping the gods. There I see Cārudatta. He must have finished worshiping, for he is now coming out of the house to throw out the offerings to the house gods.

Enter Cārudatta, engaged as described, and a maid, Radanikā.

CĀRUDATTA (*raising his eyes to heaven and sighing hopelessly*):

> Once swans and cranes came swooping down in swarms
> To snatch from my doorstep the gifts I threw;
> And now, on weedgrown steps, a wretched few
> Dry seeds lie there ignored and wait for worms. . . .

(*Very slowly he walks about the stage and sits down.*)

MAITREYA: There is Master Cārudatta. I'll go and join him. (*He walks to Cārudatta.*) Good day, sir, and good wishes!

CĀRUDATTA: Ah, there is Maitreya, friend at all times. Welcome, friend. Do sit down.

MAITREYA: As you please, sir. (*He sits down.*) Your friend Cūrṇavṛddha sends you this cloak, which is perfumed with jasmine scent, as a present. I was to give it to you after you had finished your devotions. (*He hands the cloak over. Cārudatta takes it but does not react, sunk in thought.*)

MAITREYA: Hey! What are you thinking about?

CĀRUDATTA: Friend,

> If one has suffered, oh, the joy
> Of finding happiness to light
> The blinding darkness of the dead!
> But one who fell out of old joy
> In poverty's dread dead of night
> May live perhaps, but he lives dead!

MAITREYA: Come on now, friend, what would you really prefer, being poor or being dead?

CĀRUDATTA: If I had the choice between poverty and death, I should choose death. Death is but a brief pain, but poverty means suffering without end.

MAITREYA: Now, friend, stop torturing yourself! If your friends have swallowed your fortune, so the gods swallow the nectar of the moon. But like the new moon which will grow again, your loss has its brighter side too!

CĀRUDATTA: Friend, I do not care so much about the riches I have lost.[5]

> What grieves me is that guests go by
> My house because my wealth is gone,
> Like bees that past the season shun
> The elephants whose rut is dry.

MAITREYA: Sons of bitches, that is what they are, drunk with money, all of them. Cowherd boys who are scared of wasps and go where they won't be stung!

CĀRUDATTA: I am truly not concerned because I have lost my fortune, my friend, for riches come and go as luck will have it. What pains me is that as soon as one's fortune collapses people weaken even in their friendship.

> And poverty reduces one to shame,
> And a shamed man will lose his dignity;
> Without his dignity he is despised,

And once he is despised he must despair;
Disconsolate, he falls a prey to grief,
His grievances will rob him of his mind,
And, out of mind, he is completely lost:
The lack of money brings all evils on.

MAITREYA: Friend, forget this drunken love of money and stop torturing yourself!

CĀRUDATTA: Still, poverty brings a man not only cares, but the contempt, and even hostility, of strangers, the disgust of his friends, the hatred of his kinfolk, the contempt of his wife. Till he decides to depart for the woods. And the fire of grief that burns within him, never kills, it only tortures. . . . Well, I have finished with the offering. You go, my friend, and throw an offering for the Mothers on the crossroads.[6]

MAITREYA: I am not going.

CĀRUDATTA: Why not?

MAITREYA: The gods don't help even if you worship them, so what is the use of worshiping them?

CĀRUDATTA: That is no way to talk! It is an everlasting rule for every man with a household that the gods show their favor to those of serene mind, if they are duly honored with mortifications, pure thoughts, kind words, and proper offerings. Why should you doubt it? Come on, go offer to the Mothers!

MAITREYA: No, I am not going. Order somebody else. After all, I am a Brahmin, so that everything is always the other way around, like your reflection in a mirror: what is left is right, and what is right is left. Besides, it is evening, and courtesans, libertines, and slaves will be roaming the highway, and certain persons who are favorites with the king. . . . I'll be as vulnerable as a mouse running head on into a cobra hunting for frogs!

CĀRUDATTA: All right, stay then while I do my meditation.

VOICES OFFSTAGE: Stop, Vasantasenā, stop!

Enter Vasantasenā, pursued by a Libertine, Saṃsthānaka, and a Slave.

LIBERTINE: Vasantasenā, stop at once!

Don't let your elegance be spoilt by fear,
Those feet are dancing feet, look where they go!

And those seductive eyes, fright hurts them so!
So runs, pursued by hunters, a scared deer!

SAṂSTHĀNAKA: Dear little Vasantasenā, stop now!

Where are you going, running, rushing, tripping?
Stop, little morsel, please, you are not dying!
Oh, my poor heart ablaze with love, and dripping
Like a fat chunk of meat the cooks are frying![7]

SLAVE: Ma'am, stop!

She ran away from me, all terrified,
A summer peahen with her tail plumes flashing,
And like a backwoods cockerel my dashing
Master is dancing after his brief bride!

LIBERTINE: Vasantasenā, stop at once!

Why, trembling like a young banana tree,
With wind-tossed red skirts flying do you flee,
Showering lotus buds incarnadine
Like crimson chips from a realgar mine?[8]

SAṂSTHĀNAKA: Stop, little Vasantasenā, stop!

My amor, cupid, and my love you fed,
And chased the sleep from my nocturnal bed—
In frantic frenzy do you trip and flee
And, Kuntī, find your Rāvaṇa in me!

LIBERTINE: Vasantasenā!

Why do your paces outstrip mine, why fly
As from the king of birds the serpent flies?
I could run up a storm and pass it by,
But on your shapely rear I'll feast my eyes!

SAṂSTHĀNAKA: Master! Master! Listen how I prayed to her! O Whip of Love Who Robs My Coin, O Eater of Asses, O Dancing Whore, Denosed Harlot, Perverter of Family, O Fallen Woman, Treasure Box of Lust, O Brothel Hostess, Brothel Haunter, Brothel Huntress, and Brothel Boarder—not less than ten names in all I invoked her with, and still she does not want me!

LIBERTINE:

Why then in such a terror do you run
Chafing your cheeks with earrings swinging,
Libertine's lute expertly played upon,
Crane flying from the clouds' far singing?[9]

SAṂSTHĀNAKA:

Atinkle-tinkle with your jewels ringing,
You flee as Draupadī from Rāma fled,
But just as Hanumān once took the cringing
Subhadrā I shall take you to my bed!

SLAVE: Love the king's favorite and you'll find a chunk of ass, as fine a piece of ass meat as a dog will pass up a corpse for!

LIBERTINE: My dear Vasantasenā,

Why must you run, holding the girdle up that slips,
Aglitter with its jeweled starbursts, down your hips?
And, wonder! must you with your rouge-streaked face resemble
Our City's outraged Patroness who's all atremble?

SAṂSTHĀNAKA:

We curs may chase you, jackal, swiftly
And follow you in hot pursuit,
You run as fast and quick and swiftly,
And with my bloody heart to boot!

VASANTASENĀ: Pallavaka, Pallavaka! Parabhṛtika, Parabhṛtika!
SAṂSTHĀNAKA (*terrified*): Oh master, master! A man, a man!
LIBERTINE: There is nothing to fear, . . .
VASANTASENĀ: Mādhavikā, Mādhavikā!
LIBERTINE (*laughing*): . . . she is only looking for her escorts, fool!
SAṂSTHĀNAKA: Now she is looking for a woman.
LIBERTINE: So?
SAṂSTHĀNAKA: I am a hero, I can kill a hundred women!
VASANTASENĀ (*finding herself deserted*): Aah! My servants have vanished. Now I must defend myself by myself.
LIBERTINE: Go find her now!
SAṂSTHĀNAKA: Little Vasantasenā, you can cry for your Cuckoo or

Blossom,[10] and the whole month of spring as far as I am concerned, but who is going to defend you when I am after you?

What price Bhīmasena, what of Rāma-with-the-Hatchet,
What of Arjuna or ten-faced Rāvaṇa?
My great model is the great Duḥśāsana,
You take down your hair and run, girl, I shall catch it!

Look here! Look!

My sword is keen, your skull is flying!
I'll cut your throat, unless I kill you.
Now stop this useless running, will you?
No one will live when he is dying!

VASANTASENĀ: My lord, I am only a woman!
LIBERTINE: That is why you live.
SAṂSTHĀNAKA: That is why you aren't dead yet.
VASANTASENĀ (*to herself*): Oh, this courtesy frightens me! But good, if this is the way it is. . . . (*Aloud.*) My lord, is it my jewelry you are after?

LIBERTINE: Good mercy, my dear lady! The garden vine does not deserve to have its flowers stolen. We are not after your jewels.
VASANTASENĀ: Then what do you want?

SAṂSTHĀNAKA: That you love me, me a man, a Man Divine, Vāsudeva himself!
VASANTASENĀ (*angrily*): Heaven forbid! You have gone too far! Go away, your proposition is outrageous!
SAṂSTHĀNAKA (*smiling and clapping his hands*): Look, master! In no time at all this pretty little courtesan has fallen in love with me! You hear what she says? "Heaven forthwith, you have gone so far!" But I have not left town! My dear lady, I swear on the head of my master and these two feet that your back is as far as I have been roving!
LIBERTINE (*to himself*): Ugh, the blockhead! Heaven forbid, she said and he understood, heaven forthwith! (*Aloud.*) Vasantasenā, what you are saying does not quite fit if you live in the District.[11] Look here, ma'am, living in the District means living with young men. You are a courtesan: think of yourself as a vine on the roadside, for everyone to pluck. The body you wear is up for sale and auctioned off. And you serve equally, my dear girl, the ones you like and the ones you hate. In the same pond bathe the wisest Brahmin and the most stupid pariah.

The same blossoming vine that bends under the peacock bends under the crow. The boat that ferries high-caste ferries out-caste. You are a courtesan, and like the pond, the vine, and the boat you must accommodate everybody.

VASANTASENĀ: But only quality inspires affection, not violence!

SAṂSTHĀNAKA: Master, this born slave girl has been in love with that penniless Cārudatta ever since they met in the court of the Kāma temple, and she does not want me. The fellow's home is just on the left here, so please don't let her slip from our fingers.

LIBERTINE (*to himself*): Trust a fool to say what he should keep secret! Well, so Vasantasenā is in love with the noble Cārudatta! They are right in saying that only pearls go with pearls. Let her go. What does this fool matter, after all! (*Aloud.*) There on the left, is that the merchant's house, bastard?

SAṂSTHĀNAKA: Exactly, that's his house on the left.

VASANTASENĀ (*to herself*): What? Yes, that is his house on the left! With all his impertinence the lout has done me a favor: he has arranged a rendezvous with my love!

SAṂSTHĀNAKA: Master, no sooner did I see Vasantasenā than she vanished in the pitch dark, like an ink drop in a pile of black beans!

LIBERTINE: Indeed, it is dark tonight. I have my eyes wide open but the darkness has sealed them. And when I open my eyes, it is as though the night had closed them.

The darkness seems to bathe my limbs,
The sky is raining mascara;
And like a favor to a thankless man
My eyes have lost their sense.

SAṂSTHĀNAKA: Master, I want to find Vasantasenā!

LIBERTINE: Do you see any sign of her, bastard?

SAṂSTHĀNAKA: What sign, master?

LIBERTINE: Any sign, the sound of her jewels, or the scent of her garland mingling with her perfume.

SAṂSTHĀNAKA: Yes, yes! I can clearly hear her scent, stuffed as my nose is with darkness, but I don't see her jewels ring.

LIBERTINE (*aside*): Vasantasenā!

The evening darkness may still cover you—
The womb of clouds to which the lightning clings—

Your garland's fragrance will discover you,
Shy girl, and your loquacious ankle rings.

Do you hear me, Vasantasenā?

VASANTASENĀ (*to herself*): Yes, I hear your advice, and I shall take it! (*In pantomime she takes off her bracelets and discards her garlands. She goes about groping with her hand.*) I am groping along the wall . . . then this must be the side door. But it is flush with the wall, it must be locked!

CĀRUDATTA: My friend, I have finished my prayers. Go now and offer to the Mothers.

MAITREYA: No, I am not going!

CĀRUDATTA: Aah, when a man is poor, his relatives no longer obey him and his best friends turn away from him. . . . Ill luck grows on him, and his character shrivels up, and like the moon his shining honor wanes. And all the crimes of others will be blamed on you. No one wants to consort with you, or speak politely. If you go to the mansions of the rich when they are feasting, they all turn cold eyes on you. You go in rags and idle far from the crowd, because you are ashamed to show yourself. Yes, I found that poverty is the deadly sin they forgot to count!

Poor Poverty, how do I mourn your fate!
When this wretch sheds the body which made you
Such an overindulgent host of late,
Whereto, I wonder, will you go, whereto?

MAITREYA (*uneasily*): All right, friend. If I must go, at least let Radanikā keep me company.

CĀRUDATTA: Radanikā, go along with Maitreya.

RADANIKĀ: As you please, sir.

MAITREYA: Here, take the offering and the lamp, Radanikā dear, while I open the side door. (*He does so.*)

VASANTASENĀ: The door opens to come to my defense! I must go in quickly. (*She looks.*) Look out! A lamp! (*She blows out the lamp by waving her skirts and enters.*)

CĀRUDATTA: Maitreya, what was that?

MAITREYA: The door as it opened made a draft and blew out the lamp. Radanikā dear, you go out the door, while I run back in; I'll light the lamp inside and join you. (*Exit.*)

SAṂSTHĀNAKA: I am still looking for Vasantasenā.
LIBERTINE: Carry on, carry on.
SAṂSTHĀNAKA (*doing so*): Master, I've caught her, I've caught her!
LIBERTINE: Fool, that's I!
SAṂSTHĀNAKA: Well, get out of the way and stay out of the way! (*He searches again and grabs hold of his Slave.*) Master, I've caught her!
SLAVE: My lord, it's me, your slave!
SAṂSTHĀNAKA: Master, stay where you are. Slave, stay where you are. Master. Slave. Slave. Master. Both of you stay out of the way! (*He searches again and grabs Radanikā by the hair.*) Master, now I really have got her! I've got Vasantasenā!

She walked in darkness but her scent betrayed her;
And as Cāṇakya once caught Draupadī
My groping fingers felt the night, and see!
I caught her by her thick long braids and stayed her!

LIBERTINE: So with the pride of youth you would run after a young man of noble family, my girl, and now you are dragged off by your beautiful flowery hair!
SAṂSTHĀNAKA: There you are, lassie, caught by the hair, braids, and tresses on your pretty little head! Scream, shriek, and screech for the Lord, God, or the Deity!
RADANIKĀ (*frightened*): What are you gentlemen up to?
LIBERTINE: That is not her voice, bastard!
SAṂSTHĀNAKA: Master, she has changed her voice, that slave girl's daughter, like a pussy cat that has its eyes on the whey.
LIBERTINE: Changed her voice? Well, that would be quite a feat. But why not, after all? She has acted on the stage, learned all the tricks, and become adept at deception: she should be able to imitate different voices.

Enter Maitreya.
MAITREYA: Look at this lamp! The flame trembles in the evening breeze like the heart of a goat that is being brought to be sacrificed. (*Approaches, sees Radanikā.*) Here I am, Radanikā.
SAṂSTHĀNAKA: Master, a man, a man!
MAITREYA: It is not right, no, it is not decent that Cārudatta's poverty should be reason for strangers to invade his home!
RADANIKĀ: Master Maitreya, look how they are manhandling me!

MAITREYA: Manhandling you? Both of us, I should say!

RADANIKĀ: What, you too?

MAITREYA: We are being assaulted!

RADANIKĀ: Exactly.

MAITREYA: Really?

RADANIKĀ: Really!

MAITREYA (*raising his stick wrathfully*): Avaunt! Hey you, in his own house even a dog can get fierce, let alone a Brahmin like me! I'll beat the scoundrel's head with this stick that's as crooked and mean as our kind of people's kind of fate, until it splinters like a dry bamboo!

LIBERTINE: O Great Brahmin! Pardon us, pardon us!

MAITREYA (*studying the Libertine*): It isn't you who did it. (*Studying Saṃsthānaka.*) That's him, that's the crook! Bah, Saṃsthānaka, brother-in-law to the king and a beast of a man! It isn't right! Even if my lord Cārudatta has become a pauper, are his virtues no longer the ornament of Ujjayinī that people may freely invade his house and molest his servants?

Never insult a man because he is poor: he may not be poor to fate; while a man who lacks morals, however rich he may be, is a pauper.

LIBERTINE (*uneasily*): Brahmin, please forgive us. We laid hands on you, not out of arrogance, but because we mistook you for someone else.

We chased a loving woman here.

MAITREYA: This one?

LIBERTINE: Heaven forbid!

One in the prime of youth, and free.
We erred and she could disappear
While we suggested lechery.

In any case, please accept our apologies, which are all that remains to us. (*He lets go of his sword, and with a supplicant's gesture throws himself at Maitreya's feet.*)

MAITREYA. You are an honest man. Get up, get up! I took you to task because I did not know you. Now I know you and I apologize.

LIBERTINE: Oh no! We owe you apologies. I shall get up on one condition.

MAITREYA: Explain.

LIBERTINE: That you don't mention any of this to the noble Cārudatta.
MAITREYA: I won't tell him.
LIBERTINE:

> My head bows, Sir, to your benevolence:
> You humbled swordsmen with magnificence!

SAṂSTHĀNAKA (*sulking*): Why did you humiliate yourself before this crooked fool of a Brahmin! You folded your hands and fell at his feet!
LIBERTINE: Because I am scared!
SAṂSTHĀNAKA: Scared? Of what?
LIBERTINE: Of Cārudatta's qualities.
SAṂSTHĀNAKA: What qualities? What qualities does a man have who has nothing to feed you when you come to his house?
LIBERTINE: That is no way of talking!

> The man was ruined by keeping men like me;
> He spent his fortune with humility:
> A well in summer that was full at first
> And dried by quenching every comer's thirst!

SAṂSTHĀNAKA: But who is the bastard really?

> A great brave hero? Śvetaketu the Bold?
> Or Rāvaṇa, Rādhā's son that Indra got?
> A son of Kuntī's got of Rāma, old
> Jaṭāyu, Aśvatthāman, the whole lot?

LIBERTINE: Fool! He is the noble Cārudatta! A tree of wishes to all the needy, bending down under the burden of its excellence! A host to all good men, mirror to the learned, touchstone of rectitude, ocean tide of uprightness, a benefactor without contempt, treasury of manliness, of a character both capable and generous. For he alone lives truly who is praised for his superior qualities: the others merely breathe!—Let's go.
SAṂSTHĀNAKA: Before we have caught Vasantasenā?
LIBERTINE: Vasantasenā has gone.
SAṂSTHĀNAKA: How gone?
LIBERTINE: Gone, like the sight of a blind man, the health of a sick man, the mind of a madman, the success of a lazy man, like the perfect wisdom of a slow-witted lecher! Meeting you she vanished, as love vanishes before an enemy!

SAMSTHĀNAKA: I am not going before we have caught her.

LIBERTINE: Have you never heard that to hold an elephant you need a pole, to hold a horse you need a bridle, to hold a woman you need a heart? As you don't have a heart, you might as well go.

SAMSTHĀNAKA: Go if you want to. I am not going.

LIBERTINE: Well, here I go. (*Exit.*)

SAMSTHĀNAKA: So master gives it a miss. (*To Maitreya.*) Hey, you, beggar boy with the crow's whiskers, hit bottom!

MAITREYA: I have already hit bottom.

SAMSTHĀNAKA: Who made you?

MAITREYA: Fate.

SAMSTHĀNAKA: Stand up then.

MAITREYA: So we shall.

SAMSTHĀNAKA: When?

MAITREYA: When we are back in favor with fate.

SAMSTHĀNAKA: Cry then!

MAITREYA: I have done my bit of crying.

SAMSTHĀNAKA: Who made you?

MAITREYA: Poverty.

SAMSTHĀNAKA: All right, laugh!

MAITREYA: Laugh we shall.

SAMSTHĀNAKA: When?

MAITREYA: When the noble Cārudatta is rich again.

SAMSTHĀNAKA: Well, little beggar boy, you go tell that pauper in my name that a courtesan called Vasantasenā, a girl as golden as ever an actress appearing in a heroic drama, who has been in love with him ever since they met in the yard of the Kāma temple,[12] has escaped into his house when I was courting her somewhat forcefully. If he delivers her into my hands, without my having to sue him first, and is quick to oblige me, I'll be his friend. If he does not oblige me, he has an enemy till death. And you may remind him:

Some things will never rot,
A pumpkin with the stalk in dung,
Dried vegetables and stewed meat,
A meal cooked on a winter night,
And debt, and enmity.

You will tell him in nice words, you will tell him in easy words, you will tell him in clear words, clear enough for me to hear them while I am sitting in the dovecot on the roof of my palace. And if you don't, I'll crack your head *crack!* like an elephant nut between door and doorstep!

MAITREYA: I'll tell him.

SAṂSTHĀNAKA (*stealthily*): Slave, has the master really gone?

SLAVE: Yes, he has.

SAṂSTHĀNAKA: Then let us run off.

SLAVE: Please hold the sword, sir.

SAṂSTHĀNAKA: No, you keep it!

SLAVE: Here, sir, please, sir, you hold the sword.

SAṂSTHĀNAKA (*taking it by the wrong end*):

> Cradling my barkless, radish-reddish sword
> In its sheathed sleep upon this shoulder fair,
> I rush, a jackal in a howling herd
> Of dogs and bitches, to my safer lair.

(*Circling the stage exeunt Saṃsthānaka and Slave.*)

MAITREYA: My dear Radanikā, don't mention your abuse to your master. He suffers enough already from his poverty and this will only make him suffer more.

RADANIKĀ: Master Maitreya, I am Radanikā. I know when to keep quiet.

MAITREYA: So you do indeed.

CĀRUDATTA (*addressing Vasantasenā*): Radanikā! Rohasena likes playing in the wind, but now he must be getting cold in the evening breeze. Bring him inside and wrap him in this cloak. (*He hands her the cloak.*)

VASANTASENĀ (*to herself*): He has mistaken me for his maid! (*She takes the cloak and sniffs the perfume.*) Oh, the cloak is scented with jasmine—that shows that he is not indifferent to the pleasures of his youth! (*Stealthily she wraps herself in it.*)

CĀRUDATTA: Come on, Radanikā. Take Rohasena and bring him inside!

VASANTASENĀ (*to herself*): But I have no right to go inside!

CĀRUDATTA: Come on, Radanikā! Why don't you answer me? Alas!

> When a man has been haunted by destiny
> Till he reaches the dregs of poverty
> All the friends of his wealth turn enemy
> And old servants demand their liberty!

Radanikā and Maitreya approach.
MAITREYA: Well, here is Radanikā back.
CĀRUDATTA: Radanikā? But who was the other woman?

> A woman now touched with impurity
> As she touched my cloak unknowingly—

VASANTASENĀ (*to herself*): No, touched with purity!

> And clean as the crescent moon did she rise
> That is racing the clouds of the autumn skies.

But it was not proper that I looked upon another's wife.
MAITREYA: Well, you can stop accusing yourself of having looked upon any other man's wife. That was Vasantasenā, and she has been in love with you ever since that meeting in the courtyard of the Kāma temple.
CĀRUDATTA: Ayi! Vasantasenā? (*To himself.*)

> I fell in love with her; but when one's wealth is gone,
> Love is a coward's rage with none to prey upon!

MAITREYA: Friend, the king's brother-in-law has a message for you.
CĀRUDATTA: What is it?
MAITREYA: That a courtesan called Vasantasenā, as golden a girl as ever an actress appearing in a heroic drama, who has been in love with you ever since you met in the court of the Kāma temple, has escaped into your house, when she was courted somewhat forcefully.
VASANTASENĀ (*to herself*): "Courted somewhat forcefully"—well the expression at least is flattering.
MAITREYA: If you deliver her into his hands before he needs to sue you, and are quick to oblige him, he'll be your friend; if you do not oblige him, he'll be your enemy till death.
CĀRUDATTA (*with contempt*): The ignoramus! (*To himself.*) Ayi, she is a woman to be worshiped like a goddess! When she is prodded to come into the house, she will not stir, with utter disregard for a man's position. And accustomed as she is to male society, she will say not an improper word, though she speaks often. (*Aloud.*) My lady Vasantasenā, I have insulted you by treating you unwittingly as a servant girl, for I did not recognize you. I bow my head and beg forgiveness.
VASANTASENĀ: But I did wrong by trespassing upon your Honor's threshold: with bowed head I seek your pardon!

MAITREYA: Fine. Now you are both nicely bowing like two paddy fields perpetually nodding to each other. Now I bow my head, as the camel bends its knee, and most humbly suggest that both of you get up.

CĀRUDATTA: Yes indeed, let us dispense with formalities.

VASANTASENĀ (*to herself*): How cleverly and kindly proposed! But it would not be correct for me to stay the night now that I have come to his house in the way I did. Then I should say this. (*Aloud.*) If your Honor is disposed to favor me, then I wish to leave my jewelry in your house. Those bandits pursued me because of my jewels.

CĀRUDATTA: This house is not fitted for their custody.

VASANTASENĀ: My lord, a deception! It is people one trusts with custody, not houses.

CĀRUDATTA: Maitreya, take the jewels.

VASANTASENĀ: I am favored. (*She hands over her jewels.*)

MAITREYA (*accepting them*): Thank you very kindly, my lady!

CĀRUDATTA: You blockhead, it is only for custody.

MAITREYA (*under his breath*): In that case let the burglars come and get them.

CĀRUDATTA: Only for a few days . . .

MAITREYA: . . . This is going to be ours?

CĀRUDATTA: . . . After which I shall return them.

VASANTASENĀ: My lord, now I wish to go home, if the Brahmin may escort me.

CĀRUDATTA: Maitreya, escort my lady.

MAITREYA: You escort her, and you will look like a regal flamingo in the company of this lady who walks like one. But I am only a Brahmin: anywhere people may jump on me and swallow me like dogs that get at the crossroads offerings!

CĀRUDATTA: Very well, Maitreya. I myself will accompany you, my lady. We must have torches lighted so that we may walk the king's highway with assurance.

MAITREYA: Vardhamānaka! Light torches.

SLAVE (*aside*): How am I to light them without oil?

MAITREYA (*aside to Cārudatta*): Our torches are like courtesans: they won't burn for penniless lovers.

CĀRUDATTA: Very well, Maitreya. No torches—look:

> Pale as a loving woman's cheek the moon has risen
> With its escort of planets and will light our way:

Its clear white rays are dripping on the crowding darkness,
Like drops of milk that spray the blackened dried-up mud.

(*With tenderness.*) My lady Vasantasenā, here is your house. Do enter.
(*Exit Vasantasenā, looking back tenderly.*)
CĀRUDATTA: Friend, Vasantasenā has gone. Come, we must return home.

The highway is deserted and the guardsmen prowl—
We must avoid their errors, night is always foul.

(*They walk about.*) You will guard that jewel casket by night, and Vardhamānaka by day.
MAITREYA: As you wish.

ACT TWO

Enter a Slave Girl.

SLAVE GIRL: I am looking for my mistress. Her mother has sent me with a message. I must go in and find her. (*She walks and looks about.*) There she is now, my mistress, drawing somebody's picture in her heart! I'll go to her now.

Enter Vasantasenā: she is seated, dreamy; Madanikā is with her.

VASANTASENĀ: And then, what happened, my dear?

MADANIKĀ: I was not talking, my lady! Why are you asking?

VASANTASENĀ: What did I say?

MADANIKĀ: "And then, what happened?"

VASANTASENĀ (*frowning*): Ah, of course.

The Slave Girl approaches.

SLAVE GIRL: My lady, your mother tells you to bathe and bring the offering to the gods.

VASANTASENĀ: Tell mother that I will not bathe today. Let a Brahmin take care of the offering.

SLAVE GIRL: Very good, my lady. (*Exit.*)

MADANIKĀ: Please, my lady, what is the matter? I am not being forward, only concerned.

VASANTASENĀ: How do I look to you then, Madanikā?

MADANIKĀ: Your heart is gone, and I am sure you are longing for the man who has taken it!

VASANTASENĀ: Indeed you are right to be so sure. You are an expert at reading hearts!

MADANIKĀ: How wonderful! God Kāma himself will be pleased; it'll be a feast of love for the lucky young man! Tell me, my lady, is it the king you attend, or the king's favorite?

VASANTASENĀ: I like to love, my dear, not to dance attendance!

MADANIKĀ: Have you fallen in love with a young Brahmin of distinguished learning?

VASANTASENĀ: No doubt one must honor Brahmins. . . .

MADANIKĀ: Well, then, with a merchant's heir, who has made a vast fortune by trading in many towns?

VASANTASENĀ: My dear, merchants will leave their mistresses, however much they love them, to travel abroad and inflict on them the pains of solitude.

MADANIKĀ: Not the king, not the king's favorite, not a Brahmin, and not a merchant—then who is left for my high[13] mistress to love?

VASANTASENĀ: But did you not come with me to the courtyard of the Kāma temple?

MADANIKĀ: So I did, my lady.

VASANTASENĀ: And still you pretend you know nothing?

MADANIKĀ: I know! Is it he? The one who helped you when you asked protection?

VASANTASENĀ: Say his name!

MADANIKĀ: And he lives on the Square of the Provosts?

VASANTASENĀ: Come, I asked you to say his name!

MADANIKĀ: Cārudatta is his name, and well taken it is.

VASANTASENĀ (*pleased to hear his name*): Very good, Madanikā, very good. You know things.

MADANIKĀ (*to herself*): Yes indeed! (*Aloud.*) But I hear he is *poor*, my lady.

VASANTASENĀ: I love him the more for it. People do not blame a courtesan for giving her heart to a poor man.

MADANIKĀ: But do the roving honey bees stay with the mango tree when it has lost its bloom?

VASANTASENĀ: That is the more reason to call them honey bees!

MADANIKĀ: If you love him so, why didn't you seek him out at once, my lady?

VASANTASENĀ: Well, if I had sought him out at once, he would have been difficult to approach a second time, for he couldn't possibly reciprocate. . . . And that I had to avoid.

MADANIKĀ: And therefore you left your jewelry with him?

VASANTASENĀ: Nothing escapes you, my dear.

VOICES OFFSTAGE: Folks, there's a gambler running, running with ten gold pieces owing! Catch him, catch him! Hey, stop at once! I can still see you!

Enter, brusquely through the curtain, a Masseur.

MASSEUR: Man, what a life, to be a gambler! I was thrown by a donkey throw as mean as a donkey just gotten loose, and the spear throw floored me as Karna's spear did Ghaṭotkaca! The bookmaker had his nose in his book, and when I saw that I made myself scarce. Now I am in the open street, but who is going to shelter me? There they are out looking for me, the keeper and the gambler I was playing. . . . I'll squeeze myself backwards into this temple niche and play God for a change.

(*With all manner of gesticulations he does so and stays there.*)

Enter Māthura and the Gambler.

MĀTHURA: Folks, there's a gambler running, running with ten gold pieces owing! Catch him, catch him! Hey, stop at once! I can still see you.

GAMBLER:

> Are you flying to hell?
> Seeking Indra's protection?
> Even Rudra won't save you
> From the banker's detection!

MĀTHURA:

> Where, where did you go, you blight,
> That grudge a good banker his fee?
> So you wanted to escape from me
> And ran in a frenzy of fright?
> Your family hasn't been blackened enough?
> The smooth you can take, can you take the rough?

GAMBLER (*looking at the tracks*): Here he went, and here the tracks stop.

MĀTHURA (*studying the tracks thoughtfully*): Aha! The tracks run backward! And the statue in that temple niche was missing. . . . (*Pondering.*) That crooked gambler has squeezed himself backward into the niche!

GAMBLER: Let's chase him.

MĀTHURA: Sure enough!

(*Both enter the temple, searching; they discover the Masseur and wink at each other.*)

GAMBLER: Wood, isn't it, this statue?

MĀTHURA: Wood? No, it is stone. (*He rocks the stiff Masseur to and fro, winking at his companion.*) Stone. Well, come on, let's have a game. (*Both play at dice with all kinds of gestures.*)

MASSEUR (*trying to master his obvious wish to join in the game, to himself*):

> The sound of dice affects a poor man's brain
> As beating drums a king who lost his land.
> But no, I know I shouldn't try my hand,
> I mustn't ever make a play again!
> No, I'd fall down Mount Meru. . . . Oh, the cries,
> The fascinating cuckoo cries of dice!

GAMBLER: My throw, my throw!

MĀTHURA: No, mine!

MASSEUR (*suddenly getting in from the side*): No, it is my turn now!

GAMBLER: Got the fellow!

MĀTHURA (*grabbing him*): Bah, robber, we got you! Give up your ten gold pieces.

MASSEUR: Today you get them.

MĀTHURA: I want them now!

MASSEUR: I'll pay all right, take it easy.

MĀTHURA: You pay up now!

MASSEUR: Oh, my head! (*He rolls on the floor; both kick him wildly.*)

MĀTHURA: There (*drawing a circle around the Masseur*), I've trapped you in the gambler's circle.

MASSEUR (*getting up, despairingly*): I am bound by the gambler's circle. That is the one bond a gambler can't escape from.[14] But how am I to pay you?

MĀTHURA: Come on, get bail!

MASSEUR: All right. (*He takes the Gambler aside.*) If I get bail, will you bail me out for five pieces?

GAMBLER: All right.

MASSEUR (*turning to Māthura, taking him aside*): If I have bail for five pieces, will you stand bail for another five?

MĀTHURA: No harm in it, all right.

MASSEUR (*aloud*): So you will stand bail for five gold pieces.

MĀTHURA: I'll stand bail.

MASSEUR (*aloud to Gambler*): And you'll stand bail for five gold pieces?

GAMBLER: I'll stand bail.

MASSEUR: Well, goodbye now.[15]

MĀTHURA: Hey, where are you going? Pay your ten gold pieces!
MASSEUR: Folks, watch him! You! I just got bail for five gold pieces, and you stood bail for another five. I am clean, and now you ask for ten more!
MĀTHURA (*grabbing him*): Crook! Sharp Māthura, that's me! I want a fair deal! Pay up, you robber, and all of it now!
MASSEUR: Where can I get it?
MĀTHURA: Go sell your father!
MASSEUR: Never had a father.
MĀTHURA: Go sell your mother!
MASSEUR: Never had a mother.
MĀTHURA: Go sell yourself.
MASSEUR: Do me a favor and take me to the highway.
MĀTHURA: Come along.
MASSEUR: All right. (*They walk about.*) Gentlemen! Buy me from this bookie, only ten gold pieces! (*Looking, as though at someone.*) What do you say? What can I do? I'll make a fine bearer about the house! Now he walks off without a reply! All right, I'll ask this one. (*He repeats his offer.*) The fellow goes off without even considering me! Ah, since the noble Cārudatta has lost his fortune, I've lost mine.
MĀTHURA: Pay up!
MASSEUR: How can I pay? (*He throws himself at the feet of Māthura, who thrashes him.*)
MASSEUR: People, save me, help!

Enter Dardura.[16]
DARDURA: The only thing the game of dice lacks to make it a kingdom is a throne!

The gambler never counts defeat,
His revenues keep flowing in,
And all he has goes waste.
But future bills he's sure to meet—
As to a king come bowing in
The wealthy making haste.

Play and you shall be rich,
Win wives and friends by play,
Do charity and feed yourself,
Play more and all's away.

The trey took what I had,
The deuce did dry me out,
Ace sent me to the door,
And nought sent me about.

(*Looking straight ahead.*) There's my ex-bookmaker Māthura coming. Well, I can't run away, I must hide my face. (*Trying to cover his face with his cloak in various ways, he stares at it.*)

This cloak is worn to the last thread,
This cloak boasts of one hundred tears!
This cloak is, as a garment, dead!
This cloak draws only stares!

Indeed, I am mortified! For look,

One foot is holding the floor, the other upended,
And as long as the sun shines I stay suspended![17]

MĀTHURA: Make him pay!

MASSEUR: How can I pay? (*Māthura drags him through the dust.*)

DARDURA (*to an imaginary bystander*): I say, what is going on here? (*Listens.*) You don't say! A gambler manhandled by a games master? Nobody will buy him free? I, Dardura, will buy him free! (*He approaches.*) Make way, make way! (*He looks.*) Well, Māthura the crook himself! And one mortified Masseur!

Who does not stand all day with drooping head,
Whose backside shows no scars of gravel rubbings,
Whose calves are still unchewed, erect, well-fed,
That man should stay away from gambler drubbings!

Good. I must appease Māthura. (*He walks up to him.*) Māthura, I am greeting you.

MĀTHURA: I greet you back.

DARDURA: What's wrong?

MĀTHURA: He owes me ten gold pieces.

DARDURA: A trifle.

MĀTHURA (*pulling the cloak from under Dardura's arm*): Folks, look! The man who wears such rags calls ten gold pieces a trifle!

DARDURA: Bah, fool! Must a man who has money wear it by a rope around his neck to show it? Come on! Miserable, perishing brute, for ten gold pieces you murder a man who still has his five senses?

MĀTHURA: Gentlemen, ten gold pieces are a trifle to him, but for me it's a fortune.

DARDURA: If that's how you feel, listen. Stake him ten gold pieces and throw for it.

MĀTHURA: And then what?

DARDURA: If he wins, he pays you back.

MĀTHURA: And if he doesn't?

DARDURA: He won't pay.

MĀTHURA: Then there's no use talking. You said it, you do it. Sharp Māthura, that's me. I know how to cheat myself, and I am not afraid of cheats. Smarty, you stink!

DARDURA: Hey, who stinks?

MĀTHURA: You stink!

DARDURA: Your father stinks! (*He gives the Masseur a sign to run off.*)

MĀTHURA (*who notices it*): Bullpup, is that the way you play?

DARDURA: That's the way I play.

MĀTHURA: You there, pay the ten gold pieces.

MASSEUR: I'll pay today, I'll pay for sure! (*Māthura drags him along.*)

DARDURA: Brute, you can beat him up when my back is turned, but not while I am looking!

(*Māthura drags the Masseur through the dust and punches his nose. Bleeding, the Masseur goes down and acts as though he has lost consciousness. Dardura runs in and separates them. Māthura strikes Dardura and Dardura returns the blow.*)

MĀTHURA: Ouch, you dirty son of a bitch! Now you have it coming!

DARDURA: Brute, you have assaulted me in public! See if you want to assault me in court tomorrow.

MĀTHURA: I'll see all right!

DARDURA: You'll see how?

MĀTHURA (*opening his eyes wide*): That's how! (*Dardura throws dirt in Māthura's eyes and gives the Masseur a sign to get away. Māthura falls to the ground, with eyes closed. The Masseur runs off.*)

DARDURA (*to himself*): Now I have made an enemy of the biggest games master of the city. It is not safe to stay. I am going to Prince Āryaka. My good friend Śarvilaka told me that a soothsayer has predicted that Prince Āryaka, son of the late King Gopāla, will be king. And all people of my kind have chosen his side. Yes, I'll join him too. (*Exit.*)

MASSEUR (*walks around, trembling; he looks up*): There is a house with the side door open. Whoever owns it, I'll go in! (*He enters and sees Vasantasenā.*) My lady, protect me!

VASANTASENĀ: No one has anything to fear who asks my protection. Close the door, Madanikā. (*The girl does as she is told.*) Who is threatening you?

MASSEUR: A creditor, ma'am.

VASANTASENĀ: You may open the door again now, girl.

MASSEUR (*to himself*): Yes, why should she think that there'd be anything to fear from a creditor?

For he who knows his strength
And takes what he can carry
May journey through the jungle,
He'll never stumble and die.

MĀTHURA (*rubbing his eyes, to the Gambler*): Hey you, pay up!

GAMBLER: While we were fighting with Dardura, the fellow ran off.

MĀTHURA: I broke his nose. Come on, we'll follow the blood trail. (*They follow the trail.*)

GAMBLER: He has gone into Vasantasenā's place!

MĀTHURA: Then I'll never see my money again!

GAMBLER: We'll report it to the court.

MĀTHURA: And meanwhile the crook will come out and disappear. No, we'll block the door and catch him.

Vasantasenā signals to Madanikā.

MADANIKĀ: Where are you from, sir? Who are you? Whose son are you? What is your occupation and why are you afraid?

MASSEUR: Please listen, ma'am. I was born in Pāṭaliputra, the son of a craftsman, and I make my living as a masseur.

VASANTASENĀ: That is a very delicate art you have mastered, sir.

MASSEUR: That is why I mastered it, because it was an art. But now it is only a living.

VASANTASENĀ: You sound very sad, my good sir. Please go on.

MASSEUR: Yes, ma'am. When I was still at home the stories of travelers made me curious to see strange lands and I journeyed to this country. I came to Ujjayinī and here I have served only one master—a rare one, handsome and gentle-spoken, who did not boast of what he gave to others and forgot whatever ill others did to him. In a word, he was so big-hearted that he looked on others as himself and always received with love whoever needed his help.

MADANIKĀ: But who is this splendid ornament of our city, who seems to have robbed her ladyship's lover of his virtues?

VASANTASENĀ: Well-spoken, my dear. My heart asks the same question!

MADANIKĀ: Please go on, sir.

MASSEUR: Ma'am, at present the liberal gifts which his sympathies prompted—

VASANTASENĀ: Have exhausted his fortune?

MASSEUR: How did you know before I told you, my lady?

VASANTASENĀ: It does not take much guessing. Virtue and riches rarely go together. The fullest wells are least drinkable.

MADANIKĀ: But what is his name, sir?

MASSEUR: But who does not know the name of this moon on earth? He lives on the Square of the Provosts. And he is called Master Cārudatta, whose name be blessed.

VASANTASENĀ (*coming down to him from her seat in great joy*): This house is yours, sir! Give him a seat, my dear, and wave a fan. The gentleman is suffering from fatigue!

MASSEUR: What treatment, just because I mentioned Cārudatta! Thank you, Master Cārudatta. You are the only man alive on earth, all the others just breathe! (*Dropping at Vasantasenā's feet.*) Please, please, ma'am. Do sit down again.

VASANTASENĀ (*resuming her seat*): Where is your creditor, who must be a rich man?

MASSEUR:

> But who cannot be rich? Wealth comes and goes.
> Only a good man owns a rich respect.
> If one does not know how to pay respect,
> Is it true riches that he owns, or knows?

VASANTASENĀ: Go on.

MASSEUR: So I entered the gentleman's service, as his masseur. When only nobility remained of his fortune, I made gambling my living. Luck ran against me and I lost ten gold pieces.

MĀTHURA: I am robbed! I am ruined!

MASSEUR: The games master and a gambler are after me now. You have heard all, and I leave it to you to judge.

VASANTASENĀ: When the tree is shaking, Madanikā, the birds that built their nests in it are scattered. Go, my girl, and give the games master and the gambler this bracelet; tell them that this gentleman has sent it.
MADANIKĀ (*taking it*): As you wish, my lady. (*She leaves.*)

MĀTHURA: I am robbed, I am ruined!

MADANIKĀ: Two men who are raising their eyes to heaven, sighing pitifully, and watching the door while they are talking—I take it that they are the games master and the gambler. (*She approaches them.*) Good day, sir.
MĀTHURA: And a good day to you.
MADANIKĀ: Sir, who of you is the games master?
MĀTHURA:

To whom, girl with the curving hips,
With the eye that roves so instructively,
And those meretricious love-marked lips,
Are you talking so seductively?

I have no money! Find someone else.
MADANIKĀ: Anybody who dares say such things must be a gambler! Does anyone owe you a debt?
MĀTHURA: Yes indeed! Ten gold pieces. What about him?
MADANIKĀ: My lady sends this bracelet to settle—No, no! He sends it himself!
MĀTHURA (*taking it eagerly*): Ha, you may tell the gentleman that his debt is wiped out. Let him come and enjoy another game! (*Exeunt.*)

MADANIKĀ (*returning to Vasantasenā*): The games master and the gambler have gone, they are completely satisfied.
VASANTASENĀ: Then go, sir, and reassure your family.
MASSEUR: Please, my lady, let me teach my art to the hands of your servants!
VASANTASENĀ: Rather go and, as you did before, serve the gentleman for whom you learnt your art.
MASSEUR (*to himself*): She has put me nicely in my place! But how can I repay her now? (*Aloud.*) Ma'am, those gamblers' insults move me to become a Buddhist monk. Remember the text: "The Masseur who was a Gambler turned a Friar!"
VASANTASENĀ: Please, sir, do not act rashly!
MASSEUR: My lady, my mind is made up! (*He strides about.*)

Now I have done with gambling
Which everybody hates,
And baldly I'll be rambling
With all the highway greats.

(*Confused noise offstage.*)

MASSEUR (*listening*): Hey, what is going on! (*As though addressing someone.*) What do you say? There's a mad elephant running loose, Vasantasenā's Shatter-Post? Aho! I'll gaze upon the rutting brute. I'll be a Buddha yet![18] (*Exit.*)

Enter abruptly through the curtain Karṇapūraka,[19] beaming and happy.

KARṆAPŪRAKA: Where's my lady, where is she!

MADANIKĀ: Hooligan! What are you so excited about? Can't you see her right in front of you?

KARṆAPŪRAKA (*looking*): Ma'am, I greet you.

VASANTASENĀ: Karṇapūraka, you look very pleased with yourself. What has happened?

KARṆAPŪRAKA (*with pride*): Ma'am, if you did not see Karṇapūraka's heroic act just now, you missed something!

VASANTASENĀ: What *is* the matter, Karṇapūraka?

KARṆAPŪRAKA: Listen, ma'am. Your elephant, the mean one, Shatter-Post, broke off the pillar he was chained to, killed the mahout, and bore down on the highway, creating an uproar. People shouting everywhere!

Save the children! Up the roofs! Climb a tree!
Hurry! Don't you see? A crazy elephant running free!

Anklets flying and people tripping,
The gaudiest gem-studded girdles ripping,
And starbursts of glamorous bracelets slipping!

That wild beast plunged into Ujjayinī as though it were his private lotus pond, splashing about with trunk, feet, and tusks! Until he came upon a wandering friar. The man dropped his staff, pot, and bowl, but the elephant squirted water over him and spooned him up with his tusks. And people screeching again! "Aah! He's killing a friar!"

VASANTASENĀ (*anxiously*): Oh, our carelessness!

KARṆAPŪRAKA: Don't you worry, ma'am, I was there. When I saw the animal dragging along a bunch of broken, shattered chains, carrying along a friar caught between his tusks, I, Karṇapūraka—no, this poor slave you feed on rice balls—wiped out an old gambler's debt with my left foot, snatched an iron bar from a market stand, and challenged the savage beast.

VASANTASENĀ: What then?

KARṆAPŪRAKA: Like the Vindhya Mountains[20] he towered over me, but I attacked the furious animal and hauled the friar from between his tusks.

VASANTASENĀ: You acted splendidly! And then?

KARṆAPŪRAKA: All the gentlemen could do was shout: "Bravo, Karṇapūraka, bravo!" And Ujjayinī was so full that it was tipping over like a boat that is loaded to the side. Then one gentleman felt the places where he would wear his jewels, found them empty, sighed deeply, and threw his cloak over me.

VASANTASENĀ: Karṇapūraka, find out whether that cloak is scented with jasmine!

KARṆAPŪRAKA: I can't recognize any smell with that rutting elephant's smell about me.

VASANTASENĀ: Look if there is a name on it.

KARṆAPŪRAKA: Yes, there is, You must read the name, my lady.[21] (*He holds out the cloak to her.*)

VASANTASENĀ (*reading*): "Master Cārudatta's." (*She seizes the cloak eagerly and wraps herself in it.*)

MADANIKĀ: It looks well on madam, doesn't it, Karṇapūraka.

KARṆAPŪRAKA: Yes, it looks well on madam.

VASANTASENĀ: Here is your reward, Karṇapūraka. (*She hands him a gem.*)

KARṆAPŪRAKA: Now it looks much better on madam! (*He receives the gem on his hands folded at his head and bows.*)

VASANTASENĀ: Karṇapūraka, where is Master Cārudatta now?

KARṆAPŪRAKA: Still in the street, he was about to go home.

VASANTASENĀ: Come, my dear girl, we'll go upstairs to the roof terrace and watch him pass.

ACT THREE

Enter Vardhamāna.

VARDHAMĀNA:

> A good man, kind to his servants,
> Stays a good master, poor though he be—
> A mean man, proud of his riches,
> Gets meaner and ends with cruelty.
>
> The bull that wants to graze on grain will not be stayed,
> The wife that loves another man will not be prayed,
> The gambler yearning for the game won't be delayed,
> The vice instinct in character will not be swayed.

Master Cārudatta went out a long while ago to hear a concert. Half the night is gone and still he has not come back. I'll take a nap meanwhile on the porch. (*He does so.*)

Enter Cārudatta and Maitreya.

CĀRUDATTA: Ah, Rebhila sang splendidly, splendidly! Yes, the vīṇā is the pearl that did not grow in the sea.

> To loving hearts a friend of deep compassion,
> Welcome distraction to anticipation,
> Soothing the pains that come with separation,
> Delight that heightens still a lover's passion. . . .

MAITREYA: Hey, come on! Let's go home!

CĀRUDATTA: Ah, splendidly indeed did Rebhila sing.

MAITREYA: Me, two things always make me laugh, a woman speaking Sanskrit and a man wailing a song. A woman trying to speak Sanskrit puffs like a milch cow that has her first nose ring, and a man wailing a song sounds like an ancient priest hung with faded garlands who chants the Veda. I positively did not like it!

CĀRUDATTA: Friend, Rebhila did sing splendidly today. And still you are not satisfied? Tender, and sweet, and clear was his voice, filled with emotion, and gay, and enchanting. . . . But why must I look for many compliments? In a word, I wondered if there was not a woman hidden—

> The concert's over now, but as I go I hear
> A voice most sweetly modulated; strings,
> Closely embracing it, ring through the melody
> And whisper languidly with the exhausted voice,
> To rise once more to twice-impassioned swell. . . .

MAITREYA: Why, friend, even the dogs are quietly asleep in the street between the market stands. Let us go home now! (*Looking ahead.*) Look! Our Lord the Moon has graciously made room for the darkness and come down the stairway from the terrace of the sky!

CĀRUDATTA: Yes, it is true.

> Moon leaves the heavens to the night
> And sets, with its twin horns upraised:
> Wild elephant, immersed in mud,
> But its twin tusks gleaming above.

MAITREYA: Ha, here we are home. Vardhamāna, Vardhamāna! Open up!

VARDHAMĀNA: I hear Master Maitreya's voice. Master Cārudatta is back. I'll open the door for him. (*He does so.*) I greet you, Master. And you too, Maitreya. Please sit down, the beds are made. (*Both sit down.*)

MAITREYA: Vardhamāna, call Radanikā to wash our feet.

CĀRUDATTA (*thoughtfully*): We should not wake her if she is asleep.

VARDHAMĀNA: Master Maitreya, I'll fetch the water, you wash his feet.

MAITREYA (*insulted*): What! This son of a slave girl is going to get the water, and I, a Brahmin, am to wash your feet?

CĀRUDATTA: Maitreya, my good friend, you fetch the water and Vardhamāna will wash my feet.

VARDHAMĀNA: Master Maitreya, the water, please!

(*Maitreya fetches the water. Vardhamāna washes Cārudatta's feet and walks away.*)

CĀRUDATTA: Give the Brahmin water to wash his feet.

MAITREYA: Water to wash my feet? I will have to kick around in the dirt anyway like a whipped donkey!

VARDHAMĀNA: But you are a Brahmin, Master Maitreya![22]

MAITREYA: I am a Brahmin like a grass snake is a cobra!

VARDHAMĀNA: Still I shall wash your feet, Master Maitreya. (*He does.*) Master Maitreya, I was to keep that golden box by day and you, by night. Here it is. (*He gives it and makes his exit.*)

MAITREYA (*taking it*): Is it still here? Aren't there any burglars in Ujjayinī to take this whoreson robber of my sleep? Friend, I am going to leave it inside.

CĀRUDATTA: No, you shall not leave it inside. A courtesan carried it on her person and so will you, Brahmin, until we have returned it. (*He is about to doze off and murmurs the stanza* "The concert's over now . . .")

MAITREYA: Are you sleepy?

CĀRUDATTA: Yes,

> Sleep, creeping from my forehead, furtively,
> Now seems to rest upon my eyes,
> Like age, invisibly to rise
> And grow by feeding on man's energy.

MAITREYA: Let us sleep then. (*He falls asleep.*)

Enter Śarvilaka.

ŚARVILAKA: Erudition and energy opened a hole that allowed easy ingress, and thereby the way to easy success! And now I crawl through, groveling in the gravel like a snake wriggling out of its old skin. (*He studies the sky; pleased.*) Ha! The moon is down. And Night, obscuring the Stars behind a Veil of Clouds, covers like a mother the world's greatest Hero whose nocturnal sallies, when he is bent on the Plunder of his Neighbors, moves the King's Constabulary to panic! Now I have breached the garden fence, and lo! I am in the middle grounds. There remains the house itself now to be violated. Onward! Let people decry our handiwork that flourishes during sleep, let them protest that a confidence trickster is a robber, not a clobber—but if we have a bad name, at least, it is better to be free than to kneel to a Master; and besides, Aśvatthāman has set the example by the Massacre of the Sleeping Kings.[23]

Now in what precise location do I make the breach? Where is the wall weakened by seeping water? Where will the noise go unheard? Where do I risk no gaping holes that demand to be noticed? Where is the mansion's clay emaciated by the corroding effect of saltpeter?[24]

Where may I avoid casting my gaze upon womenfolk? There indeed shall lie my success. (*He feels the wall.*) Here the ground is eaten away by perpetual exposure to the sun and the leaking of water—and also corroded by saltpeter. And a mousehole! To be sure, success is mine! This is the first sign of a burglar's success. First stage: I must now create a hole. But what kind of hole? The Lord of the Golden Lance[25] has addressed himself to this problem and suggests four methods, to wit: baked bricks are to be pried out, unbaked bricks are to be broken, clay elements are to be watered, wooden elements are to be hacked. Here we have an instance of baked bricks—the bricks are to be pried out. Next point: the nature of the hole. Lotus Cup? Sun-shaped? Crescent? Oval? Cross? Conic Pitcher? What spot is most suitable to exhibit my craftmanship and astonish on the morrow the staring citizenry? It is a baked-brick wall, therefore the Conic Pitcher looks best. Which I now create. Indeed, on all occasions when I opened at night walls that had been affected by saltpeter and embarked on difficultuous operations, the neighbors would congregate in the morning to discuss my craftmanship, noting errors as well as marking dexterity. (*He prays.*)

I bow to thee, Granter of Wishes, Kumāra Kārttikeya!
I bow to thee, God of the Golden Lance, Subrahmaṇya,
That art vowed to the Gods,
I bow to thee, Son of the Sun!
I bow to thee, Master of Magic whose first pupil I am!

The God has graciously granted my prayer and given me the Unguent of Invisibility! When I have applied it, the constables will not detect me, and swords, if they strike me, will not hurt me. (*He rubs himself with an ointment.*) Oh bother, I forgot my measuring tape! (*He thinks.*) No matter, my Brahmin's thread will replace it. Indeed a Brahmin's thread is a tool of many uses for a Brahmin, especially for one like me. If one makes a professional hole in the wall, one can use it to measure with. If one wants to lift a jewel off a body, one can use it as a lasso. If one wants to open a bolted gate, one can use it to pull the bolt. If one's bitten by an insect or a snake, one can use it as a tourniquet.—Now to measure and on with the work! (*He starts working and stops to study his progress.*) One more brick and the opening is made. Ouch, a snake has bitten me! (*He ties his Brahmin's thread around his finger and shows signs of severe pain. He applies some salve.*) I am well again. (*He finishes the hole and looks through.*) Ah, there's a lamp burning.

The flame traces a golden line,
Piercing the hole, onto the ground:
Slight beam amid the dark around,
As on a touchstone a golden shine.

(*He continues working.*) The hole is finished. Good. I'll enter now. Or rather I will not enter, but introduce my dummy.[26] (*So he does.*) Fine, nobody. Thank you, Kārttikeya! (*He enters and looks about.*) Ah, two men sleeping. Very good, I'll open the door just in case, so that I can save myself.—Why, the house is so old that the door squeaks. I shall have to get water. Now where do I find water? (*He looks right and left, finds water, and pours it over the door with great care.*) I must not let the water splash on the floor. So far so good. Now I must see if they are really sleeping or just pretending. (*He tickles them and watches for reactions.*) Splendid, they must be really asleep. Their breathing is unsuspecting, it is very clear and rhythmic. The eyes are shut tightly, both of them, and no movements behind the lids. The joints of the body are relaxed and stray limbs stick out of the bed. And no one will bear light in his face unless he is sleeping. (*He reconnoiters the surroundings.*) Ah, a drum? And a flute. And a tambourine. And here is a vīṇā too! And reeds. Books over there. Have I broken into the house of a music and dance teacher? But I came to burgle because I had the impression it was a *decent* home! Now, is he really so poor, or does he keep his treasures buried, not to have them taxed or stolen? Anything buried is mine! Very well, I'll throw some witching grain around. (*He does so.*) The seed is sown, but nothing shows up. He is really poor. All right, I'm off.

MAITREYA (*half waking*): Cārudatta, it looks as if there's a hole in the wall, there may be a thief. You take the gold box now.

ŚARVILAKA: What! He has seen me enter, and now he is mocking me, because he is too poor to be robbed! Shall I kill him off? Or does he only sleep lightly and talk in his sleep? (*He watches him.*) Oho, there really is a jewel box, wrapped in a ragged bath towel, glittering in the light of the lamp. I'll have it. Still, it is not a very honorable thing to do, robbing a well-born man as poor as I am. No, I'm off.

MAITREYA: For the love of the cow and the Brahmin! Take this gold box off my hands or be damned!

ŚARVILAKA: Well, the love of the cow and the love of the Brahmin I cannot sin against. I'll take it. But the lamp is burning still. Here I have got a fire-loving moth, big enough to blow out the flame. Time and place are perfect. I am letting it go now. Go, moth, and circle over the lamp in your artful way! There, it is blown out by the wind of its wings, and darkness is contrived by the kindly moth. But have not I contrived darkness—in my Brahmin family? I, the son of a scholar of all four Vedas, who would not accept any fees—I, Śarvilaka, have stooped to crime to gain the favors of the harlot Madanikā. But now I will do this Brahmin the favor for which he asks.

MAITREYA: You have cold fingers, friend.

ŚARVILAKA: Oh bother my carelessness! My fingers are still cold from touching the water. I'll warm them in my armpit.

(*He warms his left hand and takes the box.*)

MAITREYA: You have it?

ŚARVILAKA: A Brahmin's wish is a command. I have it.

MAITREYA: Now like the merchant who's sold out I can sleep in peace.

ŚARVILAKA: Great Brahmin, sleep for a hundred years. Alas, that a Brahmin family should be cast into darkness because of a harlot . . . But it is I who have been cast out. A curse on poverty whose powers are inscrutable: for I perform the evil deed while I decry it. Now it remains for me to go to Vasantasenā's house and buy Madanikā's freedom. (*He walks around; looks.*) Aho! That sounds like footsteps. Oh please, no constables! Very well, I'll stand like a pillar. But what are constables to a man like me? I climb like a cat, run like a deer, grab like a vulture, guess a man's strength, asleep or awake, like a dog, crawl like a snake, disguise myself like Māyā,[27] speak as many tongues as Speech, light the dark like a lamp, slip from a pinch like a lizard, a horse on land and a ship at sea! Fast as a snake, stable as a mountain, keen-eyed as an eagle, terrain-sure as a hare, thievish as a wolf, strong as a lion!

Enter Radanikā.

RADANIKĀ: What is going on? Vardhamāna was sleeping on the porch, but now he is nowhere to be seen. Well, I shall have to call Master Maitreya. (*She walks about.*)

ŚARVILAKA (*about to strike down Radanikā, checking himself when he looks more closely*): What, a woman! Then I'll go.[28] (*Exit.*)

RADANIKĀ (*continuing to walk, with terror*): Oh, what is going on! A thief has broken into our house! I must awake Maitreya! (*She approaches Maitreya.*) Master Maitreya, get up, get up! The house has been burgled and the burglar is escaping!

MAITREYA (*rising from his sleep*): What are you talking about, my little slave? The house is escaping and the burglar is burgled?

RADANIKĀ: Stop joking, you wretch! Can't you see for yourself?

MAITREYA: What are you talking about? It looks as if the house has a new door! Friend Cārudatta, get up, get up! The house has been burgled and the thief is escaping!

CĀRUDATTA: Now please stop joking!

MAITREYA: I am not joking! Look for yourself.

CĀRUDATTA: Where?

MAITREYA: There!

CĀRUDATTA (*studying it*): What an elegant hole!

> The bricks are neatly stacked and put aside—
> The hole, wide-waisted, to the head grows thinner. . . .
> It is as though from fear to touch a sinner
> This noble mansion broke its heart and died!

Indeed, even in crime there can be artistry.

MAITREYA: The burglar must be one of two people: a stranger to town, or someone training for burglary. For who in all of Ujjayinī does not know what riches your house no longer holds?

CĀRUDATTA: It must have been a foreigner who has been practicing his craft on my house, not knowing that inside people slept the confident sleep of the poor. And after the great expectations at seeing a house so grand in design, he had at last, exhausted by the labor of his breaking, to leave with no more hope left. . . . What is the poor man to tell his friends? I entered the house of a provost's son and came out empty-handed?

MAITREYA: Hey, you are not sorry for that damn thief, are you? What he thought was: this is a fine house, I'll carry a jewel box or a gold box away with me! (*When a memory strikes him, in panic to himself.*) Where is the gold box? (*Remembering the rest, aloud.*) Friend, all the time you say: Maitreya is a fool, Maitreya is no genius. But it was a good idea, wasn't it, for me to give you the gold box, else that whoreson would have made off with it.

CĀRUDATTA: Don't joke now!

MAITREYA: Well, I may be a fool, but not such a fool that I don't know the times and places for jokes.

CĀRUDATTA: When was that?

MAITREYA: Just as I told you that your fingers were cold.

CĀRUDATTA: So it could be true! (*He looks around to search, then, with pleasure.*) Maitreya, I have good news for you.

MAITREYA: It is not stolen?

CĀRUDATTA: It is!

MAITREYA: What is the good news?

CĀRUDATTA: That he did, after all, leave contented.

MAITREYA: But it was a trust!

CĀRUDATTA: Oh, a trust! (*He collapses.*)

MAITREYA: Please be calm, sir! Why must you swoon because a robber makes off with a trust?

CĀRUDATTA (*coming to*): Who will believe the truth? Everybody will suspect me. For in the world poverty has no dignity and excites suspicion. Oh, disaster! If fate has so far shown its favor to my wealth, why must it now also cruelly sully my honor?

MAITREYA: I would just deny everything. Who has been given what? Who has taken it? Any witnesses?

CĀRUDATTA: Must I now also lie? I'd rather beg so as to find the money to repay the trust! But I shall not lose my honor and lie!

RADANIKĀ: I must tell master's wife. (*Exit.*)

Enter Cārudatta's wife with Radanikā.

WIFE (*anxiously*): But my gentle husband is really unharmed? And Master Maitreya too?

RADANIKĀ: Yes, ma'am. But the courtesan's jewelry has been stolen.

Wife faints.

RADANIKĀ: Please madam, be calm!

WIFE (*coming to*): Why do you say that my gentle husband is unharmed? It were better if he had been harmed in his life than in his honor! Now all the people of Ujjayinī will say that poverty drove the honorable Cārudatta to a dishonorable deed. Destiny, great God, you play with the fortunes of the poor and they tremble like water drops on lotus petals. This pearl necklace is all I have left, I received it from my mother's family. But even this my husband's great pride will not permit him to accept. Girl, call Master Maitreya!

RADANIKĀ: As it pleases you, madam. (*She approaches Maitreya.*) Master Maitreya, madam is calling you.
MAITREYA: Where is she?
RADANIKĀ: In here. Go and see her.
MAITREYA (*approaching the wife*): Good day, madam.
WIFE: Good day, sir. Please face me, sir.
MAITREYA: I am facing you now, madam.
WIFE: Accept this gift, sir.
MAITREYA: What is this?
WIFE: I am holding a fast, the Fast of the Pearls. It is prescribed that a suitable gift, commensurate with one's wealth, be donated to a Brahmin, and that he does not keep it to himself. Therefore please accept these pearls for the sake of my fast.
MAITREYA (*accepting*): I thank you. I shall go and give it to my good friend.
WIFE: Master Maitreya, please save me from embarrassment. (*Exit.*)
MAITREYA (*astonished*): Ah, what dignity!
CĀRUDATTA: Maitreya is long. I hope he is not doing something wrong in his confusion. . . . Maitreya! Maitreya!
MAITREYA (*approaching*): Here I am. Take this. (*He holds out the pearl necklace.*)
CĀRUDATTA: What is this?
MAITREYA: The reward of marrying within your station. . . .
CĀRUDATTA: What? My Brahmin wife has taken pity on me! Alas, now I am really poor. (*Thoughtfully.*) If a man by his own ill-luck has dissipated his wealth and lies at the mercy of his wife's, the woman is the man and the man a woman. . . . But no, I am not poor—I have a wife to follow my fortunes, in you a friend in happiness and sorrow, and, rare thing among the poor, my honor is not yet lost. (*Self-possessed.*) Maitreya, take this necklace and go to Vasantasenā. Tell her in my name that in all good faith I have mistaken her gold box for mine and lost it in a game of dice; she must accept this pearl necklace in its stead.
MAITREYA: Don't do it! Why trade a pearl necklace, choicest product of four oceans, for a worthless bauble we neither ate up nor wore out, that was simply stolen by a thief?
CĀRUDATTA: That is not the way to talk. She charged us with it because she trusted us, and I merely pay this as the price of her great trust. By the body that I touch, Maitreya, I conjure you not to return before

you have made her accept it! Vardhamāna! Repair that hole with the same bricks. I must protect the constables whose errors always evoke much slander. Maitreya, my friend, you will speak not with humility but with pride!

MAITREYA: How can a pauper speak without humility?

CĀRUDATTA: I am no pauper, for I have a wife to follow my fortunes, in you a friend in happiness and sorrow, and, rare thing among the poor, my honor is not yet lost. Go now. I'll bathe and worship the dawn.

ACT FOUR

Enter a Slave Girl.

SLAVE GIRL: Her mother told me to find the mistress. There she is now, talking with Madanikā and throwing glances at a portrait. I'll go to her. (*She circles the stage.*)

Enter Vasantasenā with Madanikā as described.

VASANTASENĀ: Madanikā dear, isn't this portrait of Cārudatta an excellent likeness?

MADANIKĀ: Yes, excellent, my lady.

VASANTASENĀ: How do you know?

MADANIKĀ: By the loving glances you give it, my lady.

VASANTASENĀ: Ah, my dear, isn't this the ever complimentary courtesan who speaks?

MADANIKĀ: Ma'am, is a courtesan's compliment necessarily a lie?

VASANTASENĀ: Friendship with so many kinds of men, dear girl, makes a courtesan adept at lying.

MADANIKĀ: When your eye is in love with it and your heart, why do you ask for reasons?

VASANTASENĀ: To save myself the mockery of my friends.

MADANIKĀ: No fear of that, my lady. For women feel with the hearts of their friends.

SLAVE GIRL (*drawing near*): Ma'am, your mother sends word that a curtained coach is waiting at the side door; you must go.

VASANTASENĀ: Who has sent it, girl? Cārudatta?

SLAVE GIRL: Who would send jewels worth ten thousand gold pieces by coach. . . .

VASANTASENĀ: Who is it?

SLAVE GIRL: . . . but the king's brother-in-law, Saṃsthānaka himself?

VASANTASENĀ: Get out! (*Angrily.*) Never talk to me like that again!

SLAVE GIRL: Please, ma'am, please! I am just carrying a message.

VASANTASENĀ: It is the message I mind.

SLAVE GIRL: What shall I tell your mother then?

VASANTASENĀ: Tell her that if she wants me to live she must never send me such orders again!

SLAVE GIRL: As you think best. (*Exit.*)

Enter Śarvilaka.

ŚARVILAKA:

> To disrepute I have brought the night
> As I conquered sleep and the king's platoon,
> And fading in the sun's young light
> When the night is ruined, I am the moon.

Yea,

> Whoever glances at me when he hurries by,
> Or, as I stiffen, quickly encounters me,
> In my wicked soul I suspect them all,
> For your own crimes make you suspicious.

And I have committed a crime because of Madanikā.

When I heard a man talking to his servant, I passed his house by. And if anywhere in a house a woman was in charge, I avoided it. If the king's platoon came on from the side, I stood stiff like a doorpost, and with a hundred tricks like that I made a day of the night. (*He circles the stage.*)

VASANTASENĀ: Madanikā dear, will you put the portrait on my bed and fetch the fan? Come back quickly.

MADANIKĀ: Yes, my lady. (*She takes the portrait and makes her exit.*)

ŚARVILAKA: Here is Vasantasenā's house. I'll enter. (*He enters.*) Now where do I find Madanikā?

Re-enter Madanikā with the fan in her hand.

ŚARVILAKA (*seeing her*): Ah, there is Madanikā!

> Like Lust embodied does she strive above
> The lesser virtue of the God of Love,
> And as with sandal scents she bids depart
> The fiery pangs of this love-kindled heart!

Oh, Madanikā!

MADANIKĀ (*seeing him*): Oh, Mother, it's Śarvilaka! Śarvilaka, welcome! Where have you been?

ŚARVILAKA: I shall tell you.

(*They stare at each other, lovingly.*)

VASANTASENĀ: Madanikā is long coming back. Now where can she be? (*She looks through a round window.*) There she is, talking with a man! And with such loving eyes does she stare at him and study him silently —as though she is drinking in his presence—that I am sure he is the man who wants to set her free. Let her enjoy herself! I won't call her, I must not disturb her happiness.

MADANIKĀ: Tell me, Śarvilaka!
Śarvilaka looks about with fearful glances.
MADANIKĀ: What is the matter, Śarvilaka? Are you afraid of something?
ŚARVILAKA: Yes, I will tell you. But it is a secret. Are we alone?
MADANIKĀ: But of course!

VASANTASENĀ: Ah, a deep secret! I must not listen further.

ŚARVILAKA: Madanikā, will Vasantasenā release you, for a price?

VASANTASENĀ: He is talking about me! Then I shall listen, at this window, so he won't see me.

MADANIKĀ: Madame has promised me, Śarvilaka. She said, if she could act on her own, she would set all the slaves free, without any ransom.[29] But do you have enough money to buy me free from my mistress?
ŚARVILAKA: Darling, assailed by poverty and pursued by love I did a crime tonight.

VASANTASENĀ: And still his face is impassive! Wouldn't the cruelty show if he *had* committed a crime?

MADANIKĀ: For my sake alone you have jeopardized two things, Śarvilaka!
ŚARVILAKA: What two things?
MADANIKĀ: Your life and your honor!
ŚARVILAKA: Wealth is the neighbor of crime, my foolish girl.
MADANIKĀ: But you are an honest man, Śarvilaka! So if you did commit a crime for my sake, you cannot have gone completely against your character.
ŚARVILAKA: No, I did not pluck a jewel from a woman as one plucks a blossom from a vine. Nor did I rob a Brahmin or steal the gold reserved for a sacrifice. I did not snatch a child from the lap of its nurse for ransom money. Even if my mind is bent on theft, it still knows how to judge what is seemly! Now go and tell Vasantasenā to accept

this jewelry, which might have been fashioned with herself in mind, but not to show it in public.

MADANIKĀ: Jewelry that must not be shown, Śarvilaka, and she a courtesan? Two things that never will agree! But give it to me, I want to look at it.

ŚARVILAKA (*handing it over, circumspectly*): This is it.

MADANIKĀ (*studying it*): I believe I have seen it before. . . . Tell me, where did you get this, Śarvilaka?

ŚARVILAKA: What does it matter to you? Take it!

MADANIKĀ (*angrily*): If you don't trust me, why do you want to buy me free?

ŚARVILAKA: All right, then. If I may judge by what I heard in the Square of the Provosts this morning, it must have been at Merchant Cārudatta's.

(*Vasantasenā and Madanikā are both suddenly taken faint.*)

ŚARVILAKA: Madanikā, calm down! Here I am freeing you from dire slavery, and there you are trembling, your whole body limp with despair and your eyes wild with worry, trembling, but not for me!

MADANIKĀ (*coming to herself*): Cutthroat! When you were committing your crimes for me, did you kill, did you hurt anybody there?

ŚARVILAKA: Madanikā, a Śarvilaka does not hit a man who is afraid or asleep! I did not kill anybody, nobody got hurt.

MADANIKĀ: No, on your word?

ŚARVILAKA: No, on my word!

VASANTASENĀ (*regaining consciousness*): Oh, my heart, I have been brought back to life again!

MADANIKĀ: Oh, dear!

ŚARVILAKA (*suddenly jealous*): What "dear"?

> My heart was trapped by love, and I,
> A son of virtuous family,
> Committed theft—but still I try,
> Even if love kills honesty,
> To save my pride, while you just ran,
> Calling my darling, to another man!

(*Emphatically.*)

> The sons of noble parents are the trees
> Whose fruits are all that they have left;
> But once the whores like birds have made their nest—

Gone are the fruits, and they're bereft.
Love is a blazing fire with tongues of lust
That feed on favors, and in truth
Once that a man falls into it he burns
And with him burn his wealth and youth!

VASANTASENĀ (*smiling*): Aho! What excitement, and so unjustified!

ŚARVILAKA: I think a man must be a fool to put his trust in luck or a woman, for both go their own snaky little ways!

"Never fall in love with a girl,
If you love her, she'll be boss.
If she loves you, give her a whirl,
And if she doesn't, give her a toss!"

Quite right they are when they say:

"They laugh, they cry, but gain they must.
They make you trust them, but never trust.
If you're born high and aim still higher,
Shun them like flowers by a burning pyre!"

And

"Their faith is as firm as the waves of the sea,
Their love is as lasting as evening light.
As soon as their men have been bled quite white,
They're dropped like squeezed lacquer, and the girls run free."

Yes, women are wantons!

"There is one of whom their hearts are dreaming,
Another for whom their eyes are screaming,
A third man will make them moist with craving
As with a fourth they are lying raving!"

Someone said it, and he said it well:

"On a mountain top not a lotus will blow,
A horseload can by no donkey be borne,
Where barley is sown, no rice shall grow,
No woman is pure that is brothel-born."

(*Suddenly jealous.*) Ah, a curse on you, Cārudatta, you fiend! You are through! (*He walks a couple of paces.*)

MADANIKĀ (*holding him by the hem of his robe*): Oh, you are talking nonsense! You get angry about the most improbable things!
ŚARVILAKA: So what is improbable about this?
MADANIKĀ: Now these jewels, they were in Master Cārudatta's possession, weren't they?
ŚARVILAKA: So?
MADANIKĀ: They were left in trust with him!
ŚARVILAKA: In trust? Why?
MADANIKĀ (*speaks in his ear; alone*): That is why.
ŚARVILAKA (*put out*): Oh what an unfortunate thing! The very branch to which I clung for shade in the heat of summer I have plundered of its leaves without knowing it!

VASANTASENĀ: What? He is really sorry. Then he must have done what he did without knowing who it was.

ŚARVILAKA: Madanikā, what should I do now?
MADANIKĀ: But you are the one to know!
ŚARVILAKA: Don't say that. Look, wisdom comes naturally to women, but men have to be taught with books.
MADANIKĀ: If you will listen to what I say, Śarvilaka, return the jewels to that noble-minded man.
ŚARVILAKA: And what if he reports me to the court?
MADANIKĀ: No heat comes from the moon.

VASANTASENĀ: Well spoken, Madanikā!

ŚARVILAKA:

> Do I despair, am I afraid, of crime?
> Why must you tell me then how good he'll be?
> But yet, my infamy shames me this time. . . .
> What will the king devise for crooks like me?

But no, this would go against ordinary prudence. Think of another way.
MADANIKĀ: I know one other way.

VASANTASENĀ: What other way could there be?

MADANIKĀ: Return the jewels to Madame as though you were Cārudatta's servant.
ŚARVILAKA: And if I do?

MADANIKĀ: Then you won't be a thief, he won't owe her a debt, and she will have her jewels back.
ŚARVILAKA: Wouldn't it be too dangerous?
MADANIKĀ: Come, give it back, it will be too dangerous if you don't!

VASANTASENĀ: Bravo, Madanikā! That is spoken like a free woman!

ŚARVILAKA:

> I followed you, my love, and saw the light:
> How rare a guide is in a moonless night!

MADANIKĀ: Now wait a moment by this shrine of Kāma, while I tell Madame that you have come.
ŚARVILAKA: I will.
MADANIKĀ (*approaching Vasantasenā*): Here's a Brahmin come from Cārudatta, ma'am.
VASANTASENĀ: How do you know that he is his servant, dear?
MADANIKĀ: Wouldn't I know him? He is my own!
VASANTASENĀ (*to herself, shaking her head and smiling*): How right! (*Aloud.*) Let him enter.
MADANIKĀ: As you please, ma'am. (*Going back to Śarvilaka.*) You may go in, Śarvilaka.
ŚARVILAKA (*approaching, with embarrassment*): Luck be with you, my lady.
VASANTASENĀ: I greet you, sir. Please sit down.
ŚARVILAKA: The merchant sends you this message: "My house is too dilapidated to guard your treasure properly. Take it back." (*He hands the jewels to Madanikā, and rises to go.*)
VASANTASENĀ: I have an answer, sir, for you to carry back.
ŚARVILAKA (*to himself*): Who is going back? (*Aloud.*) What is your message?
VASANTASENĀ: Take Madanikā with you.
ŚARVILAKA: My lady, I fail to understand.
VASANTASENĀ: But I do.
ŚARVILAKA: But what do you mean?
VASANTASENĀ: Master Cārudatta asked me to give Madanikā to the man who would return these jewels. So be it well understood that it is he who has given her to you.
ŚARVILAKA (*to himself*): Ah, she has seen through me. (*Aloud.*) Well done, Cārudatta, well done!

> For on good deeds must people always set their mind:
> The rich and bad are more than matched by poor but kind!

If a man sets his mind on virtue,
There is nothing he may not dare:
For the moon by its excellent virtue
Lit on Śiva's forbidding hair![30]

VASANTASENĀ: Coachman!

(*Enter a servant with a carriage.*)

COACHMAN: The carriage is waiting, ma'am.

VASANTASENĀ: Madanikā, give me your look of luck. I have given you away to be married. Get into the carriage. Remember me.

MADANIKĀ (*weeping*): You have abandoned me![31] (*She falls at her feet.*)

VASANTASENĀ: You are now a lady who must be greeted. Go now, step into the carriage, and think of me.

ŚARVILAKA: Bless you, my lady. Madanikā, bestow the look of luck on her, and bow your head before one who has given you a rare gift, the name and the veil of a bride.

(*He gets into the carriage with Madanikā, and they start off.*)

VOICE OFFSTAGE: Is anybody there? The Heir announces that King Pālaka has taken Prince Āryaka, son of Gopāla,[32] from his village and thrown him in a ghastly dungeon, because he has become alarmed at news of the prediction that Āryaka will be king. Therefore, Gentlemen, keep prudently to your proper place in life!

ŚARVILAKA (*listening*): What? King Pālaka has imprisoned my good friend Āryaka! And I just got myself a wife. . . . Oh, what a disaster! . . . But no! There are two things a man loves most in life, his woman and his friend; but now, above a hundred beautiful women, I prefer my friend. Yes. I must get out. (*He gets out of the carriage.*)

MADANIKĀ (*in tears, folding her hands*): Yes, of course. . . . But first bring me to the house of honorable people, my husband.

ŚARVILAKA: Well spoken, my dear, well spoken, just as I hoped. (*To the coachman.*) Do you know the house of Merchant Rebhila, my man?

COACHMAN: Certainly.

ŚARVILAKA: Drive my dear lady there.

COACHMAN: As you order, sir.

MADANIKĀ: As you say, my husband. But please take care. (*Exit.*)

ŚARVILAKA: And now I shall fire the hearts of kinsmen, libertines, and soldiers of fortune, and of all those of the king's retainers who bear a grudge against their master, to rescue my friend as once Yaugandharāyaṇa rescued king Udayana![33] Indeed, I

> Shall save my friend who without cause was caught
> By evil enemies fearful of their own,
> And rush to pluck him forcefully from the jail
> Where he—moon caught in Rāhu's jaws—is thrown.

(*Exit.*)

Enter a Slave Girl.

SLAVE GIRL: Luck is with you today, ma'am. There's a Brahmin come from the noble Cārudatta.

VASANTASENĀ: Ah, my day is lucky indeed. Conduct him in, dear, with a bastard.

SLAVE GIRL: As you please, ma'am.

Enter Maitreya with a bastard.[34]

MAITREYA: Well, I never! The King of the Giants, Rāvaṇa himself, must travel in a flying chariot he has earned with the pains of self-mortification, but I, a mere Brahmin, who has not even tortured himself, travel with no less than a man and a woman!

SLAVE GIRL: Look, my lord, the gate of our house.

MAITREYA (*looking around with amazement*): Aho, the gate indeed. But the splendor of it! Sprinkled with water, brightly washed, salved with cowdung, there it stands, painted at the bottom with paintings that are devoutly worshiped with sweet-smelling flowers, and, at the top, stretching its head curiously to look into heaven. Waving garlands of jasmine, like the trunk of Airāvaṇa[35] swinging back and forth, adorn this gate which is splendid with a lofty arch of elephant's tusks and radiant with a bouquet of luck-bringing banners that, clad in the lustre of jeweled dyes, beckon me with playfully fluttering hands floating on the breeze to bid me: "This way, come!" Crystal pitchers, dotted with yellow mango shoots, are placed most decoratively at the base of the flanking columns that lift up the towering capitals, and between them the golden doors are set, thickly covered with diamonds, unbreachable like the chest of the mighty Asura. It must excite the passions of the poor! Indeed, one's glance cannot help being arrested, indifferent though one may be.[36]

SLAVE GIRL: This way, please. Here is the first court. Do enter, my lord.

MAITREYA (*entering and looking around*): Oh, wonder! A row of terraces, incandescent like the moon, or a conch shell, or the fiber of a lotus, as white as though handsful of fragrant powder had been scattered over it, and resplendent with golden steps encrusted with many-hued gems, seems to contemplate, from the full-moon faces of crystal windows from which pearl strings dangle like tear drops, the magnificence of Ujjayinī! The gatekeeper naps like a learned Brahmin who is sitting at ease. And the crows, lured by the sweet rice-gruel and curds, leave the proffered gift to the gods untouched because it looks white and pure as whitewash.[37] Show me the way, my lady!

SLAVE GIRL: This way, my lord. This is the second court, please enter.

MAITREYA (*entering and looking*): Another wonder! Here the draught bullocks are stabled, well fed on morsels of grass and chaff, their horns brightly oiled with sesamum oil. And there's a buffalo, sniffing like a well-bred person who is being slighted. And there a ram is having its neck massaged like a wrestler who just lost a match. All around they are combing the horses' manes, while a monkey is firmly tied up in their stable like a thief. (*Looking in another direction.*) And over there a couple of mahouts are feeding their elephant a mixture of boiled rice and oozing oil, kneaded into a ball. Show me the way, my lady!

SLAVE GIRL: This way, sir. Here is the third court. Please enter.

MAITREYA (*entering and looking*): More to come yet! Here the seats are made ready, to seat the well-born young gentlemen that visit this place! On this gaming table a book is lying open, half-read. There on the table the dice are waiting, genuine uncut precious stones. And there the courtesans, those expert diplomats of love's war and peace, stroll with aged libertines, showing them picture panels covered with all manner of scenes. Show me the way, my lady!

SLAVE GIRL: This way, please, my lord. We are now at the fourth court. Please enter.

MAITREYA (*entering and looking*): Oh, oh, oh! The drums are thundering like rain clouds under the hands of young women. Brass cymbals are falling like the stars that fall from heaven when their merit is exhausted, and the reed flute sighs sweetly like the humming of honey bees. There with a blow of the hand a vīṇā is made to run like a mistress enraged by her lover's jealous querulousness. And there the courtesans of the first degree, singing sweetly like honey bees drunk with the attar of flowers, are dancing, and plays are rehearsed, love plays all.

And in the round air lofts swinging water jars catch the wind. Show me farther, my lady!

SLAVE GIRL: This way, my lord. This is the fifth court, please enter.

MAITREYA (*entering and looking*): Ah, ah. The smell of resinous greens and cooking oil which excites a poor man's gluttony gets thicker and draws me on! The overheated kitchen seems to sigh through the mouths of its doors that fume with all kinds of delicious-smelling smoke. Oh, the sweet smell of all the many dishes that are being prepared only whets my appetite more! There's a handsome lad wringing out a cow's stomach like a piece of ragged cloth. The master cook is putting the finishing touch on a rich variety of dishes. Sweetmeats are put in forms, cakes are being baked. . . . (*To himself.*) Is anybody now going to give me water to wash my feet and tell me to eat what is ready? (*Looking in another direction.*) Those courtesans and bastards gaudy with so many jewels, like throngs of celestial dancers and musicians, change this house into a heaven! Hey, who are you bastards really?

BASTARDS: We,

> In strange homes cherished, on strange foods fed,
> By strange men fathered upon a strange wife,
> On strange gifts living, and only out of bed
> Unblamed, we live a gay elephant's life!

MAITREYA: Show me farther, my girl.

SLAVE GIRL: This way, sir. We are now at the sixth court. Please enter.

MAITREYA (*entering and looking*): Amazing! Gateways of craftmanship in gold and precious stones, inlaid with sapphires, seem to display the splendor of rainbows! The artisans carefully match the choicest gems, lapis lazuli, pearls, coral, topaz, sapphire, chalcedon, ruby, emeralds, and so on. Rubies are being set in gold, golden ornaments are being fashioned. Pearl necklaces are strung on red thread, beryls are polished with care, shells are pierced, corals are rubbed with hemp. Fresh saffron is spread out to dry in the sun, musk is kept damp, sandal essence is carefully extracted, and perfume compounds are being combined. Betel mixed with camphor is handed to the courtesans and their lovers. Winks are exchanged, laughter rings, and amidst amorous calls the wine flows constantly. Slaves are mixing with slave girls, and there are the men who have forgotten their sons, their wives, and their fortunes to down the cups of wine which the harlots have sipped and left. Direct me farther, my girl!

SLAVE GIRL: This way, sir. Here is the seventh court. Please enter.

MAITREYA (*entering and looking*): More to marvel at! Turtle doves in couples, which love kissing each other, are indulging their pleasure while they comfortably roost in well-fitted cages. In its cage a parrot is reciting a charm like a Brahmin whose belly is filled with curds and porridge. There a lovesick mynah is prattling without stopping, like a girl slave of the house made bold by the honor she receives. A cuckoo, reared in another's nest like a whore, is trilling away from a throat pleasurably excited by the tastes of all kinds of fruit juices. Rows of cages are hanging down from elephants' tusks along the walls. They are having a quail fight there, and over there they are making the woodcocks cackle. And here they are setting the pigeons loose from their cages. The house peacock, dancing frenziedly in the colorful splash of gemlike hues, fans with the sweeps of its wings the terrace that basks in the rays of the sun. (*Looking elsewhere.*) And there, like moonbeams rolled into balls, a couple of regal flamingoes are strutting after lovesick women as though to learn the secret of their gait. There housebroken cranes step stiffly like aging eunuchs. And look at that marvel! A courtesan chasing after a swarm of birds of many a feather! To me, really and truly, this palace of a brothel looks like the Nandana park[38] in heaven. Show me the way, my girl.

SLAVE GIRL: Come along then, sir. Here is the eighth court. Please enter.

MAITREYA (*entering and looking*): Girl, who is that man there, in his silken robe and his curious assemblage of too many baubles, who strolls about with a swagger and a wriggle?

SLAVE GIRL: That is Madame's brother, sir.

MAITREYA: What mortifications must he have endured to earn the privilege of becoming Vasantasenā's brother! But no, however splendid he may be, and glittering and scented, a body should no more go near him than to a blossoming campaka tree on the road to the burning ground! (*Looking away.*) And who is that woman in the flowery robe and with slippers on her oily feet, who is sitting on that lofty throne?

SLAVE GIRL: That, sir, is Madame's mother.

MAITREYA: The long-tressed witch certainly has a fat paunch! They must have carried her in here, like the statue of the Great God,[39] before they constructed that magnificent gate!

SLAVE GIRL: You hopeless fool, don't crack jokes about our dear little mother. She has got malaria.

MAITREYA (*with a sneer*): Oh Lord Malaria, look down upon this poor Brahmin with the same benevolence!

SLAVE GIRL: Hush your hopeless mouth, you'll die!

MAITREYA (*sneering*): Daughter of a slave girl, it'd be better if that swollen fat belly died!

> This poor little mother is a bum,
> It's the brandy plagues her, and the rum!
> If she dies, the poor little mum,
> She will last a thousand jackals some!

Tell me, my girl, do you have any ships afloat?

SLAVE GIRL: No, sir, no ships.

MAITREYA: But why should I ask? In the ocean of lust, on the clear waters of love, the breasts and buttocks and Venus' mounts are floating like enchanting ships! Now that I have seen Vasantasenā's palace with its eight courts full of adventure, I think that in truth I have gazed upon all three heavens in one place united. I don't have the power of speech to praise it fully—but is this a courtesan's house, or is it a part of the place of the God of Wealth? Where is your mistress?

SLAVE GIRL: She waits in the grove. Please enter.

MAITREYA (*entering and looking*): Oh, oh, oh! Aho, what a magnificent grove! So many lofty trees covered with marvelous blossoms! Silken hammocks, to fit the young women's buttocks, are fixed to the feet of closely spaced trees. Its beauty, with suvarṇayūthikā, śephālikā, mālitī, mallikā, navamallikā, kurabaka, atimuktikā blossoms to spread a rich carpet, makes light of the splendor of the Nandana park. (*Looking elsewhere.*) And there, covered with red lotus petals incarnadine, like the rising sun, dawns a pond. And this aśoka, robed in its blossoms, stands like a good warrior in battle cloaked in blood. But where is your mistress?

SLAVE GIRL: Lower your glance, sir, and you will see her.

MAITREYA (*seeing her and approaching*): I wish you luck, ma'am.

VASANTASENĀ (*speaking Sanskrit*)[40]: Ah, Maitreya! (*She rises.*) Welcome! Do sit down, here is a seat.

MAITREYA: Please sit down, ma'am. (*Both sit down.*)

VASANTASENĀ: Is the young merchant in good health?

MAITREYA: He is in good health, ma'am.

VASANTASENĀ: And, worthy Maitreya, this tree of nobility shooting with talent, branching with courtesy, blossoming with high prudence, rooting in trust, and fruitful in its virtues—do friendly birds still nestle in it peacefully?

MAITREYA (*to himself*): How adroit is the wretched whore in making allusions! (*Aloud.*) Of course.

VASANTASENĀ: But tell me, what is the purpose of your visit?

MAITREYA: I'll tell you, ma'am. Master Cārudatta folds his hands at his head and begs you to know . . .

VASANTASENĀ (*folding her hands*): What does he command?

MAITREYA: ". . . In all good faith I have mistaken your golden casket for my own and lost it at gambling. The games master has left town for somewhere as the king's courier, and I don't know where . . ."

SLAVE GIRL: Ma'am, you should be congratulated: the gentleman has become a gambler!

VASANTASENĀ (*to herself*): What? It has been stolen by a thief, yet his kindness compels him to take the blame . . . one must love him!

MAITREYA: ". . . and therefore, please accept this pearl necklace in exchange for it."

VASANTASENĀ (*to herself*): Shall I now show the jewels? (*She thinks.*) No, not yet.

MAITREYA: But you will not accept it, will you, ma'am?

VASANTASENĀ (*with a glance at her confidante, smiling*): Maitreya, why shouldn't I accept it? (*She takes the necklace and puts it beside her. To herself.*) The mango tree has lost its bloom, but still the juice of its fruits drips down. (*Aloud.*) Will you tell your master, Cārudatta the gambler, in my name that this evening I shall come to visit him?

MAITREYA (*to himself*): What else will she be coming to grab? (*Aloud.*) I'll tell him, ma'am. (*To himself.*) He must be stopped from loving this courtesan! (*Exit.*)

VASANTASENĀ: Take these jewels, my dear. We'll go and make Cārudatta happy!

SLAVE GIRL: But mistress, look! There's a thunderstorm coming up, most untimely!

VASANTASENĀ:

> The clouds may rise, night fall, rains shower from above,
> No more I care, for now my heart yearns for his love.

Girl, take the necklace and come back quickly!

ACT FIVE

Enter Cārudatta. He sits down and shows his longing.

CĀRUDATTA (*looking at the sky*): Out of season there is a thunderstorm gathering.

The peacocks, quick to notice, spread their plumes—
The swans indignantly, for they would start,[41]
Protest, but overhead untimely looms
The storm that bursts and fills
The heavy skies and thrills
The yearning lover's heavy heart.

Bee-black like the damp belly of a buffalo,
The Cloud, robed in the yellow silk of lightning, and
Lifting the white cranes like a conch shell in its hand,
Storms, like a second Viṣṇu, heaven from below.[42]

Like drops of fluid silver falls the rain
Out of the bursting clouds and races down,
Caught in a lightning flash and gone again,
Like trailing fringes torn off heaven's gown.

Embracing cakravāka[43] pairs, or swans in flight,
Or whirling dolphins, castles towering up high—
The wind-torn clouds build images before our sight
And cut most artful silhouettes into the sky.

The cloudy sky grows dark like Dhṛtarāṣṭra's face—
Too prideful, like Duryodhana, the peacock jeers—
The cuckoo, like Yudhiṣṭhira defeated, disappears,
The swans, like Pāṇḍu's sons, have gone and left no trace.[44]

(*He pauses and thinks.*) It has been a long while since Maitreya went to Vasantasenā, and still he has not come back.

Enter Maitreya.

MAITREYA: Well, that's a courtesan's greed and tactlessness for you! Not a compliment could she spare. How often has she not protested her love, but she did grab the necklace. And in the midst of her plenty she would not tell me: "Master Maitreya, you should take some rest. Have a cup of water before you go." I don't want to see the face of that low-born courtesan ever again! (*Discouraged.*) They're right in saying that a lotus that has not grown from a bulb, and a merchant who does not cheat, and a goldsmith who does not steal, and a village council that does not quarrel, and a courtesan who does not grab are hard to imagine. I'll find my good friend and stop him from loving that courtesan! (*He walks around and sees Cārudatta.*) Ah, my friend is sitting in the grove. I'll join him. (*Approaching.*) Luck be with you, friend. It'd better.

CĀRUDATTA (*looking up*): Ah, my good Maitreya is back. Welcome, my friend. Sit down.

MAITREYA: I am sitting already.

CĀRUDATTA: Tell me, friend, how did it go?

MAITREYA: Everything is lost!

CĀRUDATTA: Lost? She did not accept the necklace?

MAITREYA: How could we be so lucky! No, she folded her delicate little hands at her forehead and took it.

CĀRUDATTA: Then why do you say that everything is lost?

MAITREYA: Isn't it lost? For a cheap gold box, which we didn't eat or drink up, which was just stolen by a burglar, she has taken a pearl necklace that is the prize of four oceans!

CĀRUDATTA: Don't talk like that, friend. She gave us her confidence and entrusted her casket to us; we have but repaid the price of her great trust.

MAITREYA: And I have another grievance, friend. She winked at her friend and hid her face behind her shawl: she mocked me! And therefore, Brahmin though I am, I throw myself with my head at your feet and implore you to put a stop to your disastrous love for that courtesan. A courtesan is like a clod of earth that's got into your sandal: it is difficult to get rid of it. And besides, where a courtesan, an elephant, a scribe, a monk, a swindler, and a donkey live not even weeds will grow.

CĀRUDATTA: Enough now, friend, you have slandered her quite enough. My circumstances suffice to restrain me. Look,

> To rush along, a horse may make a galloping start,
> But his feet will refuse him if his breath runs out.
> And man's quicksilver nature flies about
> And sinks, exhausted, back into his heart.

And besides, my friend,

> They love a man of means, for money buys them all—

(*to himself.*)

> And virtue does not buy them at all . . .

(*Aloud.*)

> *I* lost my money, *she* no doubt her wish to call.

MAITREYA (*looking down, to himself*): He is looking at the sky and sighing deeply, a sure sign that his love has grown stronger while I was trying to stop him. . . . The proverb is right: love's left-handed. (*Aloud.*) Well, friend, she has also told me to tell you she will visit you tonight. I suppose that the necklace was not enough and she is coming to ask for more.

CĀRUDATTA: Let her come, friend. She'll go away satisfied.

SLAVE: Make way, folks!

> The more the clouds are raining,
> The more my back is dripping,
> The more the cold wind's ripping,
> The more my heart is straining!
>
> The sweet flute of the seven holes I blow,
> The clear lute of the seven strings I play,
> I sing a song that but an ass might bray,
> Not Tumbura nor Nārada can do it so!

My lady Vasantasenā has just told me: "Kumbhīlaka, you go and tell Master Cārudatta that I am coming." So to Master Cārudatta's house I go. (*He walks around and sees him while entering stage center.*) There's

Cārudatta sitting under the trees in his grove. And there's that miserable Brahmin. I'll go up to him. What, the gate to the grove is shut? I'll give that miserable Brahmin a sign. (*He throws a clod of earth at him.*)
MAITREYA: Hey, who is throwing earth at me while I am surrounded by walls like a woodapple tree?
CĀRUDATTA: The pigeons that are playing on the roof of the garden house must have dropped it.
MAITREYA: You bastard pigeons! Just wait till I have chased you off the roof to the ground with my stick like a ripe mango! (*He runs about, raising his stick.*)
CĀRUDATTA (*pulling him back by his Brahmin's thread*): Sit down, friend. What does it matter? Leave that poor pigeon alone with its dove.
SLAVE: Well, he can see the pigeon, but me he won't! All right, I hit him again. (*He does so.*)
MAITREYA (*looking around*): What, Kumbhīlaka! I'll go to him. (*He walks over and opens the gate.*) So, Kumbhīlaka, come in, and welcome.
SLAVE: I greet you, sir.
MAITREYA: Say, why have you come in such bad weather? It's dark.
SLAVE: Well, it's she, she.

MAITREYA: Who? Who?
SLAVE: She! She!

MAITREYA: You son of a whore, why are you puffing "she, she" like an old beggar during a famine?
SLAVE: And why are you hooting "who, who" like an owl?
MAITREYA: Come on, say what you have to say.
SLAVE (*to himself*): All right, I'll tell him this way. (*Aloud.*) I'll put a question to you.
MAITREYA: And I'll put my foot to your head!
SLAVE: Well, if you want to know, that's how. In what season does the mango blossom?
MAITREYA: In summer, you bastard!
SLAVE (*laughing*): Oh, no, oh, no!
MAITREYA (*to himself*): What should I say then? (*He thinks.*) All right, I'll go ask Cārudatta. (*Aloud.*) Wait a moment. (*He walks over to Cārudatta.*) I want to ask you something, friend. In what season does the mango blossom?
CĀRUDATTA: In spring, fool.
MAITREYA (*going back to the Slave*): In spring, fool.
SLAVE: I'll ask another question. Who guards the rich villages?

MAITREYA: The guards, of course.

SLAVE: Oh, no, oh, no!

MAITREYA: Now that makes me wonder. (*He thinks.*) All right, I'll ask Cārudatta again. (*He returns to Cārudatta and asks him.*)

CĀRUDATTA: The army, friend.

MAITREYA (*going back to the Slave*): The army, bastard.

SLAVE: Now we have spring (*vasanta*) and army (*senā*). Put the two together and say them fast.

MAITREYA: Senāvasanta!

SLAVE: No, the other way around.

MAITREYA (*turning around*): Senāvasanta!

SLAVE: Oh you stupid Brahmin, you should turn the parts around!

MAITREYA (*turning his feet*): Senāvasanta!

SLAVE: Turn the parts of the word around, you fool.

MAITREYA (*thinking*): Vasantasenā!

SLAVE: She has come.

MAITREYA: I must tell Cārudatta! (*He goes to him.*) Cārudatta, there's a creditor come.

CĀRUDATTA: A creditor, in our house? Why?

MAITREYA: If not into the house, at least at our door. Vasantasenā has come.

CĀRUDATTA: Are you trying to fool me, friend?

MAITREYA: If you don't believe what I say, ask Kumbhīlaka over there. Hey, Kumbhīlaka! Come here, bastard!

SLAVE (*coming*): I greet you, sir.

CĀRUDATTA: Welcome, my man. Tell me the truth. Has Vasantasenā come?

SLAVE: Yes she has come, Vasantasenā has.

CĀRUDATTA (*with joy*): Never should a kind word be without its reward, my man. Your reward, take it. (*He gives him his shawl.*)

SLAVE (*taking it and bowing with satisfaction*): I'll tell madame. (*Exit.*)

MAITREYA: Well, do you know why she has come in this bad weather?

CĀRUDATTA: I am not quite sure, friend.

MAITREYA: But I am. She found the necklace cheap and the gold box valuable, and so she wasn't satisfied and comes to ask for more!

CĀRUDATTA (*to himself*): She will go away satisfied.

Enter Vasantasenā in love, flamboyantly dressed as an abhisārikā,[45] *a girl holding her umbrella, and a Libertine.*

LIBERTINE (*referring to Vasantasenā*):

A Lakṣmī without lotus, Love's shaft of delight,
A grief to well-born women, bloom on Passion's tree,
She dances to the welcome shame of Lust's long night,
Trailed by fond followers, through Rapture's scenery.

Look, Vasantasenā, look!

Packed round the mountain peaks the looming clouds are groaning
As though of lonely wives to echo the low moaning,
And at the din the peacocks suddenly dart out
And with their jeweled feathers fan the air about!

Their faces damp with mud, the rain-blown frogs drink deep,
The peacock cries its love, the nīpa glows in bloom,
As scoundrels selflessness, so clouds obscure the moon
While lightning streaks like whores who to perdition leap.

VASANTASENĀ: Master, you have spoken well, for lo!

With roaring thunder Night wants me to stay:
"Blind woman, what are you if on my breast
Of full round clouds your man seeks love and rest!"
And like a rival in a fury blocks my way.

LIBERTINE: So it is indeed. But then, take her to task!
VASANTASENĀ: But why take one to task, master, who is so ignorant of a woman's heart?

Let clouds hurl thunderbolts, or rain, or growl,
A woman yearning for her love counts fair nor foul!

LIBERTINE: Watch that cloud, Vasantasenā!

Racing wildly with the wind, shooting shafts of rain,
Beating the drums of thunder, fire-flags flying high—
A king invading a weak enemy's domain—
It robs moon's silver from the fortress of the sky!

VASANTASENĀ: Yes, indeed! And that other cloud there!

But if the roaring clouds—gray elephants that flaunt
Their lightning banners—have already stabbed my heart,

> Must then the heron sound the drum of death to haunt
> My tardy lover, still ajourney and now doomed,
> And cry of rain! rain! casting caustic in my wound?

LIBERTINE: Indeed, Vasantasenā. Look at that one!

> And heaven's gloomy bulk, with cranes that pleat
> White headdresses on it, and lightning flying
> Like yak-tail plumes atop, seems bent on trying
> To imitate an elephant in heat!

VASANTASENĀ: Master, look!

> Between the dark tamāla leaves of clouds blooms pale the sun—
> Like arrow-showered elephants the anthills sink and fall—
> A golden torch, the lightning roams on castle roof and wall—
> And clouds abduct the daylight like a wife whose man is gone.

LIBERTINE: But watch, Vasantasenā!

> Brightly caparisoned with lightning flashes,
> A battleline of elephants that clashes,
> The javelin-throwing clouds at Indra's word
> Rescue the world as on a silver cord.

And again, watch!

> The storm-blown clouds, dark as a herd of buffalo,
> That rage like seething seas and speed on lightning-wings,
> Into the fragrant earth their diamond arrows throw
> Until the dying grass into lush verdure springs!

VASANTASENĀ: And there, master!

> Welcomed by shrilly screeching peacocks: "Here! Come here!"
> While cranes take wing to catch him in their fond embrace,
> And swans, leaving their lotuses, piqued, upward peer,
> Appears the cloud that casts collyrium on space!

LIBERTINE: Indeed, for look,

> The world now seems to sleep in day nor night,
> Staring with the blank eyes of lotus ponds,
> The dark sky-face lit up by sudden light,—
> To sleep unmoved below a thatch of clouds,
> Within a house of clouds that holds it tight.

VASANTASENĀ: Indeed, my master. And see!

Like favors to unworthy men the stars are gone;
The mountain peaks lack luster like deserted wives;
And heaven, heated by the fire of rainbows, melts,
And, liquefied, now seems to trickle down in rain.

And look!

The cloud is rising, falling, raining, roaring, darkling,
And like a new-rich man in a thousand splendors sparkling.

LIBERTINE: So it is, and behold the sky—

Blushing with lightning and smiling[46] with hundreds of cranes,
Skipping rope with the rainbow that scatters a shower of arrows,
Roaring with thunder and whirling along with the wind,
And perfuming the spaces with serpentine indigo clouds!

VASANTASENĀ:

Have you no shame, cloud, first to fail me,
While I am speeding to my love,
Roaring me down, and from above
With your wet hands now to assail me?

Ah, Indra![47]

Have you then been in love with me before
That you should roar at me to stay me?
And while I yearn for him, ought you to pour
Your showers in my path and dare delay me?

If you once for Ahalyā's sake
Lied you were Gautama, then pray,
God Indra, pity me and take
The cloud that bars my road away!

Or throw your bolt a hundred times, and groan, and rain!
A woman bound for her good love you can't detain!

The cloud may rage—for men are cruel—if it must—
But, lightning, don't you know the pangs of woman's lust?[48]

LIBERTINE: Enough, good lady. Don't blame her too much, for she is helping you. This same lightning, golden chain that swings from the chest of the king of elephants, white banner planted on a mountain peak, burning torch that lights the Dread God's inner chamber, now tells you the site of your lover's house!

VASANTASENĀ: Master, here is his house!

LIBERTINE: My lady, you are wise in all the arts, and there is nothing you still need be taught. Yet my love urges me to counsel you. When you have entered here, do not quarrel too much. There is no love where there is quarrel—but without ire there is no desire. Be angry and make him angry, but be quick to calm down and to calm him! All right, that is all. . . . Hullo! Hullo! Announce to Master Cārudatta that a woman has come at this hour that is being struck by thunder—a woman fragrant with the budding blossoms of kadamba and nīpa, excited and loving, who has rushed to her lover's house with rain-blown hair, still trembling from fear of the lightning and roaring storm which she braved to see you! A woman is waiting to wash her feet of the mud that sticks to her golden anklets.

CĀRUDATTA (*listening*): Friend, go and see what is going on!

MAITREYA: As you wish. (*Approaches Vasantasenā; with awe.*) May luck favor you, my lady.

VASANTASENĀ: I greet you, sir, you are well come! (*To the Libertine.*) Master, my umbrella girl is all yours.

LIBERTINE (*to himself*): How politely am I dismissed, and how effectively! (*Aloud.*) My dear Vasantasenā, may the market of harlots, cradle of pride, frauds, tricks, and lies, spirit of vice, playground of lust, midway of the fairs of love, thrive merrily on the commodity of dexterity! (*Exit.*)

VASANTASENĀ: Master Maitreya, where is your gambler?

MAITREYA (*to himself*): Ah, ah! Well, my dear friend can feel flattered to be called a gambler! (*Aloud.*) My lady, he is in the withered grove.

VASANTASENĀ: The withered grove? Why do you call it that?

MAITREYA: There is no food or drink to be had there, my lady. (*Vasantasenā smiles.*)

MAITREYA: Please go in, my lady.

VASANTASENĀ (*aside to her slave girl*): What am I to say when I am inside?

SLAVE GIRL: Try "Gambler, is your evening good?"

VASANTASENĀ: Shall I manage?
SLAVE GIRL: You have your opportunity.
MAITREYA: Please come in, my lady.
VASANTASENĀ (*goes in, walks over to Cārudatta, and hits him gently with a flower*): Ah, gambler, is your evening good?
CĀRUDATTA (*looking up*): Oh, Vasantasenā has come! (*He rises in great joy.*) My love—

> I waked through all the evenings that went by,
> I sighed through all the nights that passed,
> But now, my wide-eyed love, that we have met,
> The evening has spent its grief at last!

Be welcome, my lady. Here is a seat. Pray be seated.
MAITREYA: Here's a seat. Please sit down, my lady.
(*Vasantasenā sits down. The others resume their seats.*)
CĀRUDATTA: Look, friend! The kadamba blossom that is hanging from her ear has dripped some raindrops on one breast that stands consecrated like a royal prince anointed as Young King! But Vasantasenā's clothes are soaked. Fetch at once some choice gowns!
MAITREYA: As you please.
SLAVE GIRL: Stay here, Master Maitreya. I'll serve madame. (*She does so.*)
MAITREYA (*aside*): Why, friend—may I put a question to you?
CĀRUDATTA: Certainly.
MAITREYA (*aloud*): Well, why should this lady have come here on such a bad dark night without a moon?
SLAVE GIRL: The Brahmin is outspoken, madame!
VASANTASENĀ: You might call him clever.
SLAVE GIRL: Madame actually came to inquire after the value of that pearl necklace you sent.
MAITREYA (*aside*): Ah, didn't I tell you? That gold jewel box was worth less than the necklace, but she is still not satisfied. She has come to ask for more!
SLAVE GIRL: For madame has mistaken it for her own and lost it at a game. The games master has since left on an errand for the king and nobody knows where he is.
MAITREYA: Dear girl, you repeat our own words!
SLAVE GIRL: Take this gold box in its stead, while we are trying to find him. (*She shows him the jewel box. Maitreya examines it.*)

SLAVE GIRL: You are studying it closely. Have you ever seen it before?

MAITREYA: No, my girl. The craftmanship catches my eye.

SLAVE GIRL: Well, your eye deceives you. It is the same gold box.

MAITREYA (*happily*): Friend, this is the same gold box the burglars carried off out of our house!

CĀRUDATTA: But we gave that pretext first! We made it up to be able to return a substitute for the box she had deposited with us. Surely it is a fake?

MAITREYA: On my head as a Brahmin I swear the thing is real!

CĀRUDATTA: I am glad, indeed I am glad!

MAITREYA (*aside*): Shall I ask her how she got it?

CĀRUDATTA: What harm?

Maitreya whispers into the Slave Girl's ear, and she whispers in his.

CĀRUDATTA: What are you two whispering? Are we not allowed to know?

Maitreya whispers in Cārudatta's ear.

CĀRUDATTA: Tell me, good woman, is this that same gold box?

SLAVE GIRL: Yes, sir.

CĀRUDATTA: Never have I left happy news unrewarded. Here, take this ring as a gratification. (*He looks at his hand and finds that all his rings are gone; he is embarrassed.*)

VASANTASENĀ (*to herself*): That is why I love him!

CĀRUDATTA (*aside*): Alas—what use is it for a poor man to live at all? As he lacks the means to repay, both his pleasure and his anger are of no consequence. A pauper is like a clipped bird, a withered tree, a pond without fish, a snake whose fangs are drawn. Like empty houses, dry wells, moldered trees are the poor. When they meet with people they have known before, they are forgotten and their hours of contentment are frustrated. . . .

MAITREYA: Come on, don't wallow in it! (*Aloud and joking.*) Madame, you should have returned my bath towel!

VASANTASENĀ: You did me an injustice, Master Cārudatta, when you sent me that necklace. Must you be suspicious of me?

CĀRUDATTA (*with an embarrassed smile*): Look, Vasantasenā, would you have believed the truth? Everyone would suspect me. For in this world poverty has no dignity and rouses suspicion.

MAITREYA: I say, my girl, is madame going to stay the night?

SLAVE GIRL (*smiling*): You *do* show yourself an extremely outspoken man, Master Maitreya!

MAITREYA: Friend, the Rain-god is intruding again with his fat raindrops; it seems he wants to break up our pleasant party.
CĀRUDATTA: You are right—

The raindrops pierce the clouds
As lotus stalks pierce mud
And drop from heaven like tears
Over the moon's sad plight.

With drops as clear as good men's thoughts,
And sharp as Arjuna's most ruthless shafts,
The clouds as black as Baladeva's robes,
Pour down a shower of God Indra's pearls.

Darling, look!

Anointed with tamāla-colored clouds,
Fanned by its fond cool fragrant evening breeze,
The sky is lovingly embraced by lightning
Which came in haste, enraptured by the rains.

(*Vasantasenā shows her love and embraces Cārudatta.*)

CĀRUDATTA (*returning her embrace with joy*):

Cloud, roar with ever greater voice!
For by your grace my trembling limbs,
Beset by love and thrilled by lust,
Glow red like a kadamba bloom!

MAITREYA: Thunder, you bastard! Are you mean enough to frighten this lady with your lightning?
CĀRUDATTA: Don't blame him, friend. May the thunder rage, the lightning flash for a hundred years, for I am embraced by a girl who is rare to a man like me. Blessed are the lives of those who may press to theirs the moist and rain-chilled bodies of mistresses that hastened to their houses!—Vasantasenā, my darling. The roof is so old that the rafters are hardly held up by the pillars. The layer of plaster on my painted walls has crumbled and now the water is seeping through. . . . (*Looking up at the sky.*) Look, darling, the rainbow! Is it not as though

all of heaven seems to yawn and stretch drowsily, flicking its lightning-tongue between the gaping jaws of the clouds and stretching the rainbow like its arm? Come with me, we must go inside. (*He stands up and walks about.*) Listen to the raindrops, how sharp they sound on the palm leaves, and how gentle on the trees, clear on the stones, and splashing in the puddles! And together they keep time like many lutes that are being struck in concert. (*Exeunt omnes.*)

ACT SIX

Enter Slave Girl.[49]

SLAVE GIRL: What! Madame is not yet up! I must go inside and call her. (*She walks around and mimes going inside. Vasantasenā comes within view; she is sleeping; her body is covered.*)

SLAVE GIRL (*bending over her*): Wake up, madame, wake up! It's morning.

VASANTASENĀ (*awakening*): What? Night has already become morning?

SLAVE GIRL: For us it is morning. But for you still night!

VASANTASENĀ: And where is your "gambler," my dear?

SLAVE GIRL: He has left orders with Vardhamāna and then gone out to that old park, Puṣpakaraṇḍaka.

VASANTASENĀ: What orders did he leave?

SLAVE GIRL: He was to yoke the carriage before the night was out and take you out.

VASANTASENĀ: And where am I supposed to go?

SLAVE GIRL: To where Cārudatta has gone.

VASANTASENĀ (*embracing her*): Last night I could not see him too well. Now by day I shall see him very clearly. Am I here in the heart of the house?

SLAVE GIRL: Not only in the heart of the house, but in the heart of everyone who lives here.

VASANTASENĀ: But isn't Cārudatta's family vexed?

SLAVE GIRL: They will be.

VASANTASENĀ: When?

SLAVE GIRL: When you leave them, madame.

VASANTASENĀ: Then I shall be the first to be vexed. (*With a courteous gesture.*) Take this necklace, my dear, and go to my sister, the lady of this house, and give her a message. Tell her from me: "Master Cārudatta's virtues have rendered me his slave—and yours. These pearls should adorn your neck."

SLAVE GIRL: Cārudatta will be angry with you, madame.
VASANTASENĀ: Go now. He won't be angry.
SLAVE GIRL (*taking the pearls*): As you wish. (*Exit and re-enter.*) Madame, the lady of the house replies: "My husband has honored you with it, and it would therefore not be proper for me to accept it. And I wish you to know that my husband is my choicest adornment."

(*Enter Radanikā holding a little boy.*)
RADANIKĀ: Come, my child. Let's play for a bit with your little cart.
ROHASENA (*whining*): I don't want to play with a clay cart. Give me my golden cart!
RADANIKĀ (*sighing sadly*): How can we talk about gold, child? When daddy is rich again, then you'll play with a golden cart. Wait, I'll take him to Mistress Vasantasenā, to take his mind off it. (*Approaching.*) I bow, madame.
VASANTASENĀ: You are welcome, Radanikā. Who is the little boy's father? Poorly dressed as he is, with his little moonface he warms my heart!
RADANIKĀ: He is Master Cārudatta's son, he is called Rohasena.
VASANTASENĀ (*stretching out her arms to him*): Come, little boy of mine, give me a kiss! (*She takes him on her lap.*) He takes after his father in his looks.
RADANIKĀ: And not only in his looks, in character too, I fancy. He makes Master Cārudatta so happy.
VASANTASENĀ: Why is he crying?
RADANIKĀ: He has been playing with the little golden cart of the boy next door, and the boy has taken it away. When he kept asking for it, I made him a little cart of clay to play with. And now he says: I don't want a cart of clay. Give me that golden cart.
VASANTASENĀ: Oh, how horrible! That even a small child like him should suffer from other people's wealth! O God of Destiny, man's fate that is like a drop of water sticking to a lotus petal is only your plaything. . . . (*She weeps.*) Don't cry, my child. You'll have a golden cart to play with.
ROHASENA: Who is she, Radanikā?
VASANTASENĀ: The slave of your father's virtue.
RADANIKĀ: This lady is your second mother, my boy.
ROHASENA: But that can't be true! If she is my mother, how did she get all those jewels?

VASANTASENĀ: Child, with your innocent tongue you say the most cruel things! (*Weeping, she takes off her jewelry.*) Look, now I have become your mother! Here, take them. You must have a little golden cart made.

ROHASENA: Go away! I don't want them. You are crying!

VASANTASENĀ (*brushing away her tears*): I won't cry, my child. Go play now. (*She piles her jewelry in the clay cart.*) Get yourself a golden cart. (*Exit Radanikā with Rohasena.*)

Enter Vardhamāna with a bullock-drawn covered carriage.

VARDHAMĀNA: Radanikā! Radanikā! Tell Mistress Vasantasenā that a covered carriage is ready for her at the side door.

Enter Radanikā.

RADANIKĀ: My lady, Vardhamāna sends word that the carriage is waiting at the side door.

VASANTASENĀ: Let him wait a moment, my dear, I must get ready first.

RADANIKĀ (*going outside*): Wait a little, Vardhamāna. She is getting ready.

VARDHAMĀNA: Hullo! Now I have forgotten the cushions for the carriage! I'll get them in the meantime. The bullocks are restless, it must be because they have reins through their noses again. All right, I'll drive them back and forth. (*Exit.*)

VASANTASENĀ: Get me my make-up, my dear. I'll have to get ready. (*She busies herself making up.*)

Enter a coachman, Sthāvaraka, with a bullock-drawn carriage.

STHĀVARAKA: Saṃsthānaka, the king's brother-in-law, has ordered me to bring the carriage round at once to the old Puṣpakaraṇḍaka park. All right, here I go. Hurry up, beasts! (*He drives and looks around.*) What, my road blocked by village carts! Now what am I supposed to do about that? (*Haughtily.*) Hey, you! Out of my way, out of my way! (*Listening.*) What is it? Whose carriage is *this*? *This* is the carriage of Saṃsthānaka, the king's brother-in-law himself! Now out of my way and quick! (*Looking.*) Say, who was that fellow who suddenly turned his face away as soon as he saw me and darted off like a runaway gambler with the games master at his heels? Who could that be? But what do I care! I must hurry. Hey, peasants! Out of my way, out of my way! Now what is this again? Wait a minute? Lend a hand getting your wheel unstuck? Peasant! I'm coachman to Saṃsthānaka, the king's brother-in-law himself! Should *I* help get your wheel unstuck? But the poor fellow is alone. . . . I'll do it after all. I'll stop the carriage at the garden gate of Master Cārudatta. (*He stops the carriage.*) Here I am. (*Exit.*)

SLAVE GIRL: I think I hear wheels. The carriage must have come, madame.

VASANTASENĀ: Go now, girl. My heart hurries me. Show me the side door.

SLAVE GIRL: This way, madame.

VASANTASENĀ (*walking around*): You are free to take a rest.

SLAVE GIRL: As you wish, madame. (*Exit.*)

VASANTASENĀ (*her right eye twitching as she steps into the carriage*): My right eye is twitching! But the sight of Cārudatta will wipe away the bad omen. . . .

Enter Sthāvaraka.

STHĀVARAKA: I have cleared the road. Finally I can go! (*He jumps on and starts the bullocks.*) The carriage feels heavier! But perhaps it only seems so because I have worn myself out getting that cart wheel unstuck. All right, on we go. Come on, beasts, faster!

VOICE OFFSTAGE: Gatekeepers, all to your stations and look sharp! Prince Āryaka has escaped! He's broken out of jail, killed his jailer, shattered his chains, and made good his escape! Catch him, catch him!

Enter suddenly, without parting the back curtain, Āryaka. He is nervous and keeps his face covered. He walks around.

STHĀVARAKA (*to himself*): Mayhem in the city! I must go fast, fast! (*Exit.*)

ĀRYAKA:

> I've fled the unplumbed ocean of sudden death
> And vice that hides beneath the name of jails,
> And like an elephant that has broken loose
> Drag on one foot my piece of chain along.

Yes, it was I whom King Pālaka in his panic over a prediction took from his village and chained to a deadly prison. But thanks to my good friend Śarvilaka I have broken out. (*Dropping a tear.*)

> What sin of mine if 'tis my destiny?
> Should I be chained like a wild elephant?

For Fate cannot be stayed—who will dispute
That but a greater king can stay a king?

But where am I to go in my misfortune? (*Looking around.*) Here is an open side door, surely the door of an honest man:

An old collapsing house with mighty gates
Whose bolts are gone, whose hinges are worn out,
Surely a gentleman's, ill-starred like me,
Who has come to grief and fallen on hard times.

I'll go in here and hide.

VOICE OFFSTAGE: Come on, beasts, faster!

ĀRYAKA (*listening*): Ah, there is a carriage coming this way!

Is it a wagon for a company,
Unoccupied by evil-minded men?
Perhaps a lady's carriage that has come
To fetch her? Or by mere good luck a coach
Fit for a gentleman, bound for the country,
And empty—which kind Fate has sent to me?

Enter Vardhamāna with the carriage.

VARDHAMĀNA: Well, folks, I got the cushions. Radanikā! Tell Mistress Vasantasenā that the carriage is ready. Let her get in and ride to the old Puṣpakaraṇḍaka park.

ĀRYAKA (*listening*): It is a courtesan's carriage, and bound for the countryside! I'll get in. (*He sneaks to the carriage.*)

VARDHAMĀNA (*pricking his ears*): I hear her ankle rings. The lady must have come. My lady, the bullocks are shy because of their new nose reins. Please get in from the rear. (*Āryaka does so.*)

VARDHAMĀNA: The clatter of her ankle rings is silent after the last high step, and the carriage is heavy. So her ladyship must have gotten in, I take it. We'll start. Come on, beasts, go! (*He drives around.*)

Enter Vīraka.

VĪRAKA: Hey, there, hey, you, Jaya, Jayamāna, Candanaka, Mangala, Phullabhadra, and the others! How can you walk so confidently? Prince Āryaka who was in jail has broken his chains and the old king's heart and is on the loose! Hey, you, you guard the East Gate. And you the West Gate. You go to the South Gate, and you to the North

Gate. And Candanaka comes with me. We'll get on to the wall here where it has been breached. Come, Candanaka, we go!

Enter Candanaka, who is all upset.

CANDANAKA: Hey, you, Vīraka, Viśalya, Bhīmāṅgada, Daṇḍakālaka, Daṇḍaśūra, and the others!

Come here, it's safe here, but be quick, work hard,
Work fast, so that the fortune of our king
May not desert his line! Search everyone,
In gambling dens and gardens, on the road,
In town, among the markets, on the land,
Wherever your suspicions may arise!
Vīraka, you, why are you beckoning me?
Who broke his chains? Trust me and tell me all!
Who freed prince Āryaka? At whose foul birth
Stood Sol in the eighth house, Moon in the fourth,
And Venus in the sixth? And who has Mars
In his fifth house, Jupiter in the sixth,
And Saturn in the ninth? What ill-starred man
Dares free the prince while Candana is alive?

VĪRAKA:

I swear it, Candana, upon your heart
That someone has abducted him at dawn,
The sun had not yet risen half when he
Up and released Prince Āryaka from jail.

VARDHAMĀNA: Faster, beasts, faster!

CANDANAKA (*noticing the carriage*): Hey, look there! There's a covered carriage rolling in the middle of the royal highway! Find out who it belongs to and where they are going.

VĪRAKA (*looking up*): Hey, coachman, don't drive any farther. Whose carriage is this? And who's in it? Where are you going?

VARDHAMĀNA: This carriage belongs to Master Cārudatta. Vasantasenā is riding in it, I am taking her to the old Puṣpakaraṇḍaka park where she is to dally with Cārudatta.

VĪRAKA (*stepping over to Candanaka*): The coachman says that it is Cārudatta's carriage and that he is taking Vasantasenā to Puṣpakaraṇḍaka park.

CANDANAKA: Let him drive on!
VĪRAKA: Without searching the carriage?
CANDANAKA: Of course.
VĪRAKA: On whose responsibility?
CANDANAKA: Master Cārudatta's.
VĪRAKA: Who is Master Cārudatta and who is Vasantasenā that the carriage need not be searched?
CANDANAKA: What! You don't know Master Cārudatta and Vasantasenā? If you don't know them, you don't know the moon and its light[50] in the sky!

> Who does not know that bloom of virtue, moon
> Of high nobility, who saved from sorrow
> Whoever came to him—treasure of all the seas?
> But two are worth the honors of the town
> Whose beauty they point up—Vasantasenā,
> And Cārudatta, treasure of good faith!

VĪRAKA: Sure, I know Cārudatta and Vasantasenā well enough, but when I am under the king's orders, I won't know my own father!

ĀRYAKA (*to himself*): The one reveals himself an old friend, the other an old enemy.

> Though they have both been ordered to one task,
> They are not of one mind about it—fire
> Burns at a wedding and a funeral!

CANDANAKA: You are a responsible captain, and you have the king's confidence. Here, I am holding the bullocks, search the carriage.
VĪRAKA: The king trusts you too, captain. You may search the carriage.
CANDANAKA: If I search it, is it as good as though you yourself had searched it?
VĪRAKA: As good as though King Pālaka himself had searched it.
CANDANAKA: Lower the yoke, coachman.
(*Vardhamāna obeys.*)
ĀRYAKA (*to himself*): The guards are going to find me! And wretch that I am, I am unarmed! But no, I'll do as Bhīma and fight with my bare hands—it is better to die struggling than to languish in jail. But there may be no cause for violence. (*Candanaka mimes stepping into the carriage and searching it.*)
ĀRYAKA: I am at your mercy!

CANDANAKA (*speaking the Sanskrit formula*): Safety to those who seek mercy!
ĀRYAKA:

> For Victory abandons, family
> And friends desert him, and the butt of mock
> Becomes he who deserts a supplicant!

CANDANAKA: Like a bird that was frightened by a hawk, Prince Āryaka, son of Gopāla, has dropped into the birdcatcher's hand! (*Thinking.*) But he is an innocent man, he has thrown himself on my mercy, he is riding in Cārudatta's carriage, and he is the friend of the noble Śarvilaka who once saved my life. . . . On the other hand, we have our orders. . . . What is the best course? But what shall be shall be. The main thing is that I have promised him safety. A man who grants safety to a man in fear, who has the heart to do good to others, may perish if he must, but his virtue will survive on earth! (*Frightened, he gets out of the carriage.*) I saw him . . . (*He halts in mid-sentence.*) No, her, our lady Vasantasenā. She said: "Is it proper, is it right that I am molested on the royal highway when I am meeting Master Cārudatta at a rendezvous?"

VĪRAKA: But now you have raised some doubt in my mind, Candanaka!
CANDANAKA: Doubt? Why?
VĪRAKA: You started to stutter with confusion when you said you had seen *him*, and then had seen *her*. Now I don't trust you!
CANDANAKA: Why shouldn't you trust me? I am from the South, and we don't speak very clearly, because we know too many heathen tongues, of Khasas, Khaṭṭis, Kaḍas, Kadaṭṭhobilas, Karṇātas, Karṇapāvaraṇas, Dravidians, Colas, Chinese, Barbarians, Kheras, Mukhas, Madhughātas, etcetera, etcetera. We know too many tongues and we talk as we like, seen or saw, him or her.
VĪRAKA: I have to look for myself. King's orders. The king trusts me.
CANDANAKA: I'm no longer trusted?
VĪRAKA: Orders are orders.
CANDANAKA (*to himself*): If it gets known that Āryaka, son of Gopāla, was escaping in his carriage, Cārudatta will be punished by the king. Is there any way out? (*He thinks.*) I'll pick a Karṇāta[51] quarrel with him. (*Aloud.*) Who do you think you are, Vīraka? Candanaka searched this carriage and now you want to search it again.

VĪRAKA: And who do you think you are?

CANDANAKA: You may be an honored and respected man, but you forget your caste!

VĪRAKA: And what is my caste then?

CANDANAKA: Who wants to say it?

VĪRAKA: Say it!

CANDANAKA: No, I don't think I will. I know it, but I am a man of honor. But I'll keep it a secret. No use breaking a wood apple.

VĪRAKA: Say it! Say it!

Candanaka makes a meaningful gesture.

VĪRAKA: And what does that mean?

CANDANAKA: When you became a captain, you had your old flat stone in your hand, you tied up and curled people's hair and handled a razor busily![52]

VĪRAKA: You are also an honorable man, Candanaka, but you don't seem to remember *your* caste.

CANDANAKA: What is the caste of Candanaka, me pure as the moon?

VĪRAKA: Who wants to say it?

CANDANAKA: Say it! Say it!

Vīraka makes a meaningful gesture.

CANDANAKA: And what is that supposed to mean?

VĪRAKA: All right, listen. Your caste is pure enough: your mother was a kettledrum, your father a drum, and your brother a tambourine, you foulmouthed upstart. That's how you became a captain.

CANDANAKA (*angrily*): I, Candanaka, a *tanner*? Search that coach!

VĪRAKA: Hey, coachman! Turn the carriage. I want to search it. (*Vardhamāna obeys. Vīraka starts to step into the carriage, but Candanaka pulls him down by his hair, throws him down, and kicks him.*)

VĪRAKA (*getting up in a rage*): Hey, you! Here I am quietly going about the king's business and you pull me down by my hair and kick me around! Now listen to me, if I am not going to have you drawn and quartered in court, I am not Vīraka!

CANDANAKA: All right, go to the king or the judge. Who cares about you, dogface!

VĪRAKA: I will! (*Exit.*)

CANDANAKA (*looking in all directions*): Get away, coachman. If anybody questions you, tell him that Candanaka and Vīraka have searched the carriage. My lady, I'll give you a token to remember me by. (*He hands Āryaka his sword.*)

ĀRYAKA (*taking the sword to himself with joy*): I have found a sword and my right arm tenses! Everything is going well and I am safe!

CANDANAKA: My lady, I have cleared you—please remember Candanaka. It is not that I want anything, I say this in friendship.

ĀRYAKA: Today fate has made Candanaka, honorable as the moon, into a friend. Indeed I shall remember him if the prediction comes true.

CANDANAKA: May Śiva, Viṣṇu, Brahmā, Sun, and Moon grant you a safe conduct when you have slain the party of your enemies, as the Goddess once slew Śumbha and Niśumbha!

(*Exit the coachman with the carriage.*)

CANDANAKA (*looking backstage*): Look, when he rode off, my good friend Śarvilaka followed him as his faithful shadow. . . . All right, now I have made Vīraka, trusted chief constable to the king, my enemy. . . . Let me also follow this Āryaka now, with my sons and my brothers. (*Exit.*)

ACT SEVEN

Enter Cārudatta and Maitreya.

MAITREYA: Look how beautiful the old Puṣpakaraṇḍaka park really is!

CĀRUDATTA: Yes, it is beautiful, my friend.

> The blossoms are like articles displayed
> Before the boughs that do a busy trade,
> While, roving tax-collectors, sharp-eyed bees
> Are quick to levy duties on the trees.

MAITREYA: Come, sit down on this flat stone; it may not be prettied up, but it makes a nice enough seat.

CĀRUDATTA (*sitting down*): Vardhamāna is late.

MAITREYA: I told him to get Vasantasenā here at once.

CĀRUDATTA: I wonder what is keeping him. A slow cart in front of him he is waiting to pass? Perhaps he had to turn back with a broken axle, or are the reins torn? Or may he have had to come by another way because the road was blocked by a tree the lumberjacks left lying when they finished? Is he too easy on his team, or just taking his time?

Enter Vardhamāna with the carriage which hides Āryaka.

VARDHAMĀNA: Come on, bullocks! Faster!

ĀRYAKA (*to himself*):

> The king's guards startle me time and again,
> For I'm not free while I still drag my chain;
> But in this good man's coach am I kept best—
> An unknown cuckoo safe in a strange nest!

Aho! I am quite a way out of town! Shall I now get out of the carriage and hide in the park bushes? Or wait till I meet the owner of my conveyance? But why hide in the bushes? The worshipful Master Cārudatta is famed for his mercy to all who seek his help. I shall go when I have once more revealed his fame. When he sees me emerged from an ocean of disaster, the good man will be reassured. For that I have kept body and soul together despite everything I owe to the virtues of this noble man.

VARDHAMĀNA: Here is the park. I'll drive up to them. (*Approaching.*) Master Maitreya!

MAITREYA: I have good news for you. Vardhamāna is calling. Vasantasenā must have come.

CĀRUDATTA: I am very glad!

MAITREYA: You whoreson! What was keeping you?

VARDHAMĀNA: Don't rage at me, Master Maitreya. I found I had forgotten the carriage cushions and had to go and get them. That's why I am so late.

CĀRUDATTA: Vardhamāna, turn the carriage around. Maitreya, friend, help Vasantasenā descend.

MAITREYA: Bah, does she have chains on her feet that she can't get out by herself? (*He gets up and opens the carriage.*) What! That's not Mistress Vasantasenā, that is a Mister Vasantasenā!

CĀRUDATTA: Stop joking, love does not suffer delay. But I shall help her out myself. (*He gets up.*)

ĀRYAKA (*seeing him*): Ayi, there is the owner of the carriage. He looks as good as his reputation sounds!

CĀRUDATTA (*stepping into the carriage and seeing him*): Ho! Who is this man?

> His arms are like the trunks of elephants,
> His shoulders like a lion's high and broad,
> His mighty chest still broader and well-formed,
> His copper-colored eyes are great and long—
> How can a man of such an aspect ever
> Have come to such bad days that on his feet
> The shackle of a felon should be put?

Sir, who are you?

ĀRYAKA: I am Āryaka, the subject of Gopāla, who throws himself upon your mercy!

CĀRUDATTA: The one who was taken from his village and jailed by king Pālaka?

ĀRYAKA: The same.

CĀRUDATTA: Since destiny itself has brought you here and shown you to my eyes, I will give up my life, but I will not surrender you who have thrown yourself on my mercy!

(*Āryaka shows his joy.*)

CĀRUDATTA: Vardhamānaka, take the chain from his foot.

VARDHAMĀNA: As you order, sir. (*He does so.*) Master, I have taken the chain off.

ĀRYAKA: But you have put the stronger one of friendship on!

MAITREYA: Give up that chain. He is free, now we're for it!

CĀRUDATTA: Hold your tongue!

ĀRYAKA: Cārudatta, my friend, I got into your carriage in all good faith. Please forgive me!

CĀRUDATTA: I am honored that this faith was a matter of course.

ĀRYAKA: I beg your leave. I wish to go.

CĀRUDATTA: If you must.

ĀRYAKA: Well, I shall run off.

CĀRUDATTA: No, my friend, you must not run off. Your shackles have only just been removed and you will find it difficult to move about. In this part of the country you may easily run into people, but a carriage will rouse no suspicions. You must take the carriage.

ĀRYAKA: As you say, sir.

CĀRUDATTA: Bring your relatives to safety.

ĀRYAKA: But I have found another one in you!

CĀRUDATTA: Remember me in your conversations.

ĀRYAKA: I will sooner forget myself.

CĀRUDATTA: May the gods speed your travel.

ĀRYAKA: But you yourself have saved me!

CĀRUDATTA: Your destiny has saved you.

ĀRYAKA: But surely I owe my destiny to you!

CĀRUDATTA: If Pālaka is in earnest, there will be a great force of guards abroad, so make your escape quickly.

ĀRYAKA: Then, until we meet again. (*Exit.*)

CĀRUDATTA: I have committed a great offense against the king—it would not be wise to tarry another moment. Maitreya, drop that chain in an old well, for kings may watch with the eyes of their spies.

(*He indicates that his left eye twitches.*) Maitreya, my friend, your friend is longing for Vasantasenā. Look,

> Because I do not see the one I love,
> My left eyes twitches and, in fear of the evil
> This portent prophesies, my heart is trembling.

Come, let us go. (*He walks around.*) Ho! A Buddhist friar is coming this way, and his sight spells evil! (*He hesitates.*) We shall go this way. (*Exeunt omnes.*)

ACT EIGHT

Enter the Friar with a wet tunic in his hand.

FRIAR: Pile up good works, you ignoramuses!

> Be master of your bellies, stay awake
> Forever with the drum of meditation:
> Your senses, that miscreant band of thieves,
> Rob virtue of a life's accumulation!
>
> He who has killed the Five Marauding Tribes,
> Laid low the Woman, and has slain the Rogue,
> Will of a certainty find Paradise.
>
> If you have shaved your head and snout,
> But have not shaved your mind, why shave at all?
> For he who shaves his mind clean of all thought
> Has verily and truly shaved his head!

I have dyed my tunic a monkish red, so I'd better run into Saṃsthānaka's garden and rinse it in his lotus pond. And then I'll be off, and quick! (*He walks around and does so.*)

OFFSTAGE: Stop, you scurvy friar, stop!

FRIAR (*looking about, afraid*): Help! There's Saṃsthānaka coming, the king's brother-in-law! A friar offended him once, and ever since whenever he sees another friar he puts a hole through his nose as though he were a cow and chases him off. I am helpless, where am I to find help? But the Lord Buddha himself will help me.

Enter Saṃsthānaka with the Libertine, who holds a sword.

SAṂSTHĀNAKA: Stop, you scurvy monk! Stop! I'll crush your head like a radish in the tavern! (*He beats him.*)

LIBERTINE: It is not proper to beat a monk who has renounced the world and taken the red cloth, Bastard. What do you care about him? Look, sir, this garden is accessible to everyone. Ah! The very trees practice charity by granting protection to the unprotected, the park itself is as unguarded as the heart of evil men; and its pleasures are not mortgaged like those of a new-found kingdom!

FRIAR: Well met. Be gracious, servant.

SAṂSTHĀNAKA: Master, look! He is calling me names!

LIBERTINE: What does he say?

SAṂSTHĀNAKA: He is calling me a servant. I am not a barber, am I?

LIBERTINE: On the contrary, he is speaking your praise as the Buddha's Servant.

SAṂSTHĀNAKA: More praise, Friar, more praise!

FRIAR: Blest art thou and holy again!

SAṂSTHĀNAKA: Master, now he is calling me a blistered hooligan!

LIBERTINE: But he is praising you, Bastard. He says: Blest art thou and holy again!

SAṂSTHĀNAKA: What has he come here for, master?

FRIAR: To wash out my tunic.

SAṂSTHĀNAKA: Why, you scurvy monk! My sister's husband has given me personally this most beautiful park of all the parks of Ujjayinī, and here in my very own Puṣpakaraṇḍaka park, in my very own lotus pond, where the dogs and the jackals drink and I don't bathe, most eminent person and personage though I am, you are washing your foul-smelling tunic spotted like old bean soup! I'll fine you one blow.

LIBERTINE: I believe that this friar did not take his vows very long ago, Bastard.

SAṂSTHĀNAKA: How do you know?

LIBERTINE: The skin of his forehead is still white, though he is shaven. He has worn his tunic a very short time, for there is no callus on his shoulder yet. He is not yet accustomed to his red habit, for he wears it far too short; and he has too much cloth left on top, so that it is loose and does not stay on his shoulder.

FRIAR: You are right, servant. I have renounced quite recently.

SAṂSTHĀNAKA: Why didn't you renounce right at birth? (*He beats him.*)

FRIAR: Glory to Buddha!

LIBERTINE: Why must you beat the wretch? Leave him be and let him go.

SAṂSTHĀNAKA: Hey, you, stop! I want to consult.

LIBERTINE: With whom?

SAṂSTHĀNAKA: With my own heart.

LIBERTINE: What! He still has one?

SAṂSTHĀNAKA: Dear little heart of mine, dear little master, should this monk go or stay? (*To himself.*) He should neither go nor stay. (*Aloud.*) Master, I have consulted with my heart. And my heart has advised me.

LIBERTINE: What does it say?

SAṂSTHĀNAKA: He should neither go nor stay, neither breathe in nor out. In fact, he should drop dead on the spot.

FRIAR: Glory to Buddha! I crave help!

LIBERTINE: Let him go.

SAṂSTHĀNAKA: Yes, but on one condition.

LIBERTINE: What condition?

SAṂSTHĀNAKA: He must throw away the dirt in such a way that the water does not get soiled. Or he'd better pile up the water and then throw the dirt away.

LIBERTINE: Oh, stupidity! The earth is groaning under her load of fools, walking trees of flesh with rocks in their heads and topsy-turvy minds.

The Friar mocks Saṃsthānaka with gestures.

SAṂSTHĀNAKA: What does he say?

LIBERTINE: He is praising you.

SAṂSTHĀNAKA: More praise, more praise, lots more!

Friar obeys and makes his exit.

LIBERTINE: Behold the splendor of the park!

> The trees resplendent in their fruit and bloom,
> Protected by the king's keen guard from doom,
> And by the creeper vines closely embraced
> Like husbands with their women interlaced . . .

SAṂSTHĀNAKA: Well spoken, master!

> The ground is colorful with many flowers,
> Under the heavy blossoms bow the trees,
> And from the treetops hang liana bowers
> Where monkeys dart around like honey bees.

LIBERTINE: Here is a flat rock, Bastard. Sit down.

SAṂSTHĀNAKA: I am seated. (*He sits with the Libertine.*) Master, I am still thinking about Vasantasenā. She is as hard to forget as the promptings of a seducer . . .

LIBERTINE (*to himself*): So he is still dreaming of her, although she has refused him. But then, a base man falls deeper in love if the woman despises him, while with a good man love dwindles or vanishes.
SAṂSTHĀNAKA: Master, it has been quite a while now since I told Sthāvaraka to bring the carriage here as fast as possible. And he still has not come! And I have been famished for hours! And you can't go walk at noon, look,

For like a maddened ape the sun is burning
Blindingly in the middle of the sky,
And Earth is pining sadly like a mourning
Gāndhārī[53] who her hundred sons saw die!

LIBERTINE: So it is.

The cows are sleeping in the shade
Spilling mouthfuls of grass—wild deer
Drink thirstily warm water at the ponds—
No one now ventures on the road to town
For fear of sunstroke, and methinks the coach
Has left the hot road and stopped its course.

SAṂSTHĀNAKA: Master!

The sun's hot foot bears down upon my head,
The birds and feathered bipeds roost in bed,
Men, folks, and people long and hotly sigh
And from the heat into their shelters fly.

Master, the coachman still isn't coming! I'll sing a song to pass the time. (*He sings.*) Master! Master! Did you hear me sing?
LIBERTINE: You are a Gandharva,[54] what more can I say?
SAṂSTHĀNAKA: Sure I'm a Gandharva! I have been gargling the finest mouthwash, spirit of hingu, cumminum, cyperus, knot of violet, sugar, and ginger, so of course I am in very fine voice. Master, I'll now sing another song. (*He sings.*) Did you hear me sing?
LIBERTINE: You are a Gandharva, what more can a man say?
SAṂSTHĀNAKA: Of course I am a Gandharva! I have been eating stewed nightingales with spirit of hingu, dusted with pepper, dripped with oil, and mixed with butter. Of course I am in fine voice! But still the coachman has not come, master!
LIBERTINE: Do not excite yourself, please. He'll be here soon enough.

Enter Vasantasenā in the carriage with the coachman.

COACHMAN: Now I am getting scared. It's past noon—I hope that the king's brother-in-law Saṃsthānaka isn't furious. I must drive faster. Come on, beasts, faster!

VASANTASENĀ: Oh, oh! That is not Vardhamāna's voice! What has happened? Has Master Cārudatta sent another coachman with another carriage to rest his first team? My right eye is quivering. My heart is beating. I am standing up in a void. I see everything staggering around me!

SAṂSTHĀNAKA (*hearing the wheels*): The carriage has come, master.

LIBERTINE: How do you know?

SAṂSTHĀNAKA: Don't you see? You can hear it rumble like an old pig!

LIBERTINE (*looking*): Nicely observed! It's come indeed.

SAṂSTHĀNAKA: Sthāvaraka, my son, slave, so there you are?

COACHMAN: Yes, sir.

SAṂSTHĀNAKA: And so is the carriage?

COACHMAN: Yes, sir.

SAṂSTHĀNAKA: And so are the bullocks?

COACHMAN: Yes, sir.

SAṂSTHĀNAKA: And so are you?

COACHMAN (*laughing*): Yes, master, so am I.

SAṂSTHĀNAKA: Then drive up here.

COACHMAN: By which way?

SAṂSTHĀNAKA: Over the wall, where it has collapsed.

COACHMAN: But that would kill the bullocks, master, and the carriage will break down, and I'll get killed.

SAṂSTHĀNAKA: Bah, I am the king's brother-in-law! If the bullocks are killed, I'll buy others. If the carriage breaks down, I'll have another one made. If you die, I'll have another coachman.

COACHMAN: Yes, everything will be fine, only I won't be myself any more.

SAṂSTHĀNAKA: Bah, to hell with everything, you drive over the wall!

COACHMAN: Break down, carriage, break down with your master! We'll have to replace you. I'll go tell my master. (*Entering stage center.*) What! You made it without breaking! Master, the carriage is here.

SAṂSTHĀNAKA: No bullocks torn? No ropes killed? You have survived?

COACHMAN: Yes, sir.

SAṂSTHĀNAKA: Come here, master, we'll inspect our carriage. Master, you are my one and principal master, in fact I am to treat you with the

greatest consideration as a most considerate and considerable person—you be the first to step into the carriage.
LIBERTINE: So be it. (*He steps into the carriage.*)
SAṂSTHĀNAKA: Hey, wait a minute! Is this your father's carriage, that you should step into it first? I am the owner! I'll get in first!
LIBERTINE: But you told me yourself!
SAṂSTHĀNAKA: Even if I did tell you myself, you should have had the common courtesy to say: After you, my master!
LIBERTINE: After you, my master.
SAṂSTHĀNAKA: I will now ascend. Sthāvaraka, my son! Turn the carriage, slave.
COACHMAN (*turning it*): Please get in, master.
Saṃsthānaka gets into the carriage and looks around; then he shows great fear, jumps down hurriedly, and throws his arms about the Libertine's neck.
SAṂSTHĀNAKA: Master, you are lost, you are lost! There is either a ghoul or a robber in the coach. If it is a ghoul, we'll both be robbed! If it is a robber, we'll both be eaten alive!
LIBERTINE: There is nothing to fear. Why should a ghoul go for a ride in a bullock cart? I am afraid that you got blinded by the midday sun and when you saw Sthāvaraka's armored shadow mistook it for someone else.
SAṂSTHĀNAKA: Sthāvaraka, my son! Are you still alive, slave?
COACHMAN: Yes, sir.
SAṂSTHĀNAKA: Then there is a woman in the carriage, master.
LIBERTINE: What? A woman? Then let us depart at once and bow our heads like bulls which feel the rain in their eyes. For as I wish the respect of society, my eye must be shy of lighting upon a well-born lady.

VASANTASENĀ (*astonished, to herself*): What! The king's brother-in-law, who is torture to my eyes! Then I am in danger, misfortune pursues me. . . . Now my coming here will be as fruitless as seed that falls on salty soil. What can I do?

SAṂSTHĀNAKA: He's afraid, the old clerk! He does not search the carriage. . . . Master, search the carriage!
LIBERTINE: It can do no harm. All right, I will.
SAṂSTHĀNAKA: Look, the jackals fly up and the crows run off! I am getting away from here while my master is being eaten by the eyes and seen by the teeth!
LIBERTINE (*seeing Vasantasenā, to himself, in despair*): Oh, what is this? The doe that seeks the tiger! Alas, the swan has deserted her drake,

who rests like the autumn moon on the sand bars, to court a crow. . . . (*Aloud.*) Vasantasenā, this is not right! It is not proper! First you despised him nobly, and now, pressed by your mother for the money, . . .

VASANTASENĀ (*shaking her head*): No!

LIBERTINE: . . . you honor him again with all the baseness of a harlot's character. Did I not tell you to serve them equally, the ones you *like* as well as the ones you hate?

VASANTASENĀ: I have come here because I mistook the carriage. I beg protection!

LIBERTINE: Don't worry, don't worry. Well, I'll deceive him. . . . (*He goes back to Saṃsthānaka.*) You were right, Bastard, there's a ghoul in there.

SAṂSTHĀNAKA: But, master, if there is a ghoul in there, how come you haven't been robbed, or if it is a robber, why haven't you been eaten?

LIBERTINE: Why should I inquire? But why don't we walk back to Ujjayinī through the parks?

SAṂSTHĀNAKA: Whyever should we do such a thing?

LIBERTINE: For the exercise, and to give the bullocks a rest.

SAṂSTHĀNAKA: All right then. Slave, bring the carriage back. No! Wait! I should *walk* in the sight of the gods and the Brahmins? Never! If I am going in my carriage, then they'll see me from afar and say: "There goes my lord the King's brother-in-law!"

LIBERTINE (*to himself*): It is hard to make medicine out of poison! Well, I must . . . (*Aloud.*) Bastard, Vasantasenā has come to court you.

VASANTASENĀ: Heaven forbid!

SAṂSTHĀNAKA (*happily*): Me, master? Me, the great man, the little Great God myself?

LIBERTINE: Yes indeed.

SAṂSTHĀNAKA: That's an unexpected stroke of luck! At the time I made her angry, now I'll ask forgiveness at her feet.

LIBERTINE: Well spoken!

SAṂSTHĀNAKA: I throw myself at her feet! (*He approaches Vasantasenā.*) Mother of mine, listen to my prayer—

> I hurl myself at thy feet, Great-eyed One!
> My hands, Ten-toed, Clean-toothed One, are folded!
> Whatever wrong I have done in love's lunacy,
> Forgive me, nobly limbed one, I am thy slave.

VASANTASENĀ (*in anger*): Go away, your tongue is foul! (*She kicks him.*)

SAṂSTHĀNAKA: You have kicked this head that aunts and mothers kiss, that refuses to bow before the gods! You have dropped it in the dust as a jackal drops a corpse in the jungle! Hey, slave, how did you come by her?

COACHMAN: The main road was blocked by peasant carts, sir. So I left the carriage by Cārudatta's grove and got down to push one cart out of the way. I suppose she must have gotten into the carriage by mistake.

SAṂSTHĀNAKA: So she came by mistake? Not to court me? Get out! Get out of my carriage! You court a petty merchant's son, a pauper, and drive my bullocks! Get out, you slave girl, get out!

VASANTASENĀ: "You court Master Cārudatta—" yes, it is true! It is a compliment to me. Whatever may happen, let it happen.

SAṂSTHĀNAKA: With these two hands that boast ten beautiful nails, with these two hands that are as ready to caress as to whip, I shall drag you out of my carriage, pretty girl, by your hair, just as Jaṭāyu did to Vālin's mistress!

LIBERTINE: No! Women of such gifts must not be dragged by their hair—the vines of the garden don't deserve to lose their blossoms. Stand up, I shall help her down. Vasantasenā, descend.

Vasantasenā descends and stands aside.

SAṂSTHĀNAKA (*to himself*): She roused my anger with her insults, but now she has raised it to fury with her kick! Now I'll kill her. Yes, I must. (*Aloud.*) Master, wouldn't you like a nice wide cloak with a broad fringe of a hundred threads, and plenty of meat to eat your fill with, chew, chew, smack, chew?

LIBERTINE: And if so?

SAṂSTHĀNAKA: Then do me a favor!

LIBERTINE: Certainly I will, unless it is a crime.

SAṂSTHĀNAKA: Oh, master, not a ghost of a crime! There's no ghoul either.

LIBERTINE: Speak up then.

SAṂSTHĀNAKA: Kill Vasantasenā.

LIBERTINE (*stopping his ears*): Kill this young woman, the ornament of a city? This courtesan who loves like a lady? If I kill this innocent woman, what boat will ferry me across the river of hell?

SAṂSTHĀNAKA: I'll get you a raft. Besides, who is going to see you kill her? The park is deserted.

LIBERTINE:

> The Guardians of the woods will see me kill,
> And Space, and Moon and Sun with flaming rays,
> The Wind, and Justice, and the Sky, my Soul,
> And Earth who witnesses all good and sin.

SAṂSTHĀNAKA: Well, cover her up with your cloak before you kill her!

LIBERTINE: Fool, you are lost to all sense of justice!

SAṂSTHĀNAKA: Bah, the old bore is scared of crime. All right, I'll persuade my slave Sthāvaraka. Sthāvaraka, my boy, I'll give you bracelets of gold.

COACHMAN: And I'll put them on!

SAṂSTHĀNAKA: And I'll have a golden stool made for you.

COACHMAN: And I'll sit on it!

SAṂSTHĀNAKA: And I'll give you all my left-overs.

COACHMAN: And I'll eat them!

SAṂSTHĀNAKA: And I'll make you overseer of all my slaves.

COACHMAN: Master, I'll be good!

SAṂSTHĀNAKA: Then you must do what I say.

COACHMAN: Anything, master, anything bar crime.

SAṂSTHĀNAKA: There's not a ghost of a crime.

COACHMAN: Speak, sir!

SAṂSTHĀNAKA: Kill Vasantasenā!

COACHMAN: Mercy, my lord! Base as I am, I have brought the lady here only by mistake.

SAṂSTHĀNAKA: Bah, slave, even over you I hold no power?

COACHMAN: Over my body, yes; but not over my actions. Mercy, my lord, mercy! I am scared!

SAṂSTHĀNAKA: You are my slave! Why should you be afraid?

COACHMAN: Of the world hereafter, my lord.

SAṂSTHĀNAKA: What world hereafter?

COACHMAN: The world I make with my good and evil actions.

SAṂSTHĀNAKA: What do you make with good actions?

COACHMAN: A world like yours, sir, with lots of gold.

SAṂSTHĀNAKA: And what with evil?

COACHMAN: Like mine, where you have to eat the food of others. No, I'll do no crime.

SAṂSTHĀNAKA: Bah, you will not kill? (*He thrashes him thoroughly.*)

COACHMAN: Beat me, master, murder me, master, but I won't commit a crime. I have been born a slave because of the faults in my fate, and I will not buy worse—therefore I shun crime.
VASANTASENĀ: Master, I seek protection!
LIBERTINE: Bastard, pardon her! Pardon her! Well done, Sthāvaraka.

A slave, a pauper who's brought down by fate,
He craves salvation, but his master none—
Why is it fate never brings down the great
Who foster evil and who virtue shun?

Fate is a whore who chooses sides,
If he is slave and you a lord:
For he cannot enjoy your power,
And you need not obey his word.

SAṂSTHĀNAKA (*to himself*): The old jackal is afraid of injustice, that slave is afraid of the next world. But I am brother-in-law to the king! Whom should I fear, I, most eminent human male! (*Aloud.*) Hey, you, slave, son of a slave, away with you! Go to bed by yourself and rest.
COACHMAN: As you please, my lord. (*Approaching Vasantasenā.*) My lady, that is all I am capable of. . . . (*Exit.*)
SAṂSTHĀNAKA (*girding himself*): You stay, Vasantasenā, you stay. I am going to kill you.
LIBERTINE: Aah! He'll murder her before my eyes! (*He grabs him by the throat.*)
SAṂSTHĀNAKA (*falling to the ground*): Master, you are killing your lord! (*He faints and regains consciousness.*) I have fed you meat and butter at all times, but now there is something to be done you turn against me! (*Thinking.*) Good, I have found a way. The old jackal has been signaling to her with his head. I'll send him away and kill Vasantasenā when he is gone. Yes, fine. (*Aloud.*) Master, do you really think that a man like me, born in a family as great at least as a wrestler, would commit the kind of crime I mentioned? I only said that to persuade her.
LIBERTINE: Why talk of family? It is character that counts. Thorny trees thrive better on good soil.
SAṂSTHĀNAKA: Master, when you are there, she is shy and won't come around. Go now. My slave Sthāvaraka ran away when I beat him. He is escaping! Will you catch him and bring him back here, master?

VASANTASENĀ (*holding him by the hem of his cloak*): I said I need protection!

LIBERTINE: Don't worry, Vasantasenā. Bastard, I leave Vasantasenā in your hands as a sacred trust.

SAṂSTHĀNAKA: Sure, she remains in my hands for a secret thrust.

LIBERTINE: Truly?

SAṂSTHĀNAKA: Truly!

LIBERTINE (*starting, but stopping after a few steps*): But no! As soon as I am gone, he may kill her ruthlessly. I'll conceal myself and see what he wants with her. (*He stands aside.*)

SAṂSTHĀNAKA: Good! Now I'll kill her! No, wait—that Brahmin is a shrewd deceiver. The old jackal may just have gone and hidden himself, and will raise a hullabuloo like the jackal he is. There must be a way to trick him . . . yes, that's what I'll do. (*He plucks flowers and prettifies himself.*) Vasantasenā, darling, come here, my darling!

LIBERTINE: Oho! He is the great lover now. Well, I am relieved. I'll go now. (*Exit.*)

SAṂSTHĀNAKA: I am giving you gold, I am talking sweet, I fall with head and turban and all in the dust before you. And still you don't want me, with your beautiful teeth! . . . Do you think we men are made of wood?

VASANTASENĀ: Who can doubt it now? (*She lowers her face while she recites the next two stanzas.*)

Low crook for sin to use your power,
To use your gold for a vain lure . . .
But never do bees leave the flower
However straight it grow and pure.

A poor man, if well-born and good, deserves our care:
To love such a man is any public woman's pride!

Besides, since I have known the mango tree, I will not consider a palāśa!

SAṂSTHĀNAKA: Daughter of a slave! That pauper Cārudatta you compare to a mango, and me you call a sapling, not even a sap! Even while you are insulting me you keep thinking of that man Cārudatta.

VASANTASENĀ: He lives in my heart: could I forget him?

SAṂSTHĀNAKA: So he lives in your heart? Then I can strangle him at the same time! Stay there, lover of a penniless little trader, stay there!

VASANTASENĀ: Please repeat it! Repeat that praiseworthy description!

SAṂSTHĀNAKA: Let that son of a whore, Cārudatta, protect you now!

VASANTASENĀ: He would, if he could see me.

SAṂSTHĀNAKA: Who is he? Śakra? Mahendra, son of Vālin? Rambhā's son Kālanemi? Subandhu? King Rudra? Droṇa's son Jaṭāyu or Cāṇakya, Dhundhumāra or Triśanku? Even they couldn't save you! As Cāṇakya killed Sītā in the age of the Bhāratas, so I'll strangle you as Jaṭāyu strangled Draupadī! (*He reaches out to get hold of her.*)

VASANTASENĀ: Ah, mother, where are you? Oh Cārudatta, I die before my heart's desire is done. . . . I'll scream! No! I should be ashamed to have people say that Vasantasenā screamed. I bow to the noble Cārudatta!

SAṂSTHĀNAKA: That slave girl still speaks the scoundrel's name! (*Pressing her throat.*) Think of him, slave girl! Think of him now!

VASANTASENĀ: I bow to the noble Cārudatta!

SAṂSTHĀNAKA: Die, slave girl, die! (*He mimes strangling her. Vasantasenā loses consciousness and falls down: she remains motionless.*)

SAṂSTHĀNAKA (*joyfully*):

> That crooked vessel of misconduct, witch
> That wallowed in iniquity, who came
> On time to love whoever came to love—
> Need I relate my arms' heroic acts?
> Even her breath died . . . Mother, she is dead!
> As dead as Sītā in the Bhārata!
> I wanted her, she loathed me, and my rage
> Has killed her off in this deserted park
> Puṣpakaraṇḍaka—the noose of Death
> Fell suddenly to frighten her to death.
> Poor dad and brother kept at court to miss this!
> Poor mother like another Draupadī
> To miss this spectacle of resolute
> Heroic bravery of me, her son!

All right, the old jackal will be back soon. Let me get a little away from here and wait for him. (*He does so.*)

Enter the Libertine with the Coachman.

LIBERTINE: I have been coaxing Sthāvaraka along. Now I must find the Bastard. (*He walks around, looking.*) Ai, there's a tree fallen down on the road, and falling it killed a woman! Oh murderer, why did you commit this crime? You have killed me too, murderous tree, by the sight of this woman that was killed as you fell. This is a bad omen, for indeed my heart fears for Vasantasenā. But the gods will bring luck. (*He approaches Saṃsthānaka.*)

SAṂSTHĀNAKA: I am happy you came, master. And Sthāvaraka, my son, I am happy you came too.

COACHMAN: Of course.

LIBERTINE: Return my trust.

SAṂSTHĀNAKA: What trust?

LIBERTINE: Vasantasenā.

SAṂSTHĀNAKA: She is gone.

LIBERTINE: Where?

SAṂSTHĀNAKA: After you.

LIBERTINE (*suspiciously*): She did not go this way, did she?

SAṂSTHĀNAKA: Which way did you go?

LIBERTINE: East.

SAṂSTHĀNAKA: Well, she went south.

LIBERTINE: I myself went south.

SAṂSTHĀNAKA: She went north.

LIBERTINE: You're confusing me, and my heart is not at peace. Tell me the truth!

SAṂSTHĀNAKA: I swear it on your head with my own two feet. Just set your heart at peace, I killed her.

LIBERTINE (*in despair*): You really killed her?

SAṂSTHĀNAKA: If you don't believe my word, look for yourself: the first heroic deed of Saṃsthānaka, the king's own brother-in-law. (*He shows him.*)

LIBERTINE: Then I am lost, wretch that I am! (*He falls in a faint.*)

SAṂSTHĀNAKA: Well, well, master is dead!

COACHMAN: Courage, master, take courage. I killed her first by bringing the carriage here without thinking!

LIBERTINE (*regaining consciousness, sadly*):

The stream of charm at last ran dry,
And love returned to her own land. . . . Ah, thou
Beautiful woman of the sparkling gems,
Brilliantly expert in the games of love,
River of kindliness with laughing isles,
Alas, thou refuge of the likes of me . . .

The market place of love is bankrupt now
With all its piles of happiness for sale . . .

(*Weeping.*)

Ah, dire calamity!

What did you hope to gain with what you wrought?
The blackguard killed our city's charm of luck. . . .

(*To himself.*) Oh, The criminal may even put the crime on me. . . . Yes, I must get away from here. (*He circles the stage. Saṃsthānaka approaches him and tries to stop him.*)

LIBERTINE: Don't touch me, murderer! I have finished with you. I am leaving you!

SAṂSTHĀNAKA: Aha, first you assassinate Vasantasenā and now you try to blame me for it? Where do you think you are going?

LIBERTINE: Degenerate!

SAṂSTHĀNAKA: I'll give you a hundred different things, I'll give you gold, I'll give you coin, I'll give you pennies. May my criminal bravado be shared by all the people!

LIBERTINE: Fie! It must remain yours alone!

COACHMAN: Heaven help us!

Saṃsthānaka laughs.

LIBERTINE:

No love will be between us evermore.
Cease laughing! Fie, a curse on friendship which
Debases and humiliates the friend.
Would that I never had concourse with you,
I throw you off as one throws off the bow
Whose cord has snapped!

SAṂSTHĀNAKA: Please, master, be nice to me. Come on, let's go to town and have fun.

LIBERTINE:

I am no outcast, but I served with you
And now I'm deemed an outcast and debased.
Could I still follow you who killed a woman?
On whom the women look with quick dread eyes?

(*Sadly.*) Vasantasenā, may you be spared the life of a courtesan in your next birth and be reborn in a pure and virtuous family!

SAṂSTHĀNAKA: Where do you think you are going after murdering Vasantasenā in my own park Puṣpakaraṇḍaka? Come on! You'll answer for the crime before my brother-in-law the king! (*He holds on to him.*)

LIBERTINE: Ah, wait, you miserable crook! (*He bares his sword.*)

SAṂSTHĀNAKA (*stepping away in fear*): Hey, what now? You scared? All right, run!

LIBERTINE (*to himself*): I would be a fool to stay. Yes indeed, I'll join the noble Śarvilaka and Candanaka and their party. (*Exit.*)

SAṂSTHĀNAKA: Go to hell! Hey, Sthāvaraka, my boy, how did I do?

COACHMAN: You have done a great crime, my lord.

SAṂSTHĀNAKA: What, slave? You say I have done a crime. All right, come on then. (*He takes off some of his ornaments.*) Take these jewels. I give them to you. But they are mine as long as I want to wear them. The rest of the time you can have them.

COACHMAN: On you they look good, my lord. What use are they to me?

SAṂSTHĀNAKA: Go now. Take these bullocks here and wait for me in the dovecot at the palace until I am back.

COACHMAN: As you command, my lord. (*Exit.*)

SAṂSTHĀNAKA: The master has disappeared to save his own skin, and this slave I'll put in chains and I'll jail him in the dovecot. So we'll keep our counsel. Now I must go. No, one more look at her to see if she's dead. Perhaps I'll have to kill her again. (*He looks at her.*) Well, she is very nicely dead. Good. I'll cover her with my cloak. Wait a minute, my name is on it. An educated person would recognize it. Good, I'll cover her up with this pile of dry leaves which a whirlwind has blown up. (*He does so and pauses to think.*) Good, that's what I'll do. Now I'll go to the court and enter a complaint that Cārudatta the provost has trespassed on my old park Puṣpakaraṇḍaka and murdered Vasantasenā for her money. I'll play a new trick to destroy Cārudatta, a trick as heinous as killing a cow in a law-abiding town! Good, I go. (*While making his exit he sees the Friar; with fear.*) Oh, dear little mother! Wherever I go I run into this accursed friar. There he is again, with a saffron-dyed robe. I led the fellow by the nose and he'll hate me now. If he sees me he'll inform on me that I have killed her. How can I get away? (*Looking around.*) Right! I'll get out over the wall where half of it has collapsed. And flying I fly through the sky to Lankā town, as Indra flew from Hanumān's Peak through earth and hell! (*Exit.*)

Enter brusquely, without parting the curtain, the Friar.

FRIAR: I have washed my habit. Now what? Shall I hang it from a branch to dry? The monkeys will tear it to pieces. Lay it on the ground? The dust will spoil it. Now where can I put it out to dry? (*Looking around.*) I'll spread it out here on this pile of dry leaves which a whirlwind has blown up. (*He does so.*) Glory to Buddha! (*He sits down.*) Fine. Well, why don't I recite the Creed? (*He starts reciting the stanza "He who has killed the Five Marauding Tribes" but stops halfway.*) No, I am through with heaven as long as I cannot repay Vasantasenā, servant of Buddha. . . . She bought me free from those gamblers and ever since I feel she has bought me. (*He looks.*) What is this sighing under the leaves? But no, the leaves were hot from the wind and the sun and now my wet habit is dripping on them, that's why they are fluttering like wings.

Vasantasenā, regaining consciousness, puts out a hand.

FRIAR: Oho! The hand of a woman, with beautiful bracelets and rings! What is this? And another hand even! (*He studies them intently.*) I think I recognize this hand. But of course, I am sure! That's surely the same hand which granted me protection! I have to see about this. (*He mimes uncovering her, seeing her, and recognizing her.*) Yes, this is she, the servant of Buddha herself! (*Vasantasenā gestures that she wants water.*)

FRIAR: What? She asks for water. But the pond is far off. What am I to do now? But of course, I wring out my habit on top of her. (*He does so.*)

Vasantasenā, fully conscious now, tries to get up. The Friar fans her with his robe.

VASANTASENĀ: Who are you, sir?

FRIAR: The servant of Buddha does not remember me? The one you bought with ten pieces of gold?

VASANTASENĀ: Yes, I remember . . . but not what you said. Would I had died!

FRIAR: What has happened, servant of Buddha?

VASANTASENĀ (*dismally*): What would happen to a prostitute? . . .

FRIAR: Arise, arise, servant of Buddha! Hold on to this creeper, here close to this tree. (*He bows down the creeper. Vasantasenā stands up, holding on to it.*)

FRIAR: There's a monastery here where a sister in Buddha lives. There you will remain till you have come completely to your senses, disciple, then you may go home. Gently now, gently, servant of Buddha. (*He circles the stage, looking.*) Move away, gentlemen, out of the way. Just a young woman with a friar, that's all. My faith is a pure faith. Who masters his hand, who masters his mouth, who masters his senses is a man indeed. What profits him a royal palace? The world hereafter lies secure in his hand. (*Exeunt omnes.*)

ACT NINE

Enter an Usher.

USHER: I am the usher, and the gentlemen of the court have ordered me to go to the court hall and set out the chairs. So I'll go now and put the court in order. (*Circles the stage and looks about.*) Here we are at the court. I'll go in. (*He enters, cleans the chairs, and sets them out.*) Everything is in good order now, I am ready with the hall. The chairs are ready too. I'll inform the magistrates. (*He circles the stage and looks about.*) Why, there's the king's brother-in-law coming, that malicious scoundrel! I'll get out of his sight! (*He stands on the side.*)

Enter Saṃsthānaka in a flamboyant robe.

SAṂSTHĀNAKA:

> I took a bath in wet moist water
> And sat amidst my park and garden ground
> With women, ladies and young females
> Like a Gandharva smooth of limb and round.
>
> Now I wear curls, then I affect a tress,
> Unless I have a mind for youthful ringlets;
> Sometimes I wear it loose or sport a tuft:
> So various is a brother-in-law to kinglets!

Like a worm that is crawling inside a lotus bud to find some room to move I have found a lot of room to move in. . . . On whom am I going to drop this wretched business? (*He remembers.*) Ah, I remember now. This wretched business is going to fall on pauper Cārudatta's head! After all, he really is a pauper, they'll believe anything of him. Right. I'll go to the court hall and have an indictment written up against him, that he has murdered Vasantasenā by strangling her. In which case I'd better get to the court hall. (*He circles the stage and looks about.*) Here's the court of justice, I'll go inside. (*He enters and looks *around.*) Well, the chairs are set out already, so the magistrates will be in soon. Meanwhile I sit down on this lawn and wait for them to come. (*He remains.*)

USHER (*circling the stage at the other side and looking forward*): The magistrates are coming now. I must go up to them. (*He approaches.*)

Enter a Judge, surrounded by a Provost, a Scrivener, and attendants.

JUDGE: Well now, Provost and Scrivener . . .

PROVOST *and* SCRIVENER: Yes, sir?

JUDGE: In judiciary matters, gentlemen, a judge must rely on others, and that makes it difficult for him to penetrate the minds of those others. They'll bring up a mysterious matter that has already been thrown out of court, they are so fired with litigious passions that they gloss over their own weaknesses, and if there is a judicial error, which both parties are quick to inflate, the king himself becomes involved. Indeed—to sum up, it is easier to blame a judge than to find virtue in a witness. For a judge must not only know the law, but also be expert in detecting deceptions. He should be eloquent without anger, impartial to friend, foe, and kin, and pronounce judgment only when he has considered the facts. He must protect the shy and bully the clever, and he himself must be a just man and incorruptible. . . . If there is a way, he must direct his mind to the deeper truth and at the same time avoid angering the king.

PROVOST *and* SCRIVENER: As they say, even in a noble man's virtue there may be some vice. But then one might as well say: Even in moonlight there may be darkness.

JUDGE: My dear Usher, show us the way to the court.

USHER: Come this way, my lord.

They circle the stage.

USHER: Here is the court, enter, my lord.

All enter.

JUDGE: Usher, go outside and find out who has a case to be heard.

USHER: As it pleases your lordship. (*He goes outside.*) Gentlemen, the judge asks who has a case to be heard.

SAṂSTHĀNAKA (*happily*): The judge has come! (*Strutting around arrogantly.*) I, most eminent person and personage, god and brother-in-law to the king our prince, have a case to be heard.

USHER (*alarmed*): Oh, mother! The king's brother-in-law is the first one who has a case to be heard! Oh, well. . . . Sir, wait a moment. I'll announce it to the magistrates. (*Approaching.*) Gentlemen, that brother-in-law of the king has come to court with a case.

JUDGE: What! The king's brother-in-law is first with a case? This spells the fall of some great man, like an eclipse at sunrise. Usher, we are going to have a crowded list today. Go outside and tell him that he cannot be heard today and should go away.

USHER: As it pleases your lordship. (*He goes outside to Saṃsthānaka.*) Sir, the judge informs you that your case cannot be heard today and that you should go.

SAṂSTHĀNAKA (*angrily*): Aha! My case cannot be heard? If it isn't heard, I'll tell my brother-in-law King Pālaka, my sister's husband, and I'll tell my sister and my mother! Then I'll throw this judge out and put another in his place. (*He is about to go.*)

USHER: My lord brother-in-law to the king, wait a moment. I'll inform the magistrates. (*Going to the Judge.*) The king's brother-in-law is furious; he says, "If my case isn't heard, I'll tell my brother-in-law King Pālaka, my sister's husband, and I'll tell my sister and my mother! Then I'll throw this judge out and put another in his place."

JUDGE: The fool is capable of anything. Usher, tell him to come, his case will be heard.

USHER (*going to Saṃsthānaka*): Sir, the judge says that you may appear; your case will be heard. Please come in, sir.

SAṂSTHĀNAKA: First they say it won't be heard, and now it will be heard. Obviously the judge is terribly afraid of me! I can make him believe anything I want. Right, I'll go in. (*He enters and approaches.*) Thank you, I'm fine. Whether you are depends on me.

JUDGE (*to himself*): Ah, the solid polish of our litigant! (*Aloud.*) Be seated.

SAṂSTHĀNAKA: Well, these are my own grounds. So I'll sit down wherever I want. (*To the Provost.*) I want your seat. (*To the Usher.*) No, I'll sit down here. (*Patting the Judge's head.*) This is where I'll sit! (*He sits down on the floor.*)

JUDGE: You have a case, sir?

SAṂSTHĀNAKA: Of course.

JUDGE: State your case.

SAṂSTHĀNAKA: I'll whisper it in your ear. I have been born in a family as big as a wrestler. The king's brother-in-law is my own father, and the king is my father's own son-in-law. I am the king's brother-in-law and my own sister is the king's wife.

JUDGE: We know all that. Why boast of family? It is character which counts here. Thorny trees thrive best on good soil. State your case.

SAṂSTHĀNAKA (*to himself*): Yes, I'll tell him. Even if I am guilty myself, he won't dare to touch me. So now. (*Aloud.*) My sister's husband has given me, as a token of his favor, the old park Puṣpakaraṇḍaka, the best park in town, to play in and to keep. I go there every day to look at it, to have it kept dry and weeded and seeded and pruned. And as fate would have it, I saw (or I didn't) the corpse of a woman lying on the ground.

JUDGE: Do you know who the deceased woman was?

SAṂSTHĀNAKA: Alas, gentlemen of the court, would I not know indeed! Such a woman, the jewel of our city, with a hundred ornaments of gold, Vasantasenā herself! Some vile person lured her into the deserted park and made his hands into a noose to strangle her, just for some money. I didn't . . . (*He stops abruptly and hides his face in his hands.*)

JUDGE: The town guards are really too careless! Provost and Scrivener, take down as the first record of the case his statement that he didn't.

SCRIVENER: As it pleases your lordship. (*He does so.*) It is recorded, my lord.

SAṂSTHĀNAKA (*to himself*): Oh, mother! Like a man who gorges himself on rice milk and tries to cross a bridge I have got myself all wet now! All right then. (*Aloud.*) Now, gentlemen of the court, didn't I say that I only saw her? Why do you raise such a hullabuloo about it? (*He rubs out the record with his foot.*)

JUDGE: How did you know she was strangled, and for money?

SAṂSTHĀNAKA: That I deduced from her completely empty and wasted throat and from the fact that she didn't have any ornaments at the usual places.

PROVOST *and* SCRIVENER: That seems to make sense.

SAṂSTHĀNAKA (*to himself*): Thank god, I live again. Oh, mother!

PROVOST *and* SCRIVENER: Whom does this case involve?

JUDGE: In general there are two kinds of legal cases.

PROVOST *and* SCRIVENER: Which two?

JUDGE: Those which are judged from statements and those which are judged from facts. In the first instance, the case is judged by the testimony of plaintiff and defendant; in the latter, where the evidence is circumstantial, the case has to be solved by the intelligence of the judge.

PROVOST *and* SCRIVENER: This case involves Vasantasenā's mother.

JUDGE: Precisely. Usher, summon Vasantasenā's mother, but do not upset her.
USHER: Yes sir. (*He goes outside and returns with the courtesan's mother.*)
BAWD: My daughter just went to a friend's to enjoy her best years. And now this gentleman here, and a long life to him, tells me to come along because the judge is summoning me. I feel like fainting! My heart is beating fast. . . . Please, sir, show me the way to the court.
USHER: Follow me, ma'am. (*They both circle the stage.*)
USHER: Here's the court. Please go in, ma'am. (*Both enter.*)
BAWD (*approaching*): Good fortune to you, gentlemen!
JUDGE: Welcome, good woman. Sit down.
BAWD: I will. (*She sits down.*)
SAṂSTHĀNAKA (*with scorn*): So you came, old bawd, so you came!
JUDGE: Well, ma'am, you are Vasantasenā's mother, are you not?
BAWD: Yes, I am.
JUDGE: Where is Vasantasenā now?
BAWD: At a friend's.
JUDGE: What is that friend's name?
BAWD (*to herself*): Terrible! This is really too embarrassing! (*Aloud.*) This is a question for the vulgar, not for a judge.
JUDGE: No coyness now! The case poses the question.
PROVOST *and* SCRIVENER: Yes, the case poses the question. There's no harm in it. Answer the question.
BAWD: What, the case? Well, if that's so, listen, gentlemen. It's Provost Vinayadatta's grandson, Sāgaradatta's son, Master Cārudatta, whose name be honored. He lives on the Square of the Provosts. My daughter has gone to his house to enjoy herself.
SAṂSTHĀNAKA: You've heard it, gentlemen. Let the words be recorded. My quarrel is with Cārudatta.
PROVOST *and* SCRIVENER: There's nothing wrong with Cārudatta's being her friend.
JUDGE: But the case now involves Cārudatta.
PROVOST *and* SCRIVENER: Precisely.
JUDGE: Write it down, Dhanadatta. The first record of the case is that Vasantasenā went to Master Cārudatta's house. Why, now we must also summon Master Cārudatta, that is to say, the case requires his presence. My dear Usher, go and summon Master Cārudatta, but without upsetting or irritating him, gently and with due respect. Tell him the judge wants to see him.

USHER: As it pleases your lordship. (*He goes outside and re-enters with Cārudatta.*) This way, sir.

CĀRUDATTA (*thoughtfully*): The king knows me very well, my character as well as my family. This summons really raises doubts about my situation. (*To himself, conjecturing.*) Has it become known that the prisoner was abducted in my carriage and is now abroad unchained? Has it come to the king's ears by means of the spies through whose eyes he sees? Is that the reason that I have been summoned like a defendant? But there's no use guessing. I must go to the court. Good fellow, show me the way to the court.

USHER: Follow me, sir. (*They circle the stage.*)

CĀRUDATTA (*alarmed*): What is that?

> A crow is croaking with a gritting sound,
> While servants of the court are summoning me—
> My left eye trembles badly, and these signs
> Of imminent disaster trouble me.

USHER: Follow me, sir. Gently now, don't get upset.

CĀRUDATTA (*circling the stage*):

> Upon a dead dry tree toward the sun
> A crow is perched and points without a doubt
> Its left eye terrifyingly at me!

(*Looking elsewhere.*) What! A snake!

> With the black broken glitter of collyrium
> Fixing its eyes on me and quivering tongue,
> And baring four white fangs, the king of coils
> Rushes with wriggling swelling belly on
> To fall on me enraged where down the road
> My treading feet roused it from its sleep.

> My foot is slipping though the ground is dry,
> My eye is trembling and my left arm twitches
> And yonder bird is croaking on and on
> To spell a dreadful death that none can doubt.

But still, in any case the gods shall bring fortune.

USHER: Follow me, sir. Here's the court of justice. Please enter, sir.

CĀRUDATTA (*entering and looking all about*): Ah, how very beautiful is the court of justice!

Flowing with lawyers deep immersed in thought,
With waves and shells of busy messengers,
Peopled with spies like crocodiles and sharks,
And like huge whales with elephant and horse,
And whining plaintiffs imitating birds
While serpentine scribes are undulating through—
This Court, firmly embanked by policy,
Seems with its monsters equal to the sea.

So be it. (*While entering he mimes bumping his head; wonderingly.*) Ah, now this again!

My left eye twitches and a raven caws,
A snake has blocked my path—may fate protect me!

I must enter. (*He enters.*)

JUDGE: So this is Cārudatta. This face with eyes that are wide open and long, and with a proudly raised nose, cannot be party to a groundless crime. For as with elephants, cows, and horses, the countenances of men do not belie their natures.

CĀRUDATTA: Good fortune to the magistrates! And you, officials, are you well?

JUDGE (*with embarrassment*): Welcome, sir. Usher, fetch a seat for this gentleman!

USHER (*bringing a seat*): Here is a seat. Pray be seated, sir. (*Cārudatta sits down.*)

SAṂSTHĀNAKA: So you got here, woman-killer, eh? So you got here. Well, well, this is proper justice, this is right and just that the murderer of a woman is offered a seat! (*Drawing himself up.*) Fine, give him his seat.

JUDGE: Master Cārudatta, is there any attachment, or affection, or love between you and the daughter of this lady?

CĀRUDATTA: Which lady?

JUDGE: This one. (*He points at Vasantasenā's mother.*)

CĀRUDATTA (*rising*): Madame, I greet you.

BAWD: Live long, my son. (*To herself.*) So this is Cārudatta. . . . My daughter's youth is in good hands!

JUDGE: Is the courtesan your friend, sir?

(*Cārudatta shows embarrassment.*)

SAṂSTHĀNAKA: All this shyness and timidity only serves this trickster to hide his real nature. But now he has murdered a woman for money, his lordship shouldn't hide any longer!

PROVOST *and* SCRIVENER: Speak up, Master Cārudatta. Don't be embarrassed, this is a legal suit.

CĀRUDATTA (*ashamed*): That I should have to confirm that a courtesan is my friend! . . . But still, my youth is at fault here, not my character.

JUDGE: This case is full of obstacles. Please master your feelings of shame and speak the truth. Firmness is all we need, but falsehoods will not be accepted. No more shyness, please! The case poses the question.

CĀRUDATTA: Who is suing me, judge?

SAṂSTHĀNAKA (*arrogantly*): I am, man.

CĀRUDATTA: To be sued by you is insufferable!

SAṂSTHĀNAKA: Bah, woman-killer! You murdered a woman like Vasantasenā with her hundred ornaments of gold, and now you turn hypocrite and deny everything!

CĀRUDATTA: You are talking nonsense.

JUDGE: Enough of that, Master Cārudatta. Speak the truth. Was the courtesan your friend?

CĀRUDATTA: Yes, she was.

JUDGE: Where is she now, sir?

CĀRUDATTA: She has gone home.

PROVOST *and* SCRIVENER: Gone home? How? When? With whom?

CĀRUDATTA (*to himself*): Must I say that she sneaked away?

PROVOST *and* SCRIVENER: Answer, sir.

CĀRUDATTA: She has gone home. What else can I say?

SAṂSTHĀNAKA: You lured her to the Puṣpakaraṇḍaka park, my very own park to boot, and strangled her with your own hands for her money! Yes, and now you say she went home!

CĀRUDATTA: Pfui, prattler. Without benefit of raindrops your face resembles the wing-tops of white cāṣa blossoms, and you lose color like a lotus in winter, little purpose though it serves!

JUDGE (*to himself*): Accusing Cārudatta is like lifting the Himālaya, crossing the ocean, catching the wind! (*Aloud.*) This is Master Cārudatta, could he commit a crime? (*He repeats the lines:* "This face with eyes . . ." *etc.*)

SAṂSTHĀNAKA: Why is this case heard with such partiality?

JUDGE: Go away, you fool! You dare recite the Veda and your tongue does not shrivel and fall out? You face the sun at noon and your eyes are not blinded? You put your hand in a blazing fire and it is not burned? You slander Cārudatta's character and the earth does not swallow you? How could Master Cārudatta commit a crime?

> He left the ocean but its pride of waves,
> The wealth he gathered he did not regard—
> This noble-minded treasure house of good
> Would do for gain a crime which crooks abhor?

BAWD: Bah, hopeless fool! A man who first returned a priceless pearl necklace, the prize of four oceans, when thieves in the night made away with a golden box that was entrusted to him, a man like that would now commit murder for a trifling sum?

JUDGE: Master Cārudatta, did Vasantasenā go home on foot or by carriage?

CĀRUDATTA: But I never got to see her, so I don't know whether she went on foot or drove.

Enter Vīraka in a rage.

VĪRAKA: How slowly did the night pass while I was nursing my grievance and the humiliation of a kick grew to a deadly enmity! I must go to court! (*With a gesture of entering.*) Good fortune to you, gentlemen.

JUDGE: Ah, there is Vīraka, the captain of the town guards. What brings you here, Vīraka?

VĪRAKA: Well, in the confusion that followed after Āryaka broke out of jail, I chased the prisoner with Candanaka. I saw a closed carriage and that made me think. I wanted to search it but Lieutenant Candanaka said: "What, I have already searched it, must you search it again?" and he kicked me with his foot! Now you have heard it, gentlemen, and you decide!

JUDGE: Do you know, good man, whose carriage that was?

VĪRAKA: It belonged to Master Cārudatta here. The coachman said that Vasantasenā was being driven to Puṣpakaraṇḍaka park for an outing.

SAṂSTHĀNAKA: There you have heard it again!

JUDGE: It is as though Rāhu swallows the pure light of the moon, or a river bank collapses to soil the clear water! Vīraka, later we shall consider the merits of your case against Candanaka. But now you must mount the horse that is waiting at the judge's door and go to Puṣpakaraṇḍaka Park and see whether there is a woman dead there or not.

VĪRAKA: As it pleases your lordship. (*He goes outside and re-enters.*)

VĪRAKA: I went there. I saw the corpse of a woman that was mangled by beasts of prey.[55]

PROVOST *and* SCRIVENER: How did you know that it was the body of a woman?

VĪRAKA: I could judge that by the hair, hands, and feet that were left.

JUDGE: The law is a trial! The more thoroughly one investigates a case, the more pitfalls open up. All the rules of jurisprudence are exhausted, and one's mind is stuck like a cow in a swamp.

CĀRUDATTA: Just as hosts of bees converge on a flower as soon as it opens, so no sooner has a man come to grief than disasters multiply in the holes that are opened.

JUDGE: Master Cārudatta, tell the truth!

CĀRUDATTA: Must everything be credited that an evil-minded man is moved by the baseness of his birth to invent, a man jealous of virtue in others and blinded by passions, a man whose only desire is to do away with an enemy? Must it be credited without consideration?

> I would not lay my hands upon a bough
> And pull it toward me to pluck its bloom—
> Would I take hold of streaming bee-black locks
> And drag a weeping woman to her doom?

SAṂSTHĀNAKA: Hey, you gentlemen of the court, are you still so partial to the defendant in this suit as to allow the criminal to keep his seat?

JUDGE: Do as he says, Usher.

(*The Usher beckons Cārudatta to leave his seat.*)

CĀRUDATTA: Caution, gentlemen of the court, caution! (*He leaves his seat and sits down on the floor.*)

SAṂSTHĀNAKA (*to himself, enjoying himself hugely*): Aha! The crime I committed has now descended on another man's head! I am going to sit where Cārudatta sat. (*He does so.*) Look at me, Cārudatta, look at me now! Confess that you killed her, confess!

CĀRUDATTA: Judge, officers! Must everything be credited . . . (*he repeats the above lines; then to himself with a sigh*). Ah, Maitreya, my friend, see how sorely I am stricken. . . . Alas, my wife, who was born in so pure a family of Brahmins. . . . Oh, Rohasena, you have not seen my plight, and vainly do you still play happily while your father perishes. . . . Why is Maitreya so long? I sent him off to Vasantasenā's to seek news of her and to return the jewels she gave him to make a golden cart for Rohasena. Why is he so long?

Enter Maitreya with the jewels in his hand.

MAITREYA: Master Cārudatta sent me to Vasantasenā with these jewels. He told me, "Maitreya, Vasantasenā put her own jewelry on little Rohasena and sent him so to his mother. But Rohasena should give away jewels, not accept them! Return them to her." So I am on my way to Vasantasenā's. (*Circling the stage and looking about; then, to an imaginary person.*) Why, there's Master Rebhila. Well, Master Rebhila, why are you looking so upset? (*Listening.*) What, my good friend Cārudatta has been summoned to court? Then it can't be a small matter. (*He thinks.*) I'd better postpone going to Vasantasenā. I'll go first to the court. (*Circling the stage and looking.*) There's the court of justice, I'll go in. (*Entering.*) Good fortune to the gentlemen of the court! Where is my friend?

JUDGE: There he is.

MAITREYA: Good luck to you, friend.

CĀRUDATTA: May be.

MAITREYA: Are you safe and sound?

CĀRUDATTA: Again may be.

MAITREYA: Why are you looking so upset? Why have you been summoned?

CĀRUDATTA: A woman—or a goddess of love—it makes no difference, would have been—as though I were a cruel man who knows of no heaven or hell, would have been—no, let him say the word!

MAITREYA: What? What?

CĀRUDATTA: This (*whispers it in his ear*).

MAITREYA: Who says so?

CĀRUDATTA (*pointing at Saṃsthānaka with his head*): That wretch, but he is only the instrument. Fate itself indicts me.

MAITREYA (*aside*): But why didn't you say she went home?

CĀRUDATTA: I *have* said it; but in the circumstances they won't believe me.

MAITREYA: Listen, you gentlemen! This man who has made the city of Ujjayinī beautiful with civic buildings, cloisters, public parks, temples, ponds, wells, and pillars, this man would now that he is impoverished commit a murder for a trifling sum of money? (*Angrily.*) Bah, you bastard, Saṃsthānaka, brother-in-law to our king! Debased and debauched basket of slander! I dare you to say, gold-jacketed monkey, to say to my face how my good friend, who is too gentle to pull down a blossoming madhavī creeper to pluck its flowers for fear that a young shoot may get cut, now could commit a heinous crime execrated in this world and the next! Wait, you son of a bawd, wait, I say, I'll beat your head to pieces with this stick that is as crooked as your evil heart!

SAṂSTHĀNAKA (*in a rage*): Do you hear that, gentlemen? I have a quarrel or a suit going with Cārudatta! Then why do you—crowfoot! skullhead!—threaten to beat my head to pieces?

Maitreya, raising his stick, repeats his insults. Saṃsthānaka gets up in a rage and hits him. Maitreya hits back. They go on hitting one another. The jewels fall from Maitreya's belt.

SAṂSTHĀNAKA (*sweeping them up and looking at them, astounded*): Look at these jewels, gentlemen, look at them! This is the poor woman's jewelry! (*Pointing at Cārudatta.*) And for this trifle he has killed and murdered her!

All the gentlemen of the court lower their faces.

CĀRUDATTA: Such a splash of jewels falling at this time for all to see by my own bad luck will cause my downfall. . . .

MAITREYA: Why don't you tell what really happened?

CĀRUDATTA: Friend, the eyesight of a king is bad; he cannot see reality. And an ignoble death awaits him who pleads poverty.

JUDGE: Alas, Jupiter is embattled with Mars; and while it is sinking, another planet arises like a comet of doom.

PROVOST *and* SCRIVENER (*looking up, to Vasantasenā's mother*): Look closely at this golden jewel box, ma'am. Is it the same or not?

BAWD (*studying it*): It looks like it, but it is not the same.

SAṂSTHĀNAKA: Bah, old bawd, you shouted it with your eyes and now you deny it with your tongue!

BAWD: Go away, wretch.

PROVOST *and* SCRIVENER: Don't speak rashly: is it the same or not?

BAWD: Sir, the jeweler's art holds my eye, but it is not the same.

JUDGE: Do you recognize the jewels themselves, good woman?

BAWD: I said it already: no, I don't recognize them, but a jeweler may well have copied them from hers.

JUDGE: You know, Provost, different things may certainly be similar, in shape as well as in the artificial quality of jewelry. And the jewelers' guild may see such a work of art and copy it; the artfulness of their hands will deceive the eye with a resemblance.

PROVOST *and* SCRIVENER: Do these jewels belong to Master Cārudatta?

CĀRUDATTA: Indeed not, indeed not.

PROVOST *and* SCRIVENER: To whom do they belong then?
CĀRUDATTA: To this lady's daughter.
PROVOST *and* SCRIVENER: How did they get separated from her?
CĀRUDATTA: Indeed they were separated. Yes, indeed.
PROVOST *and* SCRIVENER: Master Cārudatta, here the truth must be told. Truth brings happiness. A truthful man will never sin. Truth is one syllable, don't hide it with falsehood.
CĀRUDATTA: I don't know these jewels for what they are precisely, but I do know that they were fetched from our house.
SAMSTHĀNAKA: Yes, you first lured her to the park and killed her; but now you try to hide it, hypocrite!

JUDGE: Tell the truth, Master Cārudatta. Now the hard whips will unhesitantly fall upon your gentle body, and with them our hopes will fall.
CĀRUDATTA: I have been born of a family of blameless men, and I am innocent! But if I am suspected, what does it matter whether I am innocent? (*To himself.*) And what does it matter whether I live, when Vasantasenā has gone? (*Aloud.*) To cut it short, a woman or a goddess of love—what difference does it make?—I have cruelly, ignoring heaven or hell, . . . let the other say the word!

SAṂSTHĀNAKA: Murdered! Say it: I have murdered!
CĀRUDATTA: You have said it.
SAṂSTHĀNAKA: Did you hear, did you hear, gentlemen? He has murdered her. He has solved the case himself! This pauper Cārudatta should be condemned to death.
JUDGE: Usher, the king will rule. Royal guards, seize Cārudatta.
The guards seize him.

BAWD: Mercy, gentlemen, mercy! (*She repeats*: "A man who returned . . .") If my daughter has been killed, she is killed. But this man must live. Besides, a suit is a matter between two parties. I am a party, therefore let him go.

SAṂSTHĀNAKA: Off with you, born slave! Go! What has it got to do with you?
JUDGE: You must leave, ma'am. Royal guards, take her outside.
BAWD: Oh, my child, oh, my son! (*Exit, weeping.*)
SAṂSTHĀNAKA (*to himself*): I have excelled myself! Now I'll go. (*Exit.*)
JUDGE: Master Cārudatta, a judge decides guilt, the king decides the punishment. Nevertheless, Usher, inform King Pālaka that Manu[56]

has ruled that this guilty Brahmin may not be killed, but should be exiled from this kingdom with his personal fortune intact.

USHER: As it pleases your lordship. (*Exit and re-enter in tears.*)

USHER: Sir, I have been there. King Pālaka replies: "The criminal who has murdered Vasantasenā for a trifling sum will have the jewelry for which he murdered hung around his neck, be taken to the southern burning-field with drums beating, and be broken on the pole. Whoever commits a similar crime will receive the same punishment."

CĀRUDATTA: Alas, King Pālaka acts without consideration. But then, when kings have been thrown into the fire of lawsuits they rightly come to grief. Thousands of innocent men have been and are being killed by those extraordinary violators of royal decree. . . . Maitreya, my friend, go and take my son's mother my last greetings. And protect my son Rohasena.

MAITREYA: If the roots are cut, why keep the tree?

CĀRUDATTA: Do not say that. When men have died their sons remain in their image. The friendship you have borne me should now fall to Rohasena.

MAITREYA: Must I who am your friend live on while you are gone?

CĀRUDATTA: Let my eyes dwell once more on Rohasena.

MAITREYA: Yes, that is proper.

JUDGE: Usher, remove that fool of a Brahmin.

Usher takes Maitreya outside.

JUDGE: Attendant! Send word to the pariahs!

All royal guards let go of Cārudatta and exeunt.

USHER: Come this way, sir.

CĀRUDATTA (*sadly repeats the line:* "Ah, Maitreya, my friend . . ." *aloud*): The necessary ordeals of poison, fire, weighing, and water are yet to be considered, but the saw is all ready to be applied without waiting for the outcome. . . . You kill me, a Brahmin, on the word of an enemy. I curse you to hell with your sons and grandsons! (*Exeunt omnes.*)

ACT TEN

Enter Cārudatta, followed by two Pariahs.

PARIAHS:

> Don't ask for the reason, but we know new ways
> Of killing and incarceration.
> We are past masters at crucifixions
> And rapid decapitation!

Out of the way, gentlemen! Out of the way! Here's Cārudatta coming, garlanded with oleander wreaths, led proudly by us Pariahs, perishing, drop by drop, like a lamp that is running out of oil.

CĀRUDATTA:

> Sprinkled with tears and coarsened by the dirt,
> Hung with the flowers of the burning-ground,
> This corpse is offered to the shrilling crows
> In the foul stench of blood with which it is smeared.

PARIAHS: Make way, gentlemen, make way! Why are you staring at this good man? This solid tree of a good man, nesting place of the gentle, that is now to be cut down by the axe of death? Come on, you Cārudatta, come on!

CĀRUDATTA: The ways of man's fate are inscrutable, if *I* should come to such a pass! They have laid hands all over my body that is dipped in red sandal, and they have covered it with ground meal, to make me a beast fit for slaughter, me a man! . . . (*Looking in front of him.*) Aho, see the difference in men! . . . (*Compassionately.*) There are those who shed tears when they see what has befallen me, and curse man's fate; and the people of the town, incapable of saving me, bless me: "May heaven be your lot!"

PARIAHS: Make room, gentlemen, make room. Why are you staring? There are four things a man shouldn't watch: the lowering of Indra's

Banner,[57] the birth of a calf, the shooting of stars, and a good man's death.

FIRST PARIAH: Hey, Āhinta! Look, doesn't it seem as though heaven is crying and thunder is roaring out of season, because the best man of the city is being killed on the orders of Fate?

SECOND PARIAH: No. Goha, it isn't heaven that is weeping nor is the thunder roaring out of time. It is that crowded cloud of women who are making rain with their tears! While the condemned is led away, all the people weep so much that not a speck of dust, moistened by their tears, will rise from the highway.

CĀRUDATTA (*looking pitiably*): And those women in their palaces, who crane their necks through the windows, calling out to me: "Poor Cārudatta!" send their tears down in rivulets!

PARIAHS: Come on now, Cārudatta, come on. . . . Here we've got to Proclamation Point. Sound the drum! Pronounce the proclamation! Listen, listen, you gentlefolk! This is Cārudatta, son of Sāgaradatta, grandson of Provost Vinayadatta. He is the criminal who lured Vasantasenā the courtesan into the deserted Puṣpakaraṇḍaka park and strangled her with his own hands for a trifling sum of money. He was caught with the plunder and made a full confession. Therefore our king Pālaka has ordered us to execute him. If any other person commits an equally heinous deed that sins against this world and the next, our king Pālaka will deal with him in the same manner!

CĀRUDATTA (*despairingly, to himself*):

My lineage that of old was purified
By countless sacrifices, that the sound
Of holy recitation glorified
In crowded temple or on priestly ground
Is publicly proclaimed by this low band,
Who are unworthy of my family,
With their denunciation, as I stand
To die of ignominy. . . .

(*He shudders and covers his ears.*) Ah, my darling Vasantasenā!

Your teeth resplendent as the moon's pure light,
Your lips like coral chips incarnadine!
Must I who drank your face like wine divine
Now taste the poison of insult and slight?

PARIAHS: Out of the way, gentlemen, out of the way! This treasury of gems of virtue, this bridge for honest folk to cross beyond their miseries, is now being led out of town without a single ornament of gold. . . . Everyone likes a lucky man, but where do you find a man who helps a failure?

CĀRUDATTA (*looking about him*):

> My friends conceal their faces with their shawls
> And to avoid me hasten far along,
> A stranger is a friend when one has luck,
> But out of luck one never meets a friend.

PARIAHS: They have cleared out. The highway is deserted. He has already been marked for death, so let's take him down.

CĀRUDATTA *repeats the lines*: "Ah Maitreya my friend, see how sorely I am stricken . . ." *etc.*

VOICES OFFSTAGE: Oh, Father! My friend!

CĀRUDATTA (*listening to the cries, pitifully to one Pariah*): You chief of your caste, I wish to demand a Brahmin's gift from you!

PARIAHS: What? You demand a Brahmin's gift from the likes of *us*?

CĀRUDATTA: Yes, heaven forbid! This Pariah is not as mindless as that evil Pālaka! For the sake of the life to come, I wish to look once more upon the face of my son.

PARIAH: Let it be done!

VOICE OFFSTAGE: Oh, Father! Daddy!

Cārudatta, on hearing the cries, repeats this request.

PARIAHS: You citizens! Stop a moment. Master Cārudatta wants a last glimpse of the face of his son. (*Turning toward backstage.*) This way, master! Come on here, kid, this way.

Enter Maitreya with Cārudatta's son Rohasena.

MAITREYA: Hurry now, there's a good boy. Your father is being taken down to be killed.

ROHASENA: Oh, Father!

MAITREYA: My friend, why must I see you like this?

CĀRUDATTA (*looking at his son and his friend*): My son! Maitreya! (*Pitifully.*) I shall be plagued by thirst in the afterworld, for the funeral offerings of food and drink will be very meager. . . . What have I to leave my son? (*He looks on himself and sees his Brahmin's thread.*) Yes, this I still have left, this ornament of the Brahmin unadorned with gold or pearls. With this one can give the gods and the dead their share. (*He gives his son his Brahmin's thread.*)

FIRST PARIAH: Come along now, Cārudatta!

SECOND PARIAH: Hey, you, don't you address Master Cārudatta without his title! Look, in prosperity or ruin, by day or by night, Fate, like an unbridled mare, keeps to the road to find her way. His limbs are dried up, what use is a head that must bow? Still, is the moon no longer to be honored when it is eclipsed?

ROHASENA: Pariahs, where are you taking my daddy?

CĀRUDATTA: My child,

> My shoulders hung with oleander wreaths,
> Bearing the pole upon my neck, my grief
> Within my heart, I walk the road to death,
> As at a sacrifice the goat walks down
> Toward the altar of the butcher priest.

FIRST PARIAH: Boy, we aren't pariahs, although we are born from a pariah family. The real, the evil pariahs are they who do violence to a decent man.

ROHASENA: Then why are you going to kill my daddy?

FIRST PARIAH: May your life be long! It's the king's order that's to blame, not us.

ROHASENA: Kill me and let Daddy go!

FIRST PARIAH: May you live long for saying this!

CĀRUDATTA (*embracing his son in tears*): This is the true wealth of love that the poor and the rich both share, a balm to the heart that needs no dear ingredients. (*He repeats the lines*: "My shoulders hung with oleander wreaths" *etc.*) (*He looks around, and to himself repeats the lines*: "My friends conceal their faces with their shawls" *and the next.*)

MAITREYA: Dear fellows, let my good friend Cārudatta go. Kill me instead!

CĀRUDATTA: Heaven forbid! (*Looking about him, to himself.*) Now I understand . . . (*He repeats the line* "A stranger is a friend" *and the next.*) (*And aloud he repeats*: "And the women in their palaces . . .")

FIRST PARIAH: Make way, gentlemen, make way. Why are you staring at this honest man, whose hopes for life have been killed by infamy, as at a golden pitcher whose rope broke and which now sinks into the well?

CĀRUDATTA *repeats the line*: "Your teeth resplendent . . ."
SECOND PARIAH: Come on, you must repeat the proclamation!
(*First Pariah does so.*)
CĀRUDATTA:

> So I have come to this disgrace
> Where 'tis my lot to end my life. . . .
> His crying pains my mind—that I
> Should be the one that strangled her!

(*On the top of a roof, within a dovecot, Sthāvaraka, who is manacled, comes within view.*)
STHĀVARAKA (*hearing the proclamation, in despair*): Must Cārudatta die, while he is innocent? I have been fettered by my master—all right, then I must shout! Listen, folks, listen! I am the criminal! I took Vasantasenā today to the park, because she mistook my carriage for hers. And there my master strangled her with his own hands, because she would not make love to him, Cārudatta didn't do it at all! . . . What! Nobody can hear me, I am too far away. What can I do? I'll throw myself down! (*He thinks.*) If I do that, Master Cārudatta won't be killed. Right! I'll hurl myself right through this old airloft out of this dovecot. It's better that I die than Master Cārudatta, nesting tree of well-born sons! If I die, I'll gain a better world hereafter. (*He throws himself down from the roof.*) Why! I am still alive! And my manacles are broken. I'll follow the cries of the Pariahs. (*Having looked around and drawn near.*) Hey, Pariahs! Let me through!
PARIAHS: Who wants to get through?
STHĀVARAKA *repeats the lines*: "Listen, folks, listen! I am the criminal . . ."
CĀRUDATTA: Aho! Who at this late hour, when I am already caught in the noose of death, appears like a showering cloud to drought-ridden crops? Have you heard him? I do not fear death—but my name is soiled. When my innocence has been recognized, I shall welcome death like the birth of a son. That debased dull-witted crook, with whom I had no feud, has, like a poison-dipped arrowhead, tainted me!
PARIAHS: Sthāvaraka, are you telling the truth?
STHĀVARAKA: I am telling the truth. I was fettered inside the dovecot on his roof and threw myself down.

Enter Saṃsthānaka.
SAṂSTHĀNAKA (*joyfully*):

I dined at home on tamarind sauce,
On first-class rice with extra dishes
Of meat and pea-soup and stewed greens
And candy cakes and two small fishes.

(*He cocks his ear.*) That is the sound of Pariahs chattering, clattering like busted brass cymbals! The drums for the execution are sounded and I hear the roar of the kettledrum, so I think that Cārudatta the pauper is being taken to the gallows. Let me have a look. The death of an enemy is a matter of huge satisfaction to me. Besides, I have heard that a man who watches his enemy being killed won't suffer from eye trouble in his next life. Yes, like a worm inside a poison gourd looking for a hole to crawl out, I brought about Cārudatta the Pauper's death. Now I shall ascend to my very own gazebo in my dovecot and survey my heroic achievement. (*He does so and looks out.*) Well, well, what a crowd of people on hand for Cārudatta's execution! I wonder how big a crowd would be raised if a person like me, preeminent prominent personage, were taken to *my* execution? (*He looks closely.*) Now what? Ah, prettied up like a new bullock he is taken south. Why! Why should the sound of the proclamation carry as far as my little gazebo and then suddenly stop? (*He looks around.*) What! Sthāvaraka has gone! If only he does not go and spoil my plans . . . I have to find him! (*He goes down and approaches.*)

STHĀVARAKA: Masters, he is coming!
PARIAHS: Out of the way! Clear the road! Bolt your doors and keep quiet! There he comes like a mad bull with sharp and untamed horns!
SAṂSTHĀNAKA: Hey, there, hey, there! Let me through! (*He approaches.*) Sthāvaraka, my son, come along, slave. We must go.
STHĀVARAKA: Bah, criminal! Aren't you satisfied with murdering Vasantasenā? Have you now also decided to do away with Cārudatta, the wishing tree of people with heart?
SAṂSTHĀNAKA: A man like a gem-studded pitcher like me does not kill women!
ALL: What? You killed her, Master Cārudatta didn't do it.
SAṂSTHĀNAKA: Says who?
ALL (*pointing at Sthāvaraka*): This honest man!

SAṂSTHĀNAKA (*aside, afraid*): Oh, little mother, oh, dear little mother, why didn't I tie Sthāvaraka up properly? . . . He is a witness to my crime. (*He thinks.*) I must do this. (*Aloud.*) A lie, masters! Why, I caught this slave stealing my gold and I beat and hit and fettered him. He hates me for it, so how can you believe what he tells you? (*Aside he proffers his slave a golden bracelet. In a whisper.*) Sthāvaraka, my little son, take this and change your story!

STHĀVARAKA (*taking it*): Look, masters, look! He is trying to bribe me with gold!

SAṂSTHĀNAKA (*snatching away the bracelet*): There is my gold! That is why I tied him up. (*Angrily.*) Pariahs, I had put him in charge of my gold box, and when he stole my gold, I beat him up. If you don't believe me, look at his back.

PARIAHS (*looking*): He is right. A resentful slave may say anything against his master.

STHĀVARAKA: Oh, mother, that is what it means to be a slave, not to be believed when you tell the truth! (*Pitifully.*) Master Cārudatta, this is all I could do. (*He throws himself at Cārudatta's feet.*)

CĀRUDATTA (*moved with compassion*): Rise up, my upright friend! You have pity on one who is ruined, and you try to help without self-interest. . . . You have done your best to free me, and, although fate is against us, what have you left undone?

PARIAHS: My lord, give your slave a sound beating and turn him out.

SAṂSTHĀNAKA: Get away from here (*he expels him*). Now, Pariahs, what are you waiting for? Kill him!

ROHASENA: Kill me, Pariahs, let Daddy go!

SAṂSTHĀNAKA: Kill him and his kid too!

CĀRUDATTA: With this fool anything is possible. You must go now, my son, back to your mother.

ROHASENA: What is the use of going?

CĀRUDATTA: Take your mother and go to a hermitage at once, son, lest you suffer the same fate as your father by your father's fault. Maitreya, take him and leave.

MAITREYA: Do you know how I am supposed to carry on my life without you, friend?

CĀRUDATTA: It is not right, Maitreya, to give up living when your life is in your own hands.

MAITREYA (*to himself*): But it is right that I am unable to live separated from my friend. . . . I shall deliver the boy to his mother and follow my friend into death. (*Aloud.*) I'll take him away at once. (*He embraces his friend and falls at his feet; the boy also prostrates himself weeping.*)

SAṂSTHĀNAKA: Hey, didn't I tell you to kill him with his son?

(*Cārudatta shows fear.*)

PARIAHS: The king's orders didn't say that we were to kill his son as well. Run along now, boy, run along! (*Exeunt Maitreya and Rohasena.*) Here is the third place for the proclamation. Beat the drum! (*Once more they make the proclamation.*)

SAṂSTHĀNAKA (*to himself*): The townspeople still can't believe it. (*Aloud.*) Hey, you, Cārudatta, fool of a Brahmin! The townspeople still don't believe you did it. Tell them with your own tongue that you killed Vasantasenā.

(*Cārudatta keeps silent.*)

SAṂSTHĀNAKA: Pariah Goha, Cārudatta does not want to talk. Make him talk! Thrash him over and over again with that old cane whip!

PARIAH (*raising his whip*): Talk, Cārudatta!

CĀRUDATTA (*wretchedly*):

> I have been hurled into an ocean of grief,
> But yet no shudder of despair is in my heart—
> Only the fire of infamous disgrace burns me
> That I should have to say I killed the one I loved.

(*Saṃsthānaka repeats his threats.*)

CĀRUDATTA: Listen, people of the city! A woman or goddess of love—what difference does it make?—I have cruelly, ignoring heaven and hell—let the other say the word!

SAṂSTHĀNAKA: I murdered!

CĀRUDATTA: So be it.

FIRST PARIAH: You are in charge of the execution today.

SECOND PARIAH: Oh no, you are.

FIRST PARIAH: All right, let's see who is counted out. (*They make complicated calculations.*) All right, if it is my execution today, let's wait a while.

SECOND PARIAH: Whatever for?

FIRST PARIAH: Well, when my father died, his last words were: "Vīraka my son, when you are in charge of an execution, never be in a hurry to kill a man."

SECOND PARIAH: Why not?

FIRST PARIAH: Every now and then a good man may appear and buy the condemned free. Or a son is born to the king and he grants amnesty to all the condemned at a great Feast of Prosperity. Or an elephant may break loose and in the commotion the condemned man gets free. Or there is a revolution and all the condemned are set free.

SAMSTHĀNAKA: What! Is there a revolution?

FIRST PARIAH: Come, let's figure out once more who is in charge.

SAMSTHĀNAKA: Hurry up, kill Cārudatta! (*He withdraws to the side with Sthāvaraka.*)

PARIAH: Master Cārudatta, blame the king's orders, not us! Now think your last thought.

CĀRUDATTA:

> If merit still has power, even though
> The mighty sullied me, and Luck,
> May she, in heaven or wherever, now
> Wipe out the stigma that has stuck!

Friend, where do you want me to go?

FIRST PARIAH (*pointing ahead*): Look, there you see the southern burning-ground, at the sight of which the condemned quickly breathe their last.

> The tall hyenas carry off one half of you,
> And on the pole grins back the other half of you!

CĀRUDATTA: Ah, I am lost, unfortunate. (*He sits down, nauseated.*)

SAMSTHĀNAKA: I am not going yet. First I want to see Cārudatta dead. (*He walks about and looks.*) What! He is sitting down!

PARIAH: Are you afraid, Cārudatta?

CĀRUDATTA (*rising at once*): Fool! (*He repeats the lines*: "I do not fear death—but my name is soiled *etc.*")

PARIAH: Master Cārudatta, even the sun and the moon which are in heaven have their eclipses, let alone people, who are scared of death and men. In this world it so goes that he who rises falls, and that he who falls will rise. From the corpse of him who has risen and fallen a sweet-smelling flower will grow. Think that over and compose yourself. (*To the second Pariah.*) This is the place for the fourth proclamation. Let's raise our voices.

Once more they repeat the proclamation.

CĀRUDATTA: Ah, darling Vasantasenā! (*He repeats the lines*: "Your teeth resplendent . . .")

Enter in a state of great excitement Vasantasenā and the Friar.

FRIAR: Oh, dear, wasn't I lucky to become a friar and be able to comfort Vasantasenā after her untimely collapse and bring her here! Disciple, where shall I escort you?

VASANTASENĀ: To Master Cārudatta's house. Gladden me with the sight of him, like the lotus pond with the sight of the moon!

FRIAR (*to himself*): What road shall I take? (*He thinks.*) I'll take the king's road. Come, disciple. Here's the king's road. But what is this racket on the road?

VASANTASENĀ (*peering in front of her*): There is a huge crowd! Do you know what is going on, sir? Ujjayinī seems to be tilting to one side like a ship with its cargo shifting!

PARIAH: Here we are at the place for the last proclamation. Beat the drum. Pronounce the proclamation! (*They do so.*) Well, Cārudatta, now you must wait. Don't be afraid, though. We'll kill you fast.

CĀRUDATTA: You worshipful Gods . . .

FRIAR (*listening, excited*): They are taking Cārudatta to be executed because he has killed you!

VASANTASENĀ (*dismayed*): Oh, horror, should Master Cārudatta be killed for a wretch like me? Hurry, hurry, show me the way!

FRIAR: Run, run, disciple of Buddha, and bring Cārudatta back to life! Let us through, folks, let us through!

VASANTASENĀ: Let us through!

PARIAH: Master Cārudatta, the king's orders are to blame. . . . Think your last thought.

CĀRUDATTA: Let it suffice. (*He repeats the line*: "If merit still has power . . .")

PARIAH (*drawing his sword*): Lie down on your back and don't move. We'll have you dead and in heaven with one stroke. (*Cārudatta does so.*)

PARIAH (*about to strike; then gestures to show that the sword has slipped from his hand*): Aho, what is that? I drew my sword furiously with my fist, I clasped it in my fist—now why should it fall to the ground like a terrifying thunderbolt? The way it happened, I don't think Master Cārudatta is dead yet. Have mercy, Goddess of Mount Sahya! If this means Cārudatta is free, you have shown your favor to the race of Pariahs!

SECOND PARIAH: We have got to carry out our orders.

FIRST PARIAH: All right, we will (*They are about to hoist Cārudatta on the pole. He again repeats the lines*: "If merit still has power . . .")

FRIAR *and* VASANTASENĀ (*seeing it*): Don't, sirs, don't!
VASANTASENĀ: I am the wretch for whom he is being killed!
PARIAH (*looking at her*): Who is that woman running at us with her hair all untied, raising her hands and shouting to us to stop?
VASANTASENĀ: Master Cārudatta, what happened? (*She throws herself on his breast.*)
FRIAR: Master Cārudatta, what happened? (*He throws himself at his feet.*)
PARIAH (*approaches, trembling*): What! Vasantasenā! I have not killed an innocent man, have I?
FRIAR (*getting up*): No, Cārudatta is alive.
PARIAH: Alive for a hundred years!
VASANTASENĀ (*with joy*): Then I live again!
PARIAHS: We must go and tell the king at Sacrifice Grove. (*They start off.*)
SAṂSTHĀNAKA (*trembling, as he stares at Vasantasenā*): Oh, mother! Who has brought this slave girl back to life? My life flees! I must get away from here! (*He starts running.*)
PARIAHS (*drawing close to him*): The king ordered us to execute Vasantasenā's murderer. We must chase the brother-in-law! (*Exeunt.*)
CĀRUDATTA (*astounded*): While the sword was raised and I lay in the mouth of death, who came like the rain-cloud to drought-ridden crops? . . . (*He stares at her.*) Is this another Vasantasenā, or has she descended from heaven? Has my mind gone mad that I see her? Or is she the same Vasantasenā, who never died? Has she come down from heaven because she still wanted to live? Or has another nymph taken her shape and descended?
VASANTASENĀ (*rising in tears and prostrating herself at his feet*): It is still myself, Master Cārudatta, the evil crone for whose sake you fell to this disgrace!
VOICES OFFSTAGE: A miracle, a miracle! Vasantasenā is alive! (*All the bystanders say this.*)
CĀRUDATTA (*hearing what they say, she rises at once; he shows that her touch is pleasing to him, and he speaks with closed eyes and in a stammering voice*): Darling, you are Vasantasenā!
VASANTASENĀ: Yes, I am that ill-favored woman. . . .
CĀRUDATTA (*studying her with joy*): Vasantasenā herself! (*With extreme happiness.*)

Whence, like the Art of Life itself, came she,
While I had fallen afoul of Death,
Bathing her breasts with cascades of tears?

Darling Vasantasenā!

The life that I laid down for you
You have yourself restored to me:
Behold the wondrous power of love—
For who once dead may live again?

Look, my darling—

This blood-red shroud is like a bridegroom's robe,
This wreath a bridegroom's garland since we met:
And these dread sounds of doomed men's drums
Become the festive airs of marriage!

VASANTASENĀ: What has my all-too-clever man now resolved?
CĀRUDATTA: Darling, that powerful enemy, who long has hated me and now will fall to hell, broadcast that I had killed you and almost caused my ruin!
VASANTASENĀ (*stopping her ears*): Heaven forbid! The king's brother-in-law was the one who tried to kill me!
CĀRUDATTA (*noticing the Friar*): And who is he?
VASANTASENĀ: That ignoble man tried to kill me and this noble man brought me back to life.
CĀRUDATTA: Who are you, selfless friend?
FRIAR: Doesn't your honor recognize me? I am the Masseur, who took care of your feet! I was captured by gamblers, and she bought me free with a stake of jewels, but only for your sake! I was so disgusted with gambling that I became a Buddhist Friar. This noble lady took the wrong carriage and came to the Puṣpakaraṇḍaka park. And that debased man strangled her with his own hands, because she didn't want to give in to him. I saw it myself!
(*Loud tumult offstage.*)

Hail to the Bull-bannered God who once spoilt Dakṣa's oblation!
Hail to the six-faced Kārttikeya the Cleaver of Krauñca!
Hail unto Āryaka who destroyed a most powerful foeman,
Winning the orb of the earth with its radiant crest of Kailāsa![58]

Enter suddenly Śarvilaka.

ŚARVILAKA: I have killed the evil king Pālaka and rapidly consecrated Āryaka to the Throne; and carrying his Princely Behest like a Garland of Flowers on my head, I speed to rescue Cārudatta from his Plight—Yes, I killed the king, deserted by forces and council, grandly reassured the frightened Citizenry, and obtained the Universal Rule of Earth, as Bala's Enemy Indra once obtained his. (*Peering in front of him.*) Yes, that's where he should be—where those crowds are gathered. May the first Enterprise of our new King Āryaka be crowned with the Life of the noble Cārudatta. (*He approaches very quickly.*) Out of the way, cattle! (*Looking, with joy.*) Cārudatta is alive! And so is Vasantasenā. My master's wishes have been fulfilled!

Oh, blessing that I long may look to him
Who from the Shoreless Sea of Grief was saved
As with a boat by his redeeming Love,
To rise, no more eclipsed, a radiant Moon!

But how shall I approach him, I who wronged him monstrously? However, honesty always wins out. (*He approaches him openly, with folded hands.*) Master Cārudatta!

CĀRUDATTA: Who are you, sir?

ŚARVILAKA: I am he who broke into your house and stole what was left in trust with you. A great sinner takes refuge with you!

CĀRUDATTA: Do not speak like that, my friend! Your affection redeems you! (*He embraces him.*)

ŚARVILAKA: Moreover, Āryaka of noble deeds, who guards the honor of his Line, has killed the evil Pālaka in Sacrifice Grove as a human sacrifice.

CĀRUDATTA: What!

ŚARVILAKA: The same man who rode in your carriage and sought refuge with you. He killed Pālaka as a sacrificial animal at the king's own sacrifice!

CĀRUDATTA: Śarvilaka, then you were the one who set Āryaka free when King Pālaka had had him taken from his village and without cause thrown into a dungeon?

ŚARVILAKA: It is as you say, sir.

CĀRUDATTA: Good, good!

ŚARVILAKA: Immediately upon his establishment in Ujjayinī on the bank of the Veṇā your friend Āryaka gave up his residence in Kuśāvatī.

Therefore, honor the first token of your friend's affection. (*He turns around.*) You there, bring that scoundrel here, the late king's brother-in-law!

VOICES OFFSTAGE: At Śarvilaka's orders!

ŚARVILAKA: King Āryaka sends you this message, Master Cārudatta: "I have obtained this kingdom through your virtue. Make good use of it!"

CĀRUDATTA: Obtained this kingdom through my virtue?

VOICES OFFSTAGE: Hey, you, Saṃsthānaka, come on, come on! Reap the results of your evil ways!

Enter Saṃsthānaka with his hands fettered, in the charge of several constables who precede him.

SAṂSTHĀNAKA: Like an obstinate ass I am dragged along, and I am led on a leash like a fractious dog. (*Looking all around.*) The new king's cronies have appeared on all sides! I am left alone, where can I find refuge? Then I must go to him who is kind to all that throw themselves on his mercy. (*He comes closer.*) Master Cārudatta, save me, save me! (*He falls at his feet.*)

VOICES OFFSTAGE: Let go of him! Master Cārudatta, kill him!

SAṂSTHĀNAKA (*to Cārudatta*): Grant refuge to the deserted! Rescue me!

CĀRUDATTA (*compassionately*): Hear me! Safety, safety to him who asks for refuge!

ŚARVILAKA (*dismayed*): Quick! Get him away from Cārudatta! (*To Cārudatta.*) Now tell me what we should do with that criminal. Are they to drag him away in his fetters and feed him to the dogs? Raise him on a pole? Have him sawed to pieces?

CĀRUDATTA: Will what I say be done?

ŚARVILAKA: Who doubts it?

SAṂSTHĀNAKA: Master Cārudatta, I am your supplicant! Save me, save me! Do what is worthy of you! I shall never do it again!

Vasantasenā takes the condemned man's wreath off Cārudatta's shoulders and throws it over Saṃsthānaka's.

SAṂSTHĀNAKA: Mercy, daughter of a slave girl, mercy! I don't want to die. Save me!

ŚARVILAKA: Come on, take him away. Master Cārudatta, your orders! What are we to do with this criminal?

CĀRUDATTA: Will what I say be done?

ŚARVILAKA: Who doubts it?

CĀRUDATTA: Truly?

ŚARVILAKA: Truly.

CĀRUDATTA: In that case have him at once—

ŚARVILAKA: Executed?

CĀRUDATTA: No, no! Released.

ŚARVILAKA: But why?

CĀRUDATTA: The enemy that has wronged you should not be killed by the sword, if he seeks refuge at your feet. . . .

ŚARVILAKA: Well, feed him to the dogs!

CĀRUDATTA: No, let him die of gratitude.

ŚARVILAKA: Aho, how strange! How should I do that? Tell me.

CĀRUDATTA: Release him.

ŚARVILAKA: Set him free!

SAṂSTHĀNAKA: Oh, little mother, I live again. (*Exit, with constables.*)

ŚARVILAKA: You are indeed blessed in your friends, sir.

CĀRUDATTA: By your favor.

ŚARVILAKA: My lady Vasantasenā, the king is pleased to confer on you the title of wife.

VASANTASENĀ: I am grateful, my lord.

ŚARVILAKA (*after veiling Vasantasenā, to Cārudatta*): What shall we do for the Friar?

CĀRUDATTA: What do you wish most, Friar?

FRIAR: On seeing the transitoriness of things so clearly illustrated here, my esteem for the wandering life of the monks is redoubled!

CĀRUDATTA: Then you are firm in your resolve, my friend. Let him be abbot of all the monasteries in the land!

ŚARVILAKA: As you say, sir.

FRIAR: Good, good!

VASANTASENĀ: Now I feel really restored to life!

ŚARVILAKA: And what should we do for Sthāvaraka?

CĀRUDATTA: I free you from slavery, my good man. And let those Pariahs be the chieftains of all the castes of Pariahs. Candanaka should be chief constable in the kingdom. And let the king's brother-in-law have the same office he had before.

ŚARVILAKA: It will be as you say. But only let go of that one! I'll kill him!

CĀRUDATTA: Safety to him who seeks refuge. (*He repeats the lines: "An enemy that has wronged you . . ."*)

ŚARVILAKA: Now say what I can do for you.

CĀRUDATTA: From here onward everything agrees with me. The purity of my name is restored. My enemy has humbled himself at my feet and has been set free. King Āryaka has uprooted his enemies and now my dear friend rules the country. I have found my love again, and in you I have found a good friend. What more is there left for me to desire and for you to grant?—Fate seems to love the parable of the water buckets on the irrigation wheel: it empties these and fills up those, raises some and lowers others, and others again it keeps in between; and teaching us thus how our life in the world is but an interplay of irreconcilables, it plays its endless games with us. Nevertheless, let this word from the old, old epic still be repeated:

May the cows yield milk and the soil good crops,
May the rain fall in time and the wind soothe our hearts,
May the people rejoice and the Brahmins be honored,
May the virtuous kings tame their foes and rule earth!

(*Exeunt omnes.*)

THE END

THE MINISTER'S SEAL

ascribed to Prince Viśākhadatta

CANDRAGUPTA (Chandragupta), nicknamed "the Maurya," son of a deposed Nanda king, monarch of the kingdom centered at Pāṭaliputra; in his early twenties.

CĀṆAKYA, given name Viṣṇugupta, family name Kauṭilya, plenipotentiary to Candragupta, presumed author of the *Arthaśāstra*; of retirement age.

RĀKṢASA, late minister to the Nanda dynasty; now adviser to Prince Malayaketu; middle-aged.

BHĀGURĀYAṆA, secret agent of Cāṇakya; of good family, but in Cāṇakya's employ for profit; in his thirties.

MALAYAKETU, son of the Maurya's erstwhile ally, King Parvataka, from the Northern mountain states, who has since been assassinated; now the son is adversary of Candragupta; about thirty.

VIRĀDHAGUPTA, counterpart of Bhāgurāyaṇa; loyal to the Nanda dynasty and serving as agent to Rākṣasa.

ŚĀRṄGARAVA, pupil and whipping-boy of Cāṇakya.

VAIHĪNARI, Chamberlain to Candragupta.

JĀJALI, Chamberlain to Malayaketu.

(These characters speak Sanskrit.)

SIDDHĀRTHAKA, middle-class agent of Cāṇakya.

SAMṚDDHĀRTHAKA, a friend of his.

ŚAKAṬADĀSA, a scribe, old friend of Rākṣasa, continuingly loyal.

CANDANADĀSA, a jeweler and friend of Rākṣasa; has harbored, and knows the whereabouts of, Rākṣasa's wife and children.

JĪVASIDDHI, a mendicant of the Jain sect and an astrologer; agent of Cāṇakya, posing as Rākṣasa's friend.

HUNCHBACK, a spy and runner for Rākṣasa.

PRIYAṂVADAKA, a servant of Rākṣasa.

ŚOṆOTTARĀ, female guard of Candragupta.

VIJAYĀ, female guard of Malayaketu.

(These characters speak several Prākrits.)

Other speaking parts, including two BARDS, both of whom speak Sanskrit.

Act One. Scene: The modest cottage of Prime Minister Cāṇakya in the capital Pāṭaliputra. Time: shortly after the overthrow of the Nandas and the assassinations of Sarvārthasiddhi and Parvataka.

Act Two. Scene: Rākṣasa's house in Prince Malayaketu's temporary citadel, north of Pāṭaliputra. Time: several weeks later.

Act Three. Scene: Cāṇakya's house and the royal Sugāṅga palace of Pāṭaliputra on the northern bank of the Ganges. Time: after the rainy season, late October.

Act Four. Scene: Rākṣasa's house. Time: late November.

Entr'acte and *Act Five*. Scene: Malayaketu's army camp, five days from Pāṭaliputra. Time: a week later.

Entr'acte and *Act Six*. Scene: A middle-class quarter of Pāṭaliputra, and an old park on the outskirts of the city. Time: several weeks later.

Act Seven. Scene: The execution field. Time: the same day.

PROLOGUE

BLESSING

PĀRVATĪ: Who is that lucky woman on your head?
ŚIVA: Crescent.
PĀRVATĪ: Is that her name?
ŚIVA: The word describes her. But you always knew! Did you forget?
PĀRVATĪ: No, but it is the woman that I question, not your moon!
ŚIVA: You do not trust the moon? Then ask your servant Vijayā!

May Śiva's ambiguities which served to hide
Gangā from the Goddess his Consort save you too![1]

May Our Lord Śiva's cautious dance of yore,
That celebrated Tripura's defeat,
When he most mercifully spared the world
And held the power of his thudding feet,
Which threatened earth with burial, in check
And kept the gestures of his flinging hands,
Which would have burst out of the world, in bounds
And, lest it light upon an aim and burn,
Did not allow his third dread eye to gaze,
Once more protect you from vicissitudes![2]

After the blessing has been said, enter the Director.
DIRECTOR: This will do. I have been instructed by the audience to stage a new play today, a play by the poet Viśākhadatta, the son of Mahārāja Bhāskara and the grandson of Governor Vaṭeśvaradatta. The play is a heroic drama,[3] entitled *The Minister's Seal*. In fact, I am extremely happy to stage a play for an audience like this that is so appreciative of good literature. For even a fool can reap a rich

harvest, if his seed falls on good soil; the abundance of his crop does not depend on the sower's skill. So I had better get home and call my wife, so that we can begin the performance with our troupe. (*He walks about the stage and looks around.*) Here we are. Well, well, what is going on here? It looks as if we are having a celebration. All the servants are unusually busy at their jobs. One is carrying buckets full of water, another is mixing incense, a third is fashioning garlands of all kinds of flowers, and still another is humming while she pounds with her pestle. All right, then, I'll call my wife and ask what is happening. (*He looks toward backstage.*)

Talented treasure of household economy,
Loyal promoter of Love, Wealth, and Faith!
Leave for the moment, domestic tactician, your
Science and Arts, and come here at once!

Enter an Actress.

ACTRESS: Here I am, my Lord. Be good enough to grace me with your orders.

DIRECTOR: My orders can wait. Tell me, have you invited these reverend Brahmins to grace our house, or have they come by themselves as welcome guests, since there is such a variety of dishes being prepared?

ACTRESS: No, I invited the reverend Brahmins myself.

DIRECTOR: Why?

ACTRESS: We must worship the moon today. There is an eclipse.

DIRECTOR: Whoever told you that?

ACTRESS: Someone from the City.

DIRECTOR: Madam, I have made an elaborate study of all sixty-four chapters of astrology. By all means, carry on your cooking for the Brahmins, but we are not going to have an eclipse today. Somebody has played a trick on you! Look, (*in a declamatory voice*) a Cruel Grasper[4] wants to violate the Moon's Immaculate Realm . . .

VOICE OFFSTAGE: *Who dares, while I am here!*

DIRECTOR (*continuing*): . . . but the Conjunction of Mercury will save the day!

ACTRESS: Who was that man who, safely on earth, wants to save the moon and stave off its attackers?

DIRECTOR: I could not quite catch it myself. Let me try again (*repeats the phrase:* "A Cruel Grasper . . .")

VOICE OFFSTAGE: *Who dares violate my Lord the Moon while I am here? Speak up!*

DIRECTOR (*listening*): Ah, I have got it! Kauṭilya! (*Actress shrinks with fear.*) Yes, Kauṭilya of the crooked mind,[5] who burnt the house of the Nandas in the fire of his fury. He heard that someone tried to grasp the Moon and thought that his lord Candragupta was threatened. Let us get away from here! (*Exeunt.*)

ACT ONE

Enter Cāṇakya. He is fingering his hairlock, which is untied.[6]

CĀṆAKYA: Speak up! Who dares, while I am here, to attack Candragupta? Beware my hairlock,

Black, winding cobra, killer of the House of Nanda,
Spiral of dense smoke on the embers of my anger:
What doomed enemy is left that it is still unbraided?

Who tries to overreach the power of my fire
That set the underbrush of Nanda's house ablaze?
Who fails to grasp again the measure of our strength,
And like a moth flies madly to his death?

Śārṅgarava! Śārṅgarava!

Enter Cāṇakya's Pupil.

PUPIL: Master, command me!

CĀṆAKYA: My boy, I want to sit down.

PUPIL: But, master, in the room behind these doors there are cane chairs. You might sit down there.

CĀṆAKYA: Of course, my boy. It is only my preoccupation with my work that is distracting me. I am not being obstreperous, as all teachers notoriously are.[7] (*He sits down and starts talking to himself.*) Well, it has now become public knowledge in the city that Rākṣasa, the old minister of the Nandas, enraged by the extermination of the dynasty, has joined forces with the prince Maḷayaketu, Parvataka's son. Malayaketu wants to avenge his father's assassination and has been prodded to risk all for the one great prize, the kingdom of the Nandas. And Rākṣasa is preparing to attack the Maurya with a considerable force of barbarians.[8] (*He pauses for thought.*) Still, am I not able to put down the danger, even though it is public now—I, who *publicly* vowed to exterminate the Nandas and crossed the perilous rapids of my vow safely and successfully? Why not? See,

> The smoke of ceaseless grief has blackened now
> The moonlike faces of the Nanda's women;
> The ashes of confusion have whirled up
> From his once solid, treelike councilors;
> His people have, like birds, in panic emptied
> The blazing deadwood of his dynasty:
> And like a forest fire my fury died,
> Not from fatigue, but there was nothing left.

I hurled my vow at them: "Let this same country, which once with its head bowed stifled all protest for fear of the king and mournfully watched my disgrace when I was stripped of power and dismissed from the first seat of the kingdom, now silently watch how I chase the Nanda and his brood from the throne, as the lion chases the elephant from his mountain peak." And here I am now, acquitted of my vow, still wielding the sword of power for Candragupta, whom I made king.

> For I have cured the earth of the Nine Nandas,
> As of nine maladies, and rooted Fortune
> In Maurya's House, a lotus firmly planted[9]
> In its own pond. Their Houses both saw justice
> Done as I with a mind doubly devoted
> Dealt to ally and enemy the fruit
> Of love and hate.

But still, as long as Rākṣasa is free, is the earth cured of the Nandas, and is the Maurya's fortune firm? (*He reflects.*) Beware! Rākṣasa is utterly loyal to the line of Nanda, and as long as one member of the house survives he cannot be persuaded to join Candragupta and become his minister. But once he is frustrated in his loyalties, he will become manageable. Since I was convinced of this, I had Sarvārthasiddhi, the last scion of the Nandas, assassinated, even though he had retired to a hermitage. Nevertheless, although there are no more Nandas left, Rākṣasa has now rallied to Malayaketu's side, and indeed displays the most energetic enterprise to speed our downfall. . . . (*He stares before him, as though he is facing Rākṣasa.*) Well done, Councilor Rākṣasa, well done, most learned tactician, god among statesmen! For all the world serves a king who still has a kingdom, in hope of gain—yes, they may even follow him in misfortune, if they can hope for his fortunes to return. But those who continue to carry the yoke of office even when their prince has come to grief, motivated only by gratitude for old favors in simple unselfish loyalty, those, like you, are rare indeed! And that is the reason why I am trying to win you over. . . .

How much better off would Candragupta be, if Rākṣasa consented to serve him! What use is a loyal man, if he is a fool or a coward? And what use is a man who is clever and brave, if he has no loyalty? Only those who join wisdom and courage to loyalty can increase a king's fortune. The others are mere household expenses, whether the king prospers or declines.

So I have stayed in office without resting, and done all I could to secure Rākṣasa's alliance. And what have I left undone! I have circulated the scandalous rumor that Rākṣasa used a poison-girl[10] to murder our exceedingly useful ally, the poor Parvataka, because Rākṣasa calculated that the death of either Candragupta or Parvataka would be a blow against Cāṇakya. In order to publicize the affair, and make people believe it, I had Bhāgurāyaṇa abduct Parvataka's son Malayaketu, but not without giving him privately the terrifying assurance that I myself had caused the assassination of his father. With the aid of some intelligence, we could easily capture Malayaketu, while he is abroad, even though he can now make use of Rākṣasa's talents. But I do not wish to capture him for that would wipe out the effect of Parvataka's murder, for which Rākṣasa is now being publicly blamed. Then again I have employed spies who are acquainted with different regions and local dress, languages, customs, and circumstances, and employed them under all kinds of covers, to find out which people are on which side. They have reported quite competently on the friends Rākṣasa still has here in Pāṭaliputra. At the same time I have created opportunities for the principal authorities of the city, Bhadrabhaṭa and the others, to find it profitable to side with Candragupta. I have also detailed a number of devoted and confidence-inspiring agents, who are close to the king's person and of proven loyalty, to counter any attempts at assassination. Finally, there is Induśarman, a Brahmin who was a fellow student of mine. He has acquired full mastery of all sixty-four chapters of astrology and the political handbook of Uśanas. Immediately after I had sworn the death of the Nandas, I dispatched him to Pāṭaliputra in the disguise of a Jain monk, and had him cultivate the friendship of all the Nanda's ministers. Rākṣasa especially places great trust in him. He will now have an important new mission to accomplish.

No, there is nothing that I have left undone. But Candragupta himself, who has delegated the responsibilities of administering his kingdom to his prime minister, that is, to *me*, was never implicated in all this. And that is just as well. A kingdom is a king's paradise, as long as he is spared the trouble of running it. Kings are like elephants; strong as they are by nature, they are usually unhappy if they themselves have to procure the food they like. . . .

Enter a Spy; he is carrying a canvas which pictures the exploits of Yama, God of Death.

SPY: Bow, world, to Yama! Why pray to other Gods at all?

> He gets the toiling souls of each denomination!
> Each man lives by the trouble of his God's dictation,
> But Yama gets us all, no other Gods at all!

I am going into this house here, and show Yama's picture and sing his praises. (*He walks around.*)

PUPIL (*looking up*): Don't come in here, fellow.

SPY: Oh? Who lives here?

PUPIL: My master, the worshipful Cāṇakya.

SPY: Oh, we belong to the same school! Let me come in and show Yama's picture to your master and instruct him in the Law.

PUPIL (*angrily*): Idiot! Are you better versed in the Law than he?

SPY: Don't get angry, Brahmin. Nobody knows everything. Your master knows something, and people like me know something.

PUPIL: You fool! You deny omniscience to my master?

SPY: Oho, Brahmin, if your master knows everything, he must know the people who do not like the moon!

PUPIL: What could it possibly matter whether he knows or not, you fool?

SPY: Your master himself will judge that. You yourself should know at least this much; day-blooming lotuses, for instance, do not like the moon. Behold! Lotuses are lovely but their behavior belies their loveliness, for they hate the moon, even when it is full.

CĀṆAKYA (*listening, to himself*): Ah, the man hints that he knows people who are hostile to Candragupta.

PUPIL: Idiot, why do you talk such nonsense?

SPY: Nonsense may make sense, Brahmin.

PUPIL: When?

SPY: When I find a listener who understands.

CĀṆAKYA (*looking up*): Come in, my dear man. You will find an understanding listener here!

SPY: Then I will. (*He enters Cāṇakya's area.*) Greetings, your Honor!

CĀṆAKYA (*glances at him; to himself*): Of course, this is one of the experts I assigned to explore public opinion. (*Aloud.*) Welcome, my man. Sit down.

SPY: As your Honor says. (*He squats on the floor.*)

CĀṆAKYA: Now give me a report of your assignment, my man. Are the people sympathetic to Candragupta?

SPY: Why shouldn't they be? Since your Honor has removed all causes of disaffection, the people find they have a great fondness for his Majesty, honor to his name. But there are three men in the city, old and fast friends of Rākṣasa's, who grudge Candragupta his fortune.

CĀṆAKYA (*angrily*): Who begrudge themselves their lives, you had better say! Do you know their names, man?

SPY: How could I report to you, if I did not know their names?

CĀṆAKYA: Then I want to hear them.

SPY: Please listen, your Honor. First of all there is a Jain mendicant, who has gone over to the enemy.

CĀṆAKYA (*amused, to himself*): A beggar and a heretic on the enemy's side![11]

SPY: He is Jīvasiddhi, the very one who set that poison-girl on his Majesty Parvataka, the girl Rākṣasa employed.

CĀṆAKYA (*to himself*): Jīvasiddhi is my own spy. (*Aloud.*) Who else?

SPY: A close friend of Rākṣasa's, your Honor, a scribe by the name of Śakaṭadāsa.

CĀṆAKYA (*smiling, to himself*): He is of no account, if he is only a scribe. Still, one should despise no enemy, be he ever so humble. I have already detailed Siddhārthaka to him, to pose as his friend. (*Aloud.*) My good man, let us hear who the third man is.

SPY: The third is Rākṣasa's closest friend, Candanadāsa, the provost of the jewelers' guild here in Pāṭaliputra. Rākṣasa left his family in Candanadāsa's house when he escaped from the city.

CĀṆAKYA (*to himself*): Surely Rākṣasa would not leave his family with any but his closest and most sympathetic friends. (*Aloud.*) How do you know that he left his family with Candanadāsa?

SPY: This signet ring will prove it, your Honor. (*He hands over a ring.*)

CĀṆAKYA (*taking the ring, studies the inscription—Rākṣasa's name—which is engraved on it. Gleefully to himself.*) One might say that I can now wind Rākṣasa around my finger! (*Aloud.*) How did you find this ring? I want to hear the details.

SPY: Listen, sir. When you gave me the assignment to find out what attitude the people in the city were taking, I went around with this Yama show, which would open doors to me without creating any suspicions. So I also got admitted to Provost Candanadāsa's residence. I rolled out the canvas and proceeded to sing my hymns.

CĀṆAKYA: Then what?

SPY: Then I saw a little boy, of about five years old, very handsome-looking indeed, with the wide-open eyes of the naturally inquisitive child. He was climbing out of a window into the yard where I had set up my little show. Immediately there was an outcry of women's voices at the other side of the window: "Oh, he is gone, he is gone!" Their shouts betrayed an undue concern. Then a lady showed her face at the door, very briefly, caught the boy in full flight as he was scampering off, and, scolding, pulled him back into the house. As she thrust out her creeper-like hand to catch him, this ring, which is made to fit a man's finger, slipped off her finger and fell on the doorsill. It bounced and rolled unnoticed to my feet where it came to a stop and lay motionless in an act of wifely adoration! When I saw Minister Rākṣasa's name engraved on it, I brought it here, to lay it in turn at your Honor's feet. That is how I got the ring.

CĀṆAKYA: I have heard you, my man. Go now. Soon you will get a reward commensurate with your enterprise.

SPY: As your Honor commands!

CĀṆAKYA: Śārṅgarava! Śārṅgarava!

Enter the Pupil.

PUPIL: Sir?

CĀṆAKYA: Bring me an inkwell and a sheet of palm-leaf.

Pupil does so.

CĀṆAKYA (*taking the sheet, to himself*): What shall I write? For this letter must bring me victory over Rākṣasa.

Enter a Woman (Śoṇottarā) who belongs to the king's bodyguard.[12]

GUARD: Victory, your Honor!

CĀṆAKYA (*gratified, to himself*): The wish is well taken! (*Aloud.*) Śoṇottarā, what brings you here?

GUARD: Excellency, his Majesty Candragupta folds his hands to his forehead and sends you this message: "I desire with your Honor's permission to perform the funeral rites for his Majesty Parvataka, and avail myself of the occasion to distribute among the Brahmins the jewelry that his Majesty wore."

CĀṆAKYA (*pleased, to himself*): Splendid, Candragupta! It is as though you send your message in collusion with my own thoughts. (*Aloud.*) Śoṇottarā, tell the king in my name: "Excellent, my son. You are quite adept at the ways of the world. Do as you desire. However, the jewels which Parvataka wore on his person are valuable and should be presented to valuable persons. Therefore I myself shall send you some Brahmins whose value has been proved."

GUARD: As your Honor commands. (*Exit.*)

CĀṆAKYA: Śārṅgarava, tell Viśvāvasu and his two brothers to go to the king; he will present them with certain ornaments. Afterward they must come and see me.

PUPIL: As you say, sir.

CĀṆAKYA: That takes care of the second half of my letter. Now what about the first half? (*He considers.*) Ah, I know. My spies have informed me that five princes, the most powerful among the barbarians, are the closest allies of Rākṣasa: Citravarman of Kulūṭa; Siṃhanāda of Malaya,[13] a lion of a man; Puṣkarākṣa of Kashmir; Śindhuṣena of Sindh, who has shattered the power of his enemies; and Megha, emperor of Persia, who commands a large force of horsemen. If I write down their names, not even the gods' own bookkeeper can blot them out. . . . (*He reconsiders.*) Better not write any names. Keep the first part of the letter vague. (*He finishes writing.*) Śārṅgarava!

Enter the Pupil.

PUPIL: Master?

CĀṆAKYA: My boy, the handwriting of scholars is always illegible, however much care they take over it. Therefore tell Siddhārthaka for me to have this letter copied out by Śakaṭadāsa, but with no names on the outside, just the legend "From Someone Somewhere." Let him bring the letter back here. He should not tell the scribe that it is Cāṇakya who orders the copy made.

PUPIL: As you say, sir. (*Exit.*)
CĀṆAKYA (*to himself*): This means the end of Malayaketu.

Enter Siddhārthaka with the letter.

SIDDHĀRTHAKA: Victory, your Honor! Here is the letter, Śakaṭadāsa has copied it.

CĀṆAKYA (*taking it*): What a fine hand! (*He reads through it.*) Now seal the letter with this signet ring.

SIDDHĀRTHAKA (*does so*): I have sealed the letter, sir. Can I do anything else?

CĀṆAKYA: My good man, I want to employ you on a mission that only a very reliable man can accomplish.

SIDDHĀRTHAKA (*pleased*): I am honored, sir! Please tell this slave what he should do.

CĀṆAKYA: First you must go to the execution field. Shortly Śakaṭadāsa will be taken there to be killed. When he arrives you must give the executioners a signal: close your right eye at them angrily, so that they really see it. When they have caught your signal, they will pretend to be frightened of your evil eye and run about to ward it off. In the confusion that follows, abduct Śakaṭadāsa from the field and bring him to Rākṣasa. You are free to accept any reward that he will offer out of gratitude for saving his friend's life. Remain in Rākṣasa's service for the time being, until his enemies close in on him. Then you must execute this plan (*whispers into his ear*).

SIDDHĀRTHAKA: At your command, sir!
CĀṆAKYA: Śārṅgarava!

Enter the Pupil.

PUPIL: Master?

CĀṆAKYA: Take the following message to Kālapāśika and Daṇḍapāśika the magistrates: "The king orders that the Jain mendicant Jīvasiddhi, who at Rākṣasa's instigation has assassinated Parvataka with a poison-girl, be driven from the city in disgrace, with public proclamation of his crime."

PUPIL: As you command, master. (*He starts to leave.*)

CĀṆAKYA: Wait, there is some more. "And the king orders that Śakaṭadāsa the scribe, who at Rāksasa's instigation continues to make attempts on his Majesty's life in Pāṭaliputra, be crucified with public proclamation of his crime, and that his family be jailed."

PUPIL: As you command, master. (*Exit.*)

CĀṆAKYA (*to himself, in a doubtful voice*): But will this get Rākṣasa, that scoundrel?

SIDDHĀRTHAKA: Got 'em down, sir!

CĀṆAKYA (*to himself, pleased*): So we have got him! (*Aloud.*) Got down what, my good fellow?

SIDDHĀRTHAKA: Your orders, sir. I'll be on my way to success!

CĀṆAKYA (*handing over the letter and Rākṣasa's signet ring*): And may success go with you!

SIDDHĀRTHAKA: Yes, sir! (*Exit, bowing.*)

Enter the Pupil.

PUPIL: Master, Kālapāśika and Daṇḍapāśika beg to inform you that his Majesty's orders are now being executed.

CĀṆAKYA: Splendid. Now, my boy, I want to see Candanadāsa, the provost of the jewelers' guild.

PUPIL: Yes, master. (*Exit, and re-enter with Candanadāsa.*)

PUPIL: This way, merchant.

CANDANADĀSA (*to himself*): Whenever the merciless Cāṇakya is involved, even an innocent man is frightened out of his wits by an unexpected summons, let alone one as guilty as I am. That is why I forewarned Dhanasena and the others who are staying at my house that one day the accursed Cāṇakya was bound to search the house and that they at once should smuggle Rākṣasa's family out of my place. Whatever then would happen to me, let it happen.

PUPIL: Come on, merchant! This way!

CANDANADĀSA: I am coming. (*Both turn toward center.*)

PUPIL (*approaching*): Here is Candanadāsa, sir.

CANDANADĀSA: Victory, your Honor!

CĀṆAKYA (*looking up slowly*): Welcome, merchant. Take this chair.

CANDANADĀSA (*with a bow*): Surely your Honor knows that unwonted courtesy can pain a man's heart more than an insult? I shall sit on the floor, as I should.

CĀṆAKYA: No, no, my dear sir. This is the most elementary courtesy I can show you. Please, do take the chair!

CANDANADĀSA (*to himself*): He has something afoot, the crook! (*Aloud.*) As it pleases your Honor. (*He sits down.*)

CĀṆAKYA: My dear Candanadāsa, is the interest on your loans multiplying satisfactorily?[14]

CANDANADĀSA (*to himself*): This extreme politeness is suspicious. (*Aloud.*) Why shouldn't I prosper, my lord? My business is still intact, thanks to your Lordship.
CĀṆAKYA: Then Candragupta's vices do not yet call the late king's virtues to mind?
CANDANADĀSA (*stopping his ears*): Heaven forbid, sir! All the people rejoice ever more in the king's good fortune, which rises like the full moon on the clean-washed autumn sky!
CĀṆAKYA: Indeed? Still, kings wish some return on the gratitude of their subjects.
CANDANADĀSA: Please tell me, my lord! What does the king want from me and how much?
CĀṆAKYA: But, merchant! This is not Nanda's reign, this is Candragupta's! If the greedy Nandas took their royal pleasure in money, Candragupta takes his pleasure in not having to harass you.
CANDANADĀSA (*happily*): I am honored, sir!
CĀṆAKYA: You might have asked me, merchant, how this pleasure of the king could be gratified.
CANDANADĀSA: Inform me, sir.
CĀṆAKYA: In a word, by acting without hostility toward his Majesty.
CANDANADĀSA: What unhappy man has your Honor found hostile to his king?
CĀṆAKYA: You, chiefly.
CANDANADĀSA (*stopping his ears*): Heaven forbid! Heaven forbid! What threat does straw hold for fire?
CĀṆAKYA: It is a threat that you even now lodge and shelter in your house the family of Minister Rākṣasa, who works against the king.
CANDANADĀSA: Aho! Your Honor has been misinformed!
CĀṆAKYA: There, there, merchant. No need to panic. It may happen that the creatures of unseated kings in their anguish wish their families off on, oh, surely reluctant citizens, before they flee the country. If such were the case, only continued concealment would constitute a crime.
CANDANADĀSA: That is exactly what happened. At one time Rākṣasa's family stayed at my house.
CĀṆAKYA: First it was a lie, now it is true. Your two statements contradict each other, merchant.
CANDANADĀSA: Merely a misunderstanding, your Honor.
CĀṆAKYA: In Candragupta's reign there is no room for misunderstanding. Surrender Rākṣasa's family and be less misunderstood.

CANDANADĀSA: But, your Honor, I repeat, *at one time* they were staying at my house.

CĀṆAKYA: Then where are they now?

CANDANADĀSA: I don't know.

CĀṆAKYA (*smiling*): Indeed, you do not? Merchant, there is danger overhead, and no help in sight! I might add, don't deceive yourself, that just as a Cāṇakya (*he pauses and gestures modestly*) exterminated the Nandas, so Rākṣasa will uproot Candragupta. For Who would endeavor to divorce Candragupta or the Moon from his Splendor, who at last found his Rightful Place to the Joy of the whole World? While during the Nanda's lifetime he was left to wander homeless, despite the courage and policy of able ministers like Vakranāsa? Who would dare to steal from the yawning mouth of a lion the glittering eyetooth which, crimson with the blood of the elephant it tasted, shines like the crescent moon at dawn?

CANDANADĀSA (*to himself*): His results justify his boasts.

Noise offstage.

CĀṆAKYA: Śārṅgarava! Find out what is going on outside.

PUPIL: Yes, sir. (*Exit and re-enter.*) Master, the Jain mendicant Jīvasiddhi, who has been working against the king, is being driven in disgrace from the city at the king's orders.

CĀṆAKYA: Poor man! Still, let him reap the reward of his treachery. You may observe, Candanadāsa, how severely the king bears down on traitors. Accept the advice of a friend and profit by it: surrender Rākṣasa's family, and for a long time you will enjoy the king's favor.

CANDANADĀSA: Sir, how can I surrender them when they are not in my house?

More noise offstage.

CĀṆAKYA: Śārṅgarava, find out what is happening now.

PUPIL: Yes, sir. (*Exit and re-enter.*) Master, Śakaṭadāsa the scribe is being taken away to be impaled for high treason.

CĀṆAKYA: He too reaps as he has sown. Merchant, a king who is so severe on treason will not condone your sheltering Rākṣasa's family. Sacrifice the other person's family, if you want to save your family and your life.

CANDANADĀSA: Why do you threaten me? I would not have given up Rākṣasa's family, even if they *had* been staying at my house. Could I do it then when they aren't?

CĀṆAKYA: The choice is yours, Candanadāsa.

CANDANADĀSA: Yes, it is my deliberate choice.

CĀṆAKYA (*to himself*): Bravo, man! Is there anyone left in the world after Šibi[15] who would take the hard decision, when he might have profited much more easily by giving up his friends? (*Aloud.*) It is your decision, Candanadāsa!

CANDANADĀSA: Yes.

CĀṆAKYA (*angrily*): Wait, traitor! You will suffer the king's wrath!

CANDANADĀSA: I am prepared. Your Honor must act as his responsibilities dictate.

CĀṆAKYA: Śārṅgarava, take a message to Kālapāśika and Daṇḍapāśika: "Arrest the traitor Candanadāsa at once." No, wait. Tell Vijayapālaka, the captain of the citadel, to jail him with his family and to confiscate his house and all it contains. He must detain him until I have informed the Maurya.[16] The Maurya will order his execution personally.

PUPIL: As you command, master. Come along, merchant.

CANDANADĀSA: I am following you, sir. (*To himself.*) It is my good fortune to die for a friend, not for a crime. (*Exeunt.*)

CĀṆAKYA (*joyfully*): Now I have Rākṣasa. For just as this man is prepared to give up his life, as though he hated it, so as not to endanger Rākṣasa, so Rākṣasa will hate to live when his friend is in peril.

Noise offstage.

CĀṆAKYA: Śārṅgarava!

Enter the pupil.

PUPIL: At your orders, sir.

CĀṆAKYA: What is that noise?

Exit and re-enter pupil.

PUPIL: Master, Siddhārthaka has rescued Śakaṭadāsa from the execution field, and they have made good their escape!

CĀṆAKYA (*to himself*): A good beginning, Siddhārthaka, bravo! (*Aloud.*) Escaped? (*Angrily.*) Tell Bhāgurāyaṇa to catch up with them at once!

Exit and re-enter pupil.

PUPIL (*in dismay*): It is terrible, sir! Bhāgurāyaṇa has defected!

CĀṆAKYA (*to himself*): And, let us hope, successfully. (*Aloud, in anger.*) Go tell Bhadrabhaṭa, Puruṣadatta, Hiṅgurāta, Balagupta, Rājasena, Rohitākṣa, and Vijayavarman to chase Bhāgurāyaṇa and bring the criminal back!

PUPIL: At your orders, sir.

Exit and re-enter pupil.

PUPIL (*in despair*): What a disaster! The whole system is falling apart! Bhadrabhaṭa and the others defected at the crack of dawn!

CĀṆAKYA (*to himself*): And may God speed them! (*Aloud.*) Don't despair, my boy. Those who depart with a plan that was laid before are gone indeed. And let those who remain set their mind on going, as long as my own mind stays with me. If the goal is to be reached, this mind of mine is worth more than a hundred armies. And its warlike prowess has been shown amply by the annihilation of the Nandas! (*Rising.*) Yes, I shall bring Bhadrabhaṭa back and the other defectors. (*To himself.*) Where can you go now, malicious Rākṣasa?

You are like a rogue elephant flowing with rut,
Roaming the woods in a frenzy of exuberant power:
But I shall capture you with my wits, and rope you in
For you to serve at last as the Maurya's beast of burden!

(*Exit.*)

ACT TWO

Enter a Snake Charmer.

SNAKE CHARMER: Snake charmers and ministers have a lot in common. The ones know how to administer drugs, the others their affairs. Both draw their circles, to contain their snakes or their kingdoms. And while the ones keep their spells, the others keep their counsels. (*In the air, as though addressing someone.*) You ask who I am, sir? I am a snake charmer, sir. Jīrṇaviṣa. What do you say? You want to play around with my snakes? Aha! What do you do for a living? You work for the king? But then you are already playing around with snakes, my dear sir! Why? You know what they say. There are three kinds of people sure to come to grief: snake charmers who don't know their charms and antidotes, mahouts who ride a *must* elephant, and arrogant officials who work for a king. Oh, the man has disappeared. (*Again, as though addressing someone.*) What do I keep in these boxes and baskets? Snakes, sir, with their fangs intact! They are my living. You want to see them? Sorry, sir, this is not the right place. If you are curious, you can come along. I am going to show them over there in that house. What are you saying now? That is Rākṣasa's house and people of my kind are not admitted? Run along, fellow. My business opens doors. Oh, there he goes.

(*To himself, changing to Sanskrit.*) What a puzzle! When I see that Candragupta is guided by Cāṇakya's genius, I think that all Rākṣasa's efforts must be practically useless. But when I see Malayaketu guided by Rākṣasa's genius, I believe that Candragupta's throne is tottering. The Maurya's fortune is held steady on the leash of Kauṭilya's wit, it seems, but I can see how Rākṣasa's tugs at it with his tactics. And while these two great ministers are at daggers drawn, the ancient Kingdom that the Nandas have bequeathed hangs in the balance. Yes, the Goddess of Luck is caught between two masterful men, like a she-elephant caught in the forest between two battling elephant bulls, and she must be frightened and weary, if she cannot make up her mind!—I must see Rākṣasa. (*He circles the stage and waits.*)

Enter Rākṣasa. He is seated in his house. A servant is with him. His expression betrays great anxiety.

RĀKṢASA (*with a tear*): Calamity upon calamity!

The Nandas, who had pacified their foes
With wit and bravery skilfully employed,
Must like the Vṛṣṇis, through their deadly fate,
Still perish in the vastness of their race.[17]
But left awake, my mind ridden with fright,
I stayed to paint the last scenes in, and find
The canvas gone.

Why do I try? Not that the old faith is lost,
Not that I yearn for more sensations, or
Fear for the failing of my breath, or care
To rise to might again. Why do I try
A mind reduced to utter impotence
On subtler schemes but that the king I served
May in his heaven graciously accept
The slaughter of his foes?

(*He stares before him, tears in his eyes.*) Thou Goddess on thy lotus throne, divinely ignorant of virtue!

Why didst thou leave the Nanda, he a God,
A fountainhead of bliss, to court his foeman,
Son of a king begotten on a slave!
Why, wanton, wouldst thou tarry, woman, and
Not vanish like the last drops of the rut
That drove the elephant to death?

Harlot, are all the kings of famous stock
Now burnt to ashes that you should elect
A baseborn Maurya for a lord? The mind
Of woman flutters like a flower petal
And by its nature hates to recognize
A man's true virtue! Yet I shall defeat,
Woman, your man, and with your man your lust!

(*He pauses and reflects.*) Yes, I did well to leave my family with my closest friend, Candanadāsa, before I departed from Pāṭaliputra. For as long as people think that Rākṣasa still has a stake in recapturing the city, our partisans there who are working for our king will not slacken in their efforts. I have posted Śakaṭadāsa in the city and left him with large funds to give aid and comfort to the assassins we are using to kill Candragupta, and also to buy intelligence of the enemy's plans. Other friends, like Jīvasiddhi, have been given the task of collecting day-to-day information of the enemy's doings, and sabotaging them. And so I could go on.

> Our king, who loved his sons, died with them all
> When he had reared the alien tiger cub.
> But now, unless invisible Fate become
> His coat of mail, the arrow of my mind
> Will find the Maurya's weakness out, and strike.

Enter a Chamberlain.

CHAMBERLAIN:

> Just as Cāṇakya's art killed off the Nanda,
> Old age has killed Desire in me, and in
> The fortress of my body Piety rises
> As Maurya in the citadel of state.
> But Greed, like Rākṣasa, has found a way
> To prey upon our growing virtue, and
> Attempts to carry off a victory
> That fails!

(*He circles the stage and approaches center.*) Here is Rākṣasa's residence. I am going in. (*Enters and looks around.*) May your Honor prosper!

RĀKṢASA: I greet you, my lord. Priyaṃvadaka, bring in a seat.

SERVANT: Here is a seat, sir. Please sit down.

CHAMBERLAIN (*sits down*): Prince Malayaketu sends you this message, your Excellency: "My heart is distressed that your Lordship has refused to adorn his person for such a long time. Although it may not be possible at once to forget the great virtues of your late king, nonetheless your Lordship may be pleased to honor my request." (*He shows*

Rākṣasa some jewelry.) The prince has taken these jewels from his own person. Pray wear his gift.
RĀKṢASA: My lord Jājali, tell his Highness in my name that I have already forgotten the late king's virtues since I chose to revere his own. However,

> I will not grace with the most simple jewel
> This body that fails in strength and wretchedly
> Lies at the mercy of the enemy;
> Not till, most gracious lord, you have defeated
> The closing circle of your foeman's forces
> And grace Sugāṅga's golden lion-throne.[18]

CHAMBERLAIN: It will be easy for the prince, as long as your Excellency guides him. Therefore honor this first token of his Highness' gratitude!
RĀKṢASA: My lord, the prince's word must not be ignored. Nor yours. I shall obey his order.
CHAMBERLAIN (*putting the jewels on Rākṣasa's person*): May your Honor prosper. I shall leave now.
RĀKṢASA: I greet you, my lord. (*Exit Chamberlain.*)
RĀKṢASA: Priyaṃvadaka, see who is waiting at the door to see me.
SERVANT: Yes, my lord. (*He circles the stage and notices the snake charmer.*) Who are you, sir?
SNAKE CHARMER: I am a snake charmer, my dear fellow. Jīrṇaviṣa is my name. I want to perform for the minister with my snakes.
SERVANT: Wait, I'll tell him. (*Approaches Rākṣasa.*) Sir, there's a snake charmer wants to show you his snakes.
RĀKṢASA (*a spasm contracting his left eye,*[19] *to himself*): Ah! An exhibition of snakes at the very start! (*Aloud.*) Priyaṃvadaka, I have no interest in snakes. Give him what he wants and send him on his way.
SERVANT: As you wish, sir. (*Approaches.*) His Excellency graciously sends you your fee, but he is not disposed to watch your show.
SNAKE CHARMER: Good man, will you tell his Excellency that I am not only a snake charmer, but also a poet in the vernacular? If his Excellency is not disposed to watch my show, he might read this verse.
SERVANT (*taking the sheet and approaching Rākṣasa*): Sir, he begs to inform you that he is not only a snake charmer, but also a poet in the vernacular; and if your Excellency is not disposed to watch his show, you should read this verse.

RĀKṢASA (*takes the sheet and reads aloud*):

What the Honey Bee gives up
When it has taken with its art
The Elixir of the Flower Cup
May give another's art a start.

(*Thinking, to himself.*) Of course, the verse means that he is a spy of mine, and that he has news from the City of Flowers. My preoccupation with my affairs, and the large numbers of spies I employ, made him momentarily slip my mind. I remember now. He must be Virādhagupta, who goes about in the guise of a snake charmer. (*Aloud.*) Priyaṃvadaka, let him come in. He is a competent rhymester and his verses are worth hearing.

SERVANT: As you command, sir. (*Approaches Snake Charmer.*) Come in, sir.

VIRĀDHAGUPTA (*draws near and looks around; to himself, in Sanskrit*): There is his Excellency Rākṣasa,

And fearful of his importunities,
Luck even now holds only half embraced
Her Maurya—one arm loose about his neck,
The other on her lap, or resting lightly
Upon his shoulder. Still she turns her face
Away, and does not yet allow the nipple
Of her right breast to touch his chest in love's
Most intimate embrace.

(*Aloud.*) Victory, your Excellency!

RĀKṢASA (*looking up*): My dear Virādha . . . (*Stops in mid-sentence.*) Why, he has grown a beard![20] Priyaṃvadaka, I want to amuse myself for a while with his snakes. The servants may leave and take some rest. You yourself may attend to your own affairs.

SERVANT: As you please, your Excellency. (*Exit with servants.*)

RĀKṢASA: My friend Virādhagupta! Please take this seat.

Virādhagupta sits down.

RĀKṢASA (*studying his appearance*): To this then are the king's men reduced! (*Tears start to his eyes.*)

VIRĀDHAGUPTA: Don't be concerned about me, my lord. Soon you will raise us again to our former ranks!

RĀKṢASA: Friend, tell me the news from the City of Flowers.

VIRĀDHAGUPTA: It is a long story, sir. Where should I begin?

RĀKṢASA: First I want to hear what my agents accomplished with the poison, and so on, after Candragupta formally entered the city.

VIRĀDHAGUPTA: This is the story. Pāṭaliputra was surrounded by the armies of Parvataka and Candragupta, who were guided by Cāṇakya's strategy. There were Scythians among their hordes, and Greeks, Gurkhas and Cambodians, Persians and Bactrians, and they were like the oceans that will flood the world at doomsday.

RĀKṢASA (*drawing his sword, tensely*): Who shall beleaguer Pāṭaliputra as long as I am here? Pravīraka! Pravīraka! Deploy the archers at once along the walls, station our elephants at the gates to break the lines of the enemy elephants, and those who like me want glory and are willing to defy death and attack the weak opposing forces follow me outside the gates!

VIRĀDHAGUPTA: Please, your Excellency! Don't agitate yourself! The things I am describing are in the past now!

RĀKṢASA (*sighing*): Yes, it is history now, unfortunately. But for a moment I relived the past. (*He drops his sword.*) Nanda, my king, how well do I remember how you favored me almost to excess. . . . At the time of the battle you sent me order after order: Get Rākṣasa to the looming line of elephants, let Rākṣasa beat off the horsemen who threaten to flood us, Rākṣasa has got to stop the foot soldiers. . . . And your confidence in me made you believe that there were a thousand Rākṣasas in the city.

VIRĀDHAGUPTA: When King Sarvārthasiddhi saw that the city was completely surrounded, he decided he should no longer permit his people to suffer the hardships of an extended siege, after all the long days of privation that had gone before. Even at a time like that he thought only of his people! He left the city through a secret tunnel and retired to a hermitage. When the king had gone, your forces lost heart. But in the city itself your partisans made their presence felt by the violence with which they resisted the Maurya's solemn proclamation of victory. When you yourself had escaped through the tunnel to prepare for the restoration of the Nandas, and the luckless Parvataka was killed by the poison-girl that you had employed to assassinate Candragupta . . .

RĀKṢASA: See the wonder of it, my friend! I had kept that poison-girl, who could kill only a single man, just in order to assassinate Candragupta; and then, to that accursed Cāṇakya's undeserved good luck, she had to meet Parvataka and kill him! . . .

VIRĀDHAGUPTA: It was a whim of destiny, your Excellency. What can one do?

RĀKṢASA: Go on. What happened?

VIRĀDHAGUPTA: Prince Malayaketu was thrown into a panic by his father's accidental assassination and he fled. But his uncle Vairodhaka, a brother of Parvataka's, was given assurances of personal safety and stayed. When it had been announced that Maurya was to make a triumphal entry into the city, Cāṇakya summoned all the carpenters of Pāṭaliputra and told them that Candragupta, on the advice of his astrologers, would enter the palace of the Nandas at midnight. He ordered the carpenters to build fitting decorations at the Eastern Gate of the palace and elsewhere on the route. The carpenters replied that it had already been done. A certain carpenter Dāruvarman, as soon as he heard that Candragupta was preparing to enter the palace, had erected gilt arches at the main gate as well as other ornamentations; so they would confine themselves to the interior decorations. When Cāṇakya heard that Dāruvarman had decorated the palace drive on his own initiative, without awaiting any orders, he delivered a long speech in praise of the carpenter's enterprise and acted as if he were sincerely pleased. "Soon," he concluded, "Dāruvarman will receive a reward commensurate with his enterprise."

RĀKṢASA (*disturbed*): But why should Cāṇakya have been pleased? I gather that Dāruvarman's efforts either were wasted or backfired. It was a miscalculation on his part, or misguided devotion to the late king, if he did not wait till orders were given, for he must have raised Cāṇakya's worst suspicions. What happened?

VIRĀDHAGUPTA: As I said, Cāṇakya had passed information to craftsmen and townspeople that Candragupta would enter the Nanda's palace at midnight, because that was an auspicious hour. When the hour came, he set Parvataka's brother Vairodhaka on the throne next to Candragupta and divided the kingdom between them.

RĀKṢASA: What? He had promised half the kingdom to Parvataka, and then gave it away to his brother?

VIRĀDHAGUPTA: Exactly.

RĀKṢASA (*to himself*): Surely Cāṇakya was too cunning not to have contrived a way to do away with the fellow secretly. He must have taken advantage of the situation to build up enough good will among the people to cover up the scandal of Parvataka's assassination. (*Aloud.*) Then what?

VIRĀDHAGUPTA: As I said, it had already been announced that Candragupta would ceremonially enter Nanda's palace at midnight. But since Vairodhaka was to share the kingdom, they first had him undergo a consecration rite. His body was decked with an armor of snow-white pearls and gems that were woven in a cross pattern to form a flamboyant coat of mail. The crown of his head fairly glowed with a closely fitted diadem of rubies, and fragrant garlands of flowers colorfully crossed the wide expanse of his chest. Not even his best friends could have recognized him. At Cāṇakya's orders, Vairodhaka mounted Candragupta's own state elephant, Crescent Moon. And so, followed in state by Candragupta's vassals, Vairodhaka rode into the gates of King Nanda's palace. As Dāruvarman saw him approach the Eastern Gate he started the mechanism that was set up at your directive to bring the entire triumphal arch down on his head. Just before the gate Candragupta's vassals reined in their horses. Then things started happening. Behind Vairodhaka sat your man Barbaraka, Candragupta's own backrider; when the elephant was about to pass under the arch, Barbaraka groped with his hand for the golden goad which was hanging from a golden chain, to pull out the dagger that was hidden inside.

RĀKṢASA: Their timing was completely off!

VIRĀDHAGUPTA: The elephant expected a blow on the rear and changed to a trot. But the trap in the arch was timed to the animal's original speed and when Dāruvarman dropped the beam, it fell off the mark and crushed Barbaraka. The poor fellow perished with dagger in hand before he had time to reach Vairodhaka, whom he, too, had mistaken for the Maurya. Dāruvarman, knowing that he would have to die anyway, went for the iron pin on which the mechanism turned and beat Vairodhaka on the elephant to death.

RĀKṢASA: Two misfortunes at once! Fate saved Candragupta, and killed Vairodhaka and Barbaraka. What happened to Dāruvarman?

VIRĀDHAGUPTA: He was stoned to death by the soldiers that led the parade.

RĀKṢASA (*with a tear*): Alas for Dāruvarman. We have been robbed of a sincere friend! How did our physician finish, Abhayadatta?

VIRĀDHAGUPTA: Entirely, your Excellency.

RĀKṢASA (*with joy*): What? He killed Candragupta?

VIRĀDHAGUPTA: Fate would not have it.

RĀKṢASA (*in despair*): Then why do you say with satisfaction that he finished entirely?

VIRĀDHAGUPTA: Your Excellency, he prepared a draught for Candragupta mixed with a magic powder. But that accursed Cāṇakya inspected the golden cup and noticed that the gold had changed color. "Don't take that draught, Maurya! It is poisoned" he said.

RĀKṢASA: He is a clever fellow. What happened to the physician?

VIRĀDHAGUPTA: He had to drink the draught and died.

RĀKṢASA (*in dismay*): Ah, a great scientist lost! But what became of Pramodaka, who was in charge of the royal bedchamber?

VIRĀDHAGUPTA: The same as became of the others.

RĀKṢASA (*upset*): What do you mean?

VIRĀDHAGUPTA: He was a fool. When he had received the large sum you had paid out to him in advance, he began spending it in chunks. So Cāṇakya interrogated him and asked where all that money came from. The fellow told a confused and contradictory story. Upon which Cāṇakya had him tortured to death.

RĀKṢASA (*dismayed*): So here too chance has got the better of us. And what happened to Bhībhatsaka and the other killers who were to assassinate Candragupta in bed? Weren't they already posted in a tunnel inside the walls of the royal bedchamber before Candragupta set foot in the palace?

VIRĀDHAGUPTA: It is a dreadful story, your Excellency.

RĀKṢASA (*impatiently*): What is a dreadful story? Surely they weren't found out by Cāṇakya?

VIRĀDHAGUPTA: What else, sir? Before Candragupta entered the palace, the unholy Cāṇakya himself inspected the bedchamber the moment he was inside the palace. He noticed a thin line of ants on the wall which carried food out of a minute crack in the plaster, and he immediately concluded that there must be people inside. He burned the entire pavilion down. While the palace was burning, Bhībhatsaka and the others were blinded by the smoke and could not find the exit, which had been plastered shut provisionally. They ran into the raging fire.

RĀKṢASA (*with a tear*): Friend, see how fate conspired to aid the ursurper Candragupta!

> The poison-girl, whom we had secretly employed
> To murder Candragupta, was by destiny
> To kill Parvataka who held half his realm.
> And all the other men I set upon the king

Died by the very means they were to use on him.
My stratagems have borne the Maurya ample fruit!

VIRĀDHAGUPTA: Yet, Your Excellency, a man must go on when he has begun.

The lowest do not even start, for fear
Of obstacles; those in between *do* start,
But stop as soon as obstacles arise;
The best, however, will, like you, not rest
Until their work, however much beset
By obstacles, is carried to the end.

Does Śeṣa[21] go on carrying the earth
Because he does not feel the burden?
Or does the sun rise every day
Because it never feels fatigue?
No, for the great ones are ashamed
To act the coward and hang back:
It is their one ancestral vow
To do as they have said they would.

RĀKṢASA: Friend, it should be plain to you that we shall continue what we have begun. What happened afterward?

VIRĀDHAGUPTA: Afterward the accursed Cāṇakya became a thousand times more careful where Candragupta was concerned. And when he discovered from whom these attempts originated, he arrested your agents in Pāṭaliputra.

RĀKṢASA (*impatiently*): Whom did he arrest?

VIRĀDHAGUPTA: In the first place a Jain mendicant, Jīvasiddhi. He was driven in disgrace from the city.

RĀKṢASA (*to himself*): This is still bearable. A man who has no place of his own should not mind losing it. (*Aloud*.) For what crime was he exiled?

VIRĀDHAGUPTA: He was found guilty of having been paid by Rākṣasa to kill Parvataka with a poison-girl.

RĀKṢASA (*to himself*): Splendid, Kauṭilya, splendid! You neatly avoided all blame yourself and heaped it on us, while the king who owned half the kingdom stayed safely dead! One seed of statecraft, and many fruits ripen. (*Aloud*.) And further?

VIRĀDHAGUPTA: Criers proclaimed throughout the city that it had been Śakaṭadāsa who had employed Dāruvarman and the other assassins to murder the king, and he was impaled.

RĀKṢASA (*weeping*): Ah Śakaṭadāsa, my friend! You should not have had to die! But perhaps I must not mourn you, for you at least died for your master. If there is anyone to be mourned it is I, who wanted to live on even after the house of Nanda had perished!

VIRĀDHAGUPTA: Please do not speak like that, sir! For the Nanda's cause is still to be served.

RĀKṢASA: No, my friend,

> We used that cause to justify our will to live,
> And, ingrates, stayed behind when he, our king, had gone.

VIRĀDHAGUPTA: No, your Excellency,

> You did not need that cause to justify your life:
> You stayed behind only to show your gratitude!

RĀKṢASA: Continue, my friend. I am prepared to hear what fate had in store for my other friends.

VIRĀDHAGUPTA: When Candanadāsa learnt that all your friends were being rounded up, he evacuated your family.

RĀKṢASA: He was wrong to act against Cāṇakya!

VIRĀDHAGUPTA: Should he have betrayed his friend, your Excellency?

RĀKṢASA: Go on, go on!

VIRĀDHAGUPTA: Candanadāsa refused to deliver your family, in spite of Cāṇakya's insistence. Cāṇakya was furious and had him . . .

RĀKṢASA (*alarmed*): Not executed?

VIRĀDHAGUPTA: No, not executed, but jailed with his entire family and deprived of house and wealth.

RĀKṢASA: Then how can you say confidently that he evacuated my family? You should have said that he made me and my family his slaves forever!

Enter the Servant.

SERVANT: Victory, your Excellency! Śakaṭadāsa is waiting at your gate, sir.

RĀKṢASA (*with joy*): Can it be true?

SERVANT: Have your servants ever lied to you?

RĀKṢASA: Virādhagupta, how is it possible!

VIRĀDHAGUPTA: Perhaps it is true. Fortune helps the fortunate!

RĀKṢASA: Priyaṃvadaka, what are you waiting for! Show him in and reassure me!

SERVANT: As you command, sir. (*Exit.*)

Enter Śakaṭadāsa, followed by Siddhārthaka.

ŚAKAṬADĀSA (*to himself*):

> I saw the pole planted in the earth—
> But I had seen Maurya planted on earth.
> I watched the wreath put around my neck—
> But I had watched Maurya's maddening luck.
> I heard the horns blowing for my death—
> But I had heard Nanda's destruction blown.
> And so my heart, toughened long before,
> By crueler strokes, lived as it had before.

(*Now first noticing his surroundings, with joy.*) There is Minister Rākṣasa alive and well! Even when the Nandas had perished, his loyalty lived on. And he has carried on their cause, to be on earth the standard-bearer of devotion!

RĀKṢASA (*noticing him now too, with joy*): My friend Śakaṭadāsa! How happy I am! Embrace me! (*They embrace.*) Here is a seat. Sit down!

ŚAKAṬADĀSA: As you please, sir. (*He sits down.*)

RĀKṢASA: Śakaṭadāsa, I am overjoyed! Whom must I thank?

ŚAKAṬADĀSA (*pointing at Siddhārthaka*): My good friend Siddhārthaka. He chased the executioners away and carried me off from the execution field.

RĀKṢASA (*with joy*): Siddhārthaka, excellent fellow, no reward is good enough for you, but please take this. (*He takes off his jewels and hands them to him.*)

SIDDHĀRTHAKA (*taking the jewels and throwing himself at the Minister's feet, to himself*): My master said I could; all right, I am obeying! (*Aloud.*) Your Excellency, I have just arrived and I don't know anybody here well enough to trust him with these jewels and feel happy about it. I should like to seal them with this signet ring and leave them in your Excellency's treasury. I shall take them when I need them.

RĀKṢASA: That is perfectly all right, my man. Śakaṭadāsa, will you take care of things?

ŚAKAṬADĀSA: As you wish, sir. (*He looks closely at the ring. Aside to Rākṣasa.*) That ring has your name on it, sir!

RĀKṢASA (*examining the ring, to himself*): That is right. The woman of my house took it from me when I left the city, to soften her longings for me. How can it have got to him? (*Aloud.*) Siddhārthaka, how did you obtain this ring?

SIDDHĀRTHAKA: There is a jewel dealer in Pāṭaliputra, Candanadāsa. I found it at his door.

RĀKṢASA: That is right.

SIDDHĀRTHAKA: What is right, sir?

RĀKṢASA: That one might find baubles like this at a rich man's door.

ŚAKAṬADĀSA: Siddhārthaka, the ring has the minister's name on it. His Excellency will reward you richly for returning it to him. Give him the ring.

SIDDHĀRTHAKA: It will be reward enough if his Excellency is pleased to accept it . . . (*He hands over the ring.*)

RĀKṢASA: Śakaṭadāsa, you may use the ring for your duties.

ŚAKAṬADĀSA: As you command, sir.

SIDDHĀRTHAKA: My lord, I have a request to make.

RĀKṢASA: Speak freely.

SIDDHĀRTHAKA: Your Excellency knows that nobody who has worked against that devil Cāṇakya can ever return to Pāṭaliputra. Therefore if your Excellency is pleased to favor me, I should like to remain in your service.

RĀKṢASA: I shall be pleased. Only my ignorance about your own plans prevented me from extending an offer to you myself. You may remain.

SIDDHĀRTHAKA (*with joy*): I am honored!

RĀKṢASA: Śakaṭadāsa, see that Siddhārthaka takes a rest.

ŚAKAṬADĀSA: Yes, your Excellency. (*Exit with Siddhārthaka.*)

RĀKṢASA: Virādhagupta, my friend, now tell me the rest of the news from Pāṭaliputra. Do Candragupta's subjects lend a willing ear to our suggestions?

VIRĀDHAGUPTA: Indeed they do, sir. Don't they follow us in growing numbers?

RĀKṢASA: Why this disaffection?

VIRĀDHAGUPTA: The cause, as I see it, is this. Ever since Malayaketu's escape Cāṇakya has been under pressure from Candragupta. Cāṇakya himself, in his utter conceit, cancels Candragupta's orders whenever it pleases him, and the king is very vexed with him.

RĀKṢASA (*with joy*): Virādhagupta, go back again to Pāṭaliputra, in the same disguise of snake charmer. There is a very good friend of mine who lives in town in the disguise of a bard. Stanakalaśa is his name. Give him the following message: "Whenever Cāṇakya acts against Candragupta's orders, you must praise the king's prowess in verses that play on his hurt pride." He should send word in the utmost secrecy through the Hunchback.

VIRĀDHAGUPTA: As you command, sir.

Enter the servant.

SERVANT: Victory, your Excellency! Sir, Śakaṭadāsa wants you to know that these three pieces of jewelry are for sale and he asks you to look them over.

RĀKṢASA (*studying them, to himself*): Aho! These gems are priceless! (*Aloud.*) Tell Śakaṭadāsa to buy them at the asking price.

SERVANT: As you wish, sir. (*Exit.*)

RĀKṢASA (*to himself*): Now I must send the Hunchback to Pāṭaliputra. (*He rises.*) Would it be possible to alienate the accursed Cāṇakya from Candragupta? But why not?

Now is the Maurya master of all kings
And swells with power; yet Cāṇakya knows
That Candragupta reigns by his sole grace,
And smiles. One is self-satisfied with power
Regally swayed, the other with a vow
Grandly fulfilled. And their self-satisfaction
Will surely find an opportunity
To turn old friends into new enemies.

(*Exeunt omnes.*)

ACT THREE

Enter Candragupta's Chamberlain.

CHAMBERLAIN:

> My senses, which feed themselves on the objects that feed you, Desire,
> Have lost their power to perceive their objects any more.
> The limbs, which once I commanded, have lost their vigor now, Desire—
> Old age has put its foot upon your head and vainly do you pine!

(*He circles the stage, looks about, and continues as though addressing people present.*) Listen, ye servants of Sugāṅga Palace! His Majesty Candragupta, whose name be honored, sends you his orders: "I wish to watch the City of Flowers in all the splendor which the celebration of the Full Moon Festival today will lend to it. See to it that the upper terraces of the palace are made ready to receive my presence." (*He listens.*) What are you saying? You ask if his Majesty does not know that the festival has been canceled? Ah, dupes of fate, how dare you suggest such a thing! It may cost you your head! Hurry now!

> Let the beauty of yak plumes that rival the luster
> Of the Kaumudī[22] Festival's shining full moon
> Now commingling with blossoms embrace all these columns
> Which are fragrant with incense that burns at their feet.
>
> Let the flowery sprinkle of sandal perfumes
> Now quickly revive with its favors this earth
> Which so long now has carried the lion-claw throne
> That it seems to have dropped in a swoon!

(*Listening.*) What do you say? You are running already? Run, good men, run! King Candragupta is arriving, the king,

Who has resolved to shoulder with a will
The yoke that, heavy though it was, had long
Been borne before him by his royal sire.
But while the father trod with certain step
A well-known path, unstumbling in the rough,
The son, in the uncertainty of youth,
Still stumbles, though he holds the burden light.

VOICE OFFSTAGE: This way, your Majesty.

Enter the King and a female Bodyguard.

KING (*to himself*): To a king who himself is not masterful enough to plot his own course of royal duties, royalty is indeed a cause of great displeasure. If he acts in other people's interest, his own interest must suffer; and a king who has forsaken his own cause is king no longer. If the cause of others counts more with him than his own, why, he has become their servitor. And how can a man who serves others savor the taste of pleasure?

The fortune of kings is hard to placate, even for kings who possess themselves.

She flees from the severe, but does not stay
With those whose meekness is inspired by fear.
She hates the foolish but no more does love
The very learned. Trembling for the bold,
She mocks the overcautious. Alas!
Luck, like a courtesan in great demand,
Demands the utmost to be served and pleased!

Now my minister has instructed me that I should quarrel with him and, for a short time at least, rule independently. I agreed, but with great reluctance, as though I had agreed to a crime. Still, as long as our thoughts are elevated by his guidance, we are always independent. For a pupil who does the right thing is never restrained. Only when he foolishly strays from his path, does he feel the teacher's goad. Good pupils therefore are never corrected, if they want to be good; for, averse as they are from acting independently, they never reach the point where they are made to feel their dependence! (*Aloud.*) My lord Vaihīnari, conduct me to Sugāṅga Palace.

CHAMBERLAIN: This way, your Majesty.
They circle the stage.
CHAMBERLAIN: Here is the palace. Ascend gently, your Majesty, very gently.
King ascends the stairs to the upper terrace. Upstairs he looks out into space.
KING: Oh the unsurpassed beauty of a sky resplendent with the loveliness of autumn!

The autumn sky flows like a river, slowly,
And pure, with here and there a late white cloud
Emerging like a sandbank. All around
The skies are noisy with the gabbling cries
Of cranes, and when night falls clusters of stars
Dot the heavenly pond with lotuses.

Fall shows the swollen waters of the rivers
Their humbler place, and makes the paddy fields
Bow under the proud burden of their ears.
It cures the peacocks of their frenzied lust
As of a poison, and to all the world
It thus imparts its old propriety.

The autumn, like a messenger of love,
At last has taken Gaṅgā[23] down from heaven
Where she had quarreled with her Lord,
A God of many mistresses, and leads
Her, glibly telling many tales of love,
Grown calm but thin from suffering,
To her new husband, all the rivers' lord!

(*He scans the panorama.*) Aho! I see that the city has not yet begun the celebrations. Why not? My lord Vaihīnari, has the Full Moon Festival not been proclaimed in the city as I ordered?
CHAMBERLAIN: But certainly, your Majesty! The festival has been proclaimed in the city as you ordered.
KING: My lord, have the citizenry ignored our command?
CHAMBERLAIN (*stopping his ears*): Heaven forbid, your Majesty! Your commands have nowhere on earth ever been disregarded! Would your own subjects fail to obey?

KING: My lord Vaihīnari, why then do I see that no celebrations have been started in the city? Look,

No courtesans do grace with lazy steps,
Slowed by the burden of their hips, the streets
In the gay company of libertines,
Bandying jokes and witty compliments.

Nor do the wealthy rival one another
With mansions festively displayed, nor shed
Their wonted caution to indulge the whims
This feast brings thought of with their womenfolk.

CHAMBERLAIN: Your Majesty, the thing is . . .
KING: What is it?
CHAMBERLAIN: Yes, your majesty. The thing is . . .
KING: Speak up, my lord!
CHAMBERLAIN: Your Majesty, the festival has been canceled!
KING (*angrily*): Ah! By whom?
CHAMBERLAIN: Beyond this I am unable to enlighten your Majesty.
KING: Surely my lord Cāṇakya has not robbed the spectators' eyes of a perfectly lovely sight?
CHAMBERLAIN: Who else, your Majesty, could countermand your orders and live?
KING: Śoṇottarā! I wish to sit down!
GUARD: Here is the throne, your Majesty. Pray be seated.
KING (*sitting down*): My lord Vaihīnari, I wish to see my lord Cāṇakya!
CHAMBERLAIN: As your Majesty commands. (*Exit.*)

Enter Cāṇakya. His face betrays concern mixed with anger. He is at home and seated.

CĀṆAKYA (*to himself*): How dare that evil-minded Rākṣasa erect himself as my rival! Indeed he presumes to overreach the power of my genius, thinking that just as I, a Kauṭilya, departed from the city after my humiliation, dangerous as an angry cobra, to exterminate the Nanda and make the Maurya, his bastard, king in his stead, so he, Rākṣasa, will now eclipse the lustre of Maurya the Moon! . . . (*Fixing his gaze straight before him, as though Rākṣasa is standing there.*) Rākṣasa, Rākṣasa! Give up your useless resolution! You are not dealing with an arrogant Nanda whose affairs are looked after by incompetent councilors, but with a Candragupta! You are no Kauṭilya. The only thing we have in common, and to which you may rightly aspire, is hatred of the principal enemy. (*He reflects.*) But I need not trouble my mind too much with this. Parvataka's son Malayaketu is completely surrounded by my agents, whom I have shown their opportunities. Siddhārthaka and my other spies are already at work carrying out their missions. And now that I am starting a quarrel with Candragupta, as a diversionary manoeuvre, I am master enough in the art of estrangement to alienate the enemy king from my enemy minister.

Enter the Chamberlain.

CHAMBERLAIN (*aside*): To serve is to invite trouble! He who serves a king dreads first of all the king himself, then the king's minister, then the king's favorite, and whatever other parasites happen to be in the king's favor. Poverty forces one to earn one's daily ball of rice with obsequious looks and hypocrisies. No wonder that the prudent call such a degrading living a dog's life! (*He circles the stage and looks up.*) Here is Cāṇakya's house. Let us enter. (*He enters the gate and looks about him.*) Oho! Is this the splendor in which an imperial minister lives?

A broken stone to break up cowdung cakes;
A mound of sacred grass his students brought;
And kindling sticks laid out to dry that bend
The roof skirts of a cottage near collapse!

Yes, he can well afford to call his Majesty Candragupta simply the Maurya!

For even those who always speak the truth
Are tempted by their poverty to seek
Their gain and praise the king with tireless tongues
For all his nonexistent qualities.
Such is the potent working of desire.
But those who have relinquished all desire
Look on their king with no more interest
Than they might show for one stray stalk of straw.

(*Looking straight ahead, overawed.*) Oh, there is his Excellency Cāṇakya himself,

He who took hold of the world and taught two kings,
Maurya and Nanda, to rise and set at once,
And with his all-pervading light surpassed

The thousand-rayed light of a briefer sun
Whose spells of heat must take their turn with cold!

(*Kneeling on the floor.*) Victory, your Honor!

CĀṆAKYA: Vaihīnari! What brings you here?

CHAMBERLAIN: My lord, his Majesty Candragupta, whose lotuslike feet are crimsoned by the ruby rays of the diadems that tremble on the bowing heads of kings, prostrates himself before your Honor's feet and requests to see you whenever your duties permit it.

CĀṆAKYA: The Maurya wants to see me? Vaihīnari, my cancellation of the Kaumudī celebrations has not yet reached his ears, has it?

CHAMBERLAIN: It has, my lord.

CĀṆAKYA (*angrily*): Who told him?

CHAMBERLAIN (*frightened*): Please, my lord! His Majesty noticed with his own eyes that no festivities were going on in the city when he came to Sugāṅga Palace.

CĀṆAKYA: Of course, I see it now, rascal! You set the Maurya up against me while I was gone, what else?

Chamberlain remains silent and bows his head in fear.

CĀṆAKYA: It is amazing how the king's retinue conspires against Cāṇakya! Where is the Maurya?

CHAMBERLAIN: His Majesty sent for you from the Sugāṅga Palace, my lord.

CĀṆAKYA (*rises*): Conduct me to Sugāṅga Palace.

CHAMBERLAIN: This way, my lord.

Both circle the stage.

CHAMBERLAIN: Here is the palace. Please ascend gently, your Honor, very gently.

CĀṆAKYA (*ascending the stairs; looking up. To himself, with joy*): Ah, the Maurya is seated on his throne. Excellent, excellent!

The Lion Throne is empty of the Nandas
Who had abused their royal privileges,
And taken by the Maurya, chief of princes,
'Tis graced at last by one who equals it!
And these three virtues of this throne do now
Triple the pleasure that I find in it.

(*He approaches.*) Maurya, victory be yours!

KING (*rising from his throne and touching Cāṇakya's feet*): My lord, Candragupta bows to you!
CĀṆAKYA (*taking the king's hand*): Rise up, my son!

May hundred upon hundred of awed kings
Approach thee and approach thee from
The remote ranges of Himālaya
Where Gaṅgā's iridescent cascades play
And cool the mountains with their waterfalls,
Down to the southern ocean's farthest shore,
Bright with the hues of many-splendored gems,
To rest the jewels of their diadems
Humbly upon thy feet!

KING: And so it has befallen by your grace. It needs no further wishes. Sit down, my lord. (*They both sit down, their seats arranged according to rank.*)[24]
CĀṆAKYA: Maurya, why have you summoned us?
KING: To favor ourselves with your presence, my lord.
CĀṆAKYA (*smiling*): Enough courtesies, Maurya. Kings do not summon their officers without purpose. Tell me your purpose.
KING: What is your Honor's purpose in prohibiting the Full Moon Festival?
CĀṆAKYA (*smiling*): Then you have summoned me to reprimand me, Maurya?
KING: No, not to reprimand you.
CĀṆAKYA: Why then?
KING: To address a request to you.
CĀṆAKYA: If that is so, Maurya, should a pupil not respect the whims of those to whom he only may address requests?
KING: I do not doubt it. But your Honor has never indulged a whim without a reason, so there seems to be occasion for a question.
CĀṆAKYA: Maurya, you know quite well that Cāṇakya never acts without reason, even in his dreams!
KING: And therefore my curiosity makes me loquacious.
CĀṆAKYA: Listen, Maurya! The authorities on politics describe three kinds of government: that which depends on the king alone; that which depends on the minister alone; and that which devolves equally on both the king and the minister. Your government, Maurya, depends entirely on your minister. And since I am in complete charge, why

need you tire both tongue and mind by inquiring into my motives?

King averts his face in anger. Offstage two Bards begin to sing.

FIRST BARD:

The Autumn cleans the heavens as with ashes
That mirror white the whiteness of the kāsas,[25]
Washing the dark hide of the nightly sky,
Spotted by clouds, with moon's wide net of rays;
It wears the moon like a white skull about,
And smiles with the white flecks of swarming swans:
May Autumn, wondrously resembling Śiva,
No less divinely, wipe away your cares!

May Viṣṇu's half-closed eyes that open slowly,
A little red at the first break of sleep,
When he awakes on his broad serpent couch
And rises from his pillow, Śeṣa's hoods—[26]
At first they shun the sudden glare of light
That shines in gems, their task seems heavy, tears
Bud as he yawns and stretches out his limbs—
Now wakefully watch over you for ever!

SECOND BARD:

Sire, kings of your mettle
By the creator created
As vessels of valor,
Lords of all world,
Who defeat with their might
Enemy elephants
Streaming with rut,
Will no more than a lion
Suffers the breaking
Of his powerful teeth,
Suffer the breaking
Of any commandment
At any occasion,
But prove their contempt
For the other's conceit.

No king is a king for the jewels he may wear,
If it is not for his word that others must fear!

CĀṆAKYA (*listening, to himself*): The first is a blessing, which praises the beauties of the season by lending them the form of a revered God. But the second? I don't understand it . . . (*He ponders.*) Ah, I see, a trick of Rākṣasa's! You are discovered, evil genius! Kauṭilya is still awake!

KING: My lord Vaihīnari, give these bards a hundred thousand gold pieces.

CHAMBERLAIN: As your Majesty commands. (*He rises and circles the stage.*)

CĀṆAKYA (*angrily*): Wait, Vaihīnari, don't go yet. Maurya, why spend a fortune for nothing?

KING: Am I a king or a prisoner that all my deeds have to be checked by you?

CĀṆAKYA: Maurya, kings who won't apply themselves will commit errors. If you will not suffer reproof, attend to your duties.

KING: I am attending to my duties.

CĀṆAKYA: That suits us. We are attending to ours.

KING: If that is true, I wish to hear what results you expect from the cancellation of the festival.

CĀṆAKYA: And I, Maurya, should like to hear what results you expect from having the festival at all.

KING: In the first place, obedience to my orders!

CĀṆAKYA: And my first purpose in canceling the festival, Maurya, was disobedience. Your orders are like garlands of unfading flowers worn on their heads by hundreds of kings as far as the shores of the four oceans whose coasts are dark with tamāla blossoms and whose waters are churned by whales. But if your decree meets in me an obstacle, it proclaims to the world that your sovereignty is tempered with humility!

KING: Is there another reason? I want to hear it.

CĀṆAKYA: There is.

KING: Speak.

CĀṆAKYA: Śoṇottarā, tell Acala, the scribe, to give you the document listing Bhadrabhaṭa and the other defectors.

GUARD: As you command, your Honor. (*Exit and re-enter.*) Here is the list.

CĀṆAKYA (*taking it from her*): Listen, Maurya.

KING: I am all attention.

CĀṆAKYA (*reading aloud*):
"This list contains the names of prominent citizens, who first sided with his Majesty Candragupta but have now defected to Malayaketu:

"Bhadrabhaṭa, commander of the elephants.
"Puruṣadatta, commander of the horse.
"Hiṅgurāta, nephew to Candrabhānu, the Grand Chamberlain.
"Prince Balagupta, distant kin to His Majesty.
"Rājasena, His Majesty's governor, when His Majesty was prince.
"Bhāgurāyaṇa, younger brother to Siṃhala, commander of the armies.
"Rohitākṣa, son of the King of Malava.
"Vijayavarman, chieftain of a warrior clan."

So far the list.
KING: I want to know, my lord, why they have defected.
CĀṆAKYA: Listen, Maurya. Bhadrabhaṭa, commander of the elephants, and Puruṣadatta, commander of the horses, were addicted to women, wine, and hunting, and neglected their elephants and horses. So I dismissed them and put them on a subsistence allowance. They changed their allegiance and went over to Malayaketu where they now have their old commands. Hiṅgurāta and Balagupta were both greedy, and considered the allowance you granted them too small. So they went over to Malayaketu, in the hope of getting more. Rājasena, your old governor, came suddenly into great wealth on your ascension, with the gold, elephants, and horses you gave him. He went over to Malayaketu because he was afraid that you would take everything back. Now Bhāgurāyaṇa. He is General Siṃhala's younger brother. At the time he was a crony of Parvataka's, and when Parvataka was assassinated, he abducted Malayaketu and invented the story that I, Cāṇakya, had caused the prince's father to be killed. When the clique of Candanadāsa etc., who were working against you, had been punished, Bhāgurāyaṇa fled in fear that his own crimes would be visited on him and went over to Malayaketu. The prince lived up to the gratitude he owed him for saving his life and raised him at once to the rank of minister. Rohitākṣa and Vijayavarman, finally, were too proud to bear the fact that you gave their relatives gifts as great as you had bestowed upon them, and, piqued, went over to Malayaketu. These are the causes of their disaffection.

KING: But if you knew the causes, why did you not at once take counter-measures?

CĀṆAKYA: No counter-measures were feasible, Maurya.

KING: Why not? Were you incompetent to find any, or were there other motives?

CĀṆAKYA: Would I have been incompetent to think of any? Indeed, there were other motives.

KING: I wish to know what motives you had for not acting in time.

CĀṆAKYA: Listen, Maurya, and keep my words in mind.

KING: I shall do both. Proceed.

CĀṆAKYA: As you know, there are two courses of action in dealing with disaffected subjects, Maurya—benevolence and punishment. Consider benevolence. It would have meant restoring Bhadrabhaṭa and Puruṣadatta to their old offices, after they had been dismissed from them. In the case of individuals like them, negligent in their discharge of their responsibilities because of their addiction to vices, reinstatement would have meant the collapse of the entire foundation of the kingdom; for the elephants and the horses are a kingdom's foundation. How could we have dealt benevolently with Hiṅgurāta and Balagupta? They are so greedy they would not have been satisfied had I given the entire kingdom away to them. What difference would agreeableness have made in the case of Rājasena and Bhāgurāyaṇa, the one afraid to forfeit his wealth, the other to forfeit his life? And what kind of favoritism could have won back the sympathies of Rohitākṣa and Vijayavarman, who were so proud that your equal gifts to their relatives enraged them? The first alternative, benevolence, was therefore precluded. So was punishment. Before all, we had to avoid losing the confidence of those subjects who were still attached to the Nanda dynasty, and we most certainly would have lost it if, so soon after taking over from the Nandas, we had borne down severely on a group of prominent citizens who had been on our side all along.

Now Malayaketu has secured the allegiance of our old partisans. Aided by their prestige, as well as by Rākṣasa's counsel, Malayaketu presently stands ready with a considerable force of barbarian kings to attack us and revenge his father's death. This is a time to labor, not to play! So I called off the Full Moon Festival. The citadel must be fortified at once. Are we to waste time feasting?

KING: Many questions remain, my lord.

CĀṆAKYA: Ask freely, Maurya. Much remains to be explained.

KING: Then I shall ask.

CĀṆAKYA: And I shall answer.

KING: The cause of all this unpleasantness is Malayaketu. Why did you fail to prevent his escape?

CĀṆAKYA: Had we prevented him from escaping, two courses would have been open to us. Either to punish him, or to give him half the kingdom as we had promised his father. If we had punished him, we would have demonstrated our ingratitude. The conclusion would obviously be that we had also killed his father. On the other hand, what possible advantage was there in handing over half the kingdom to him, except just as a demonstration of gratitude? So I chose to let him get away.

KING: So far so good. But can you answer why you failed to act against Rākṣasa, when he was still in the city?

CĀNAKYA: Rākṣasa has an undying loyalty for his master; he also has lived in this town a long time. With the complete confidence which people who value character, or still follow the Nandas, would have had in him, with the genius and resourcefulness he possesses, the multitudes of allies he can call up, and the funds he can dispose of, he would most certainly have provoked a serious revolt in the city had he remained here. But if removed far enough, even though he might cause some disturbances abroad, he would not be too hard to handle. So we let him get away.

KING: But why not take care of him somehow, as long as he was here?

CĀṆAKYA: Did we not take care of him? Surely we "somehow" pulled him out and discarded him, like a thorn that is lodged in the heart!

KING: Why did you not capture him by force?

CĀṆAKYA: Maurya, he is a demon![27] If we had tried to capture him, he would either have killed himself or have finished off our men. And both would have been bad. You would have lost either a great man or the flower of your army. A man like Rākṣasa has to be approached like a wild elephant; we must manage to tame him.

KING: We cannot surpass your argument with one of ours, my lord. In any case, Rākṣasa emerges as a more admirable man.

CĀṆAKYA (*angrily*): Than I, should I add? No more of this nonsense! What has he accomplished?

KING: Listen, if you don't know! This very admirable man stayed in the city as long as it pleased him, even after we had captured it. He put his foot on our throat. When our victory was proclaimed throughout the town, he resisted our forces with all his might. And with the grand display of his tactical skill he has driven our mind to such a confusion that now I no longer dare trust My own men, however much they may deserve My trust.

CĀṆAKYA (*laughing*): And that is all he has done, Maurya?

KING: Is it not enough?

CĀṆAKYA: I thought perhaps he had uprooted you, as the Nandas were uprooted; or had raised Malayaketu to the ascendancy on earth to which you have been raised!

KING: That was another's doing. What has it to do with you, my lord?

CĀṆAKYA: Ingrate!

> Who did untie his hair with fingertips
> That shook with the tremors of mounting rage,
> And swore, for all the world to hear, a long,
> Long vow to finish a whole dynasty?
> And who took on the nine heroic Nandas,
> Whose treasuries were inexhaustible,
> And slaughtered them like sacrificial beasts
> While Rākṣasa looked on?
>
> The fires that burnt their corpses blaze today
> And cast upon the sky, where patient vultures
> Circle about on wide unhurried wings,
> A cloud of smoke that obfuscates the sun,
> And with their tempting smell of dripping marrow
> Gladden the beasts that haunt the burning-grounds!

KING: That was the doing of fate, which hated the Nandas.

CĀṆAKYA: Only the stupid believe in fate!

KING: But the wise do not abuse it!

CĀṆAKYA (*in a rage*): Maurya, you want to ride me like a serf!

> Beware! My hand runs to my hair again,

(*He stamps the ground.*)

> My foot starts moving on another vow!
> You light my fury's fire again which died
> Only with time and all the Nanda's race!

KING (*alarmed, to himself*): Ayi! He is really enraged!

The bloodshot glitter of his eyes sparks fire
Under the dark smoke of his frowning brow,
Although the cleansing water of his tears,
Quivering on his lashes, tempers it.

And Earth shook with so great a vehemence
Under his stamping foot that she methinks recalled
How Śiva once did stage the Mood of Dread,
And stamped her boards in his fierce dance of death.[28]

CĀṆAKYA (*controlling his pretended fury*): Maurya, Maurya, enough of words! If you think better of Rākṣasa, give him my sword of state! (*He throws down his sword, rises, and stares before him as though at some one present. To himself.*) Rākṣasa, Rākṣasa, don't be misled by the swoop of your genius which seeks to defeat a Kauṭilya's mind. For the entire plan you set afoot to alienate the king from me, because you could easily defeat a Maurya no longer loyal to Cāṇakya, will, my shrewd diplomat, end in your own accusation!

KING: My lord Vaihīnari, make it known to my subjects that henceforth Candragupta himself shall personally discharge his government, without any regard to Cāṇakya.

CHAMBERLAIN (*to himself*): What no honorific even? No "my lord" Cāṇakya, plain Cāṇakya! Why, he has for a fact lost his power. Still, I must not blame the king for the mistake he is making. If the king errs, it is the minister's fault. An elephant gets the name of being vicious through the carelessness of its handler.

KING: Do you entertain doubts, my lord?

CHAMBERLAIN: No doubts at all, your Majesty. My only thought is how fortunate it is that at last your Majesty is king!

KING (*to himself*): As long as we are wronged in this fashion, my lord Cāṇakya will be able to bring his plans to a successful end. (*Aloud.*) Śoṇottarā! This exhausting difference has given me a headache. Conduct me to my bedchamber.

GUARD: Come, your Majesty.

KING (*rising from his throne, to himself*): Now that I have denied my teacher the respect that I owe him, I feel as though my heart is buried in the earth. How must shame rend the hearts of those who *really* abuse their teachers! (*Exeunt omnes.*)

ACT FOUR

Enter a Hunchback in traveler's garb.

HUNCHBACK: Oof! What man would willingly travel back and forth for over a hundred leagues, if he weren't under king's orders which he had to respect even when the going was rough? I must go now and see Minister Rākṣasa. (*Circles the stage, wearily.*) Here is the house. Hey! Who is at the door? Tell his Excellency that the Hunchback has arrived, running all the way like a dromedary!

Enter a Doorkeeper.

DOORKEEPER: Don't shout like that, man! The minister has had sleepless nights over the cares of state and is suffering from a headache. He is still in bed. Wait here for the time being. As soon as I have a chance, I shall mention that you have arrived.

HUNCHBACK: Whatever you think best, fellow.

Enter Rākṣasa. He is lying on a bed, oppressed with cares; Śakaṭadāsa, seated on a chair, is with him.

RĀKṢASA (*to himself*): I have been thinking about the waywardness of fate at the very outset of my enterprise, and I have been trying to fathom Kauṭilya's naturally tortuous mind. I have lain awake wondering how I might frustrate his scheming and bring off my own designs—and night upon night has passed me by. My troubles are like a playwright's: first to sow the seeds of the plot, coax them, tiny as they are, to grow, and gradually to cultivate the hidden and mysterious fruits of those fertile seeds, make them ramify, and finally bundle all the branches, however remote, into the climax of the play. . . . Cāṇakya, evil genius! Is it possible that in the end you will find . . .

DOORKEEPER (*approaching*): Victory, victory . . .

RĀKṢASA: . . . you are outwitted?

DOORKEEPER: . . . Your Excellency!

RĀKṢASA (*as a spasm contracts his left eye, to himself*): So Cāṇakya will find victory, and I am outwitted! . . . (*Aloud.*) What did you want to say, my man?

DOORKEEPER: Your Excellency, here is a Hunchback who has arrived from Pāṭaliputra and wants to see you.

RĀKṢASA: Show him in at once.

DOORKEEPER: As you command, your Excellency. (*Exit and re-enter with the Hunchback.*) You may approach his Excellency now. (*Exit.*)

HUNCHBACK: Victory, your Excellency!

RĀKṢASA: Sit down, my man.

HUNCHBACK: As you command, your Excellency. (*Sits down on the floor.*)

RĀKṢASA (*to himself*): I have so many projects afoot that I cannot remember on what project I have detailed this fellow. (*Falls to thinking.*)

Enter a man with a staff in his hand.

MAN: Make room, masters! Out of the way! Strange! Don't you know that wretches like you are hardly supposed to set eyes upon kings, those gods on earth and treasures of noble virtues, let alone bother them with your propinquity? (*As though addressing some passers-by.*) What do you say, masters? Why must the road be cleared? But his Highness Malayaketu is coming! He is going to pay a visit to his Excellency Rākṣasa, who is suffering from a headache. That is why the road must be cleared! (*Exit.*)

Enter Malayaketu, followed by Bhāgurāyaṇa and his Chamberlain.

MALAYAKETU (*with a sigh, to himself*): It is ten months today since father passed away, and still, with all the bravery we vainly boast of, we have not offered him the funerary libation. . . .

> I vowed that not before the enemy's wives
> Should beat the jewels on their breasts to pieces,
> And tear their silken bodices, and shriek
> Their pitiable plaints, and let their hair
> Disheveled sweep the dust up from the floor,
> As once *his* wives had done, would I prepare
> To offer up the water to his soul.

But why enlarge?

> For either I will tread my father's path,
> Bearing the yoke that's worthy of the brave,
> And on the battlefield find death at last,

Or from the lashes of his womenfolk
Shall chase the tears and shower them upon
The eyes of his foe's wives.

(*Aloud.*) My lord Chamberlain, I wish to surprise his Excellency Rākṣasa and visit him alone and unannounced. Tell the kings of my suit on my behalf to withdraw.

CHAMBERLAIN: As you command, your Highness. (*Walking around, to imaginary persons.*) Ye lieges! His Highness orders that no one is to accompany him any further. (*Glancing about him, with satisfaction.*) The chiefs are turning back at the first sound of your Highness's orders! Look, your Highness,

Some chieftains check their steeds so forcefully
Their stalwart withers crouch before the reins
That sharply bridle them and their fast hoofs
Paw wild before them in the empty air.
And others on their splendid elephants
Have stopped so quickly that the collar bells
Are stricken dumb: like ocean tides, my Lord,
They halt before the flood line of your word!

MALAYAKETU: You too, my lord, retire with the bearers of my palanquin. Only Bhāgurāyaṇa shall follow me.

CHAMBERLAIN: As your Highness commands. (*Exit with the palanquin bearers.*)

MALAYAKETU: Bhāgurāyaṇa, my friend. I was informed by Bhadrabhaṭa and the others who have joined me here that they have not approached me through the intermediary of his Excellency Rākṣasa. No, they rather sought the good offices of my commander Śikharasena, when they became disaffected from Candragupta, because that king is in the power of his evil councilor. And they joined me to serve under me, because I would have the virtues that attract interlopers. I have given much thought to this statement of theirs, but the real meaning has not become clear to me.

BHĀGURĀYAṆA: The meaning is not entirely unfathomable, your Highness. It is only proper that they should join a conqueror of proven virtue through the mediation of one who wishes him well.

MALAYAKETU: But surely, my friend Bhāgurāyaṇa, his Excellency Rākṣasa is my most devoted and loyal follower?

BHĀGURĀYANA: Undoubtedly. Nevertheless, Rākṣasa's feud is with

Cāṇakya, not with Candragupta. If Candragupta should ever grow weary of Cāṇakya's imperiousness and dismiss him from his post, Rākṣasa might conceivably make common cause with Candragupta, both because of his loyalty to the dynasty of the Nandas, to which the king also belongs, and because of his devotion to his friends in town. If that were to happen, they themselves would not betray your trust. That is their meaning.
MALAYAKETU: That follows, indeed. Show me Rākṣasa's residence.
BHĀGURĀYAṆA: This way, your Highness. (*Walking around.*) Here is his residence. Pray enter, your Highness.
MALAYAKETU: I will.

RĀKṢASA (*to himself*): Ah, now I remember! (*Aloud.*) Did you meet with Stanakalaśa, the bard, in Pāṭaliputra?
HUNCHBACK: Yes, I did, your Excellency.

MALAYAKETU (*overhearing their conversation*): Bhāgurāyaṇa, they are discussing the affairs of Pāṭaliputra. We shall not go nearer. Let us first listen. For ministers have one way of talking before their kings, lest they discourage their master, and quite another when they speak confidentially and put things plainly.
BHĀGURĀYAṆA: As you wish, your Highness.

RĀKṢASA: Did you succeed?
HUNCHBACK: Thanks to your Excellency, we did.

MALAYAKETU: Succeed in what, Bhāgurāyaṇa?
BHĀGURĀYAṆA: The minister's strategy is so complex that it is impossible to encompass it with so little information. Pray follow his conversation closely, your Highness.

RĀKṢASA: I want to hear the details.
HUNCHBACK: Listen, your Excellency. Your instructions were for me to travel to Pāṭaliputra and tell the bard Stanakalaśa in your name to praise Candragupta with incendiary verses that would cause the king to become exasperated with Cāṇakya's repeated cancellations of his royal decrees.
RĀKṢASA: And?
HUNCHBACK: So I went to Pāṭaliputra and passed your orders on to the bard Stanakalaśa. Meanwhile Candragupta had announced that the Full Moon Festival would again be celebrated this year, and this announcement was very well received by the townspeople who so far

had been in mourning for the death of the Nandas. Now that the festival was again to be celebrated after such a long time they appreciated it the more, like a reunion with a well-loved kinsman.

RĀKṢASA (*with tears in his eyes*): Ah, Nanda, my king,

> Although the Moon now reigns, delight of lotuses,
> What kind of Full Moon Festival is worth its name
> As long as you, once joy of all the world,
> Moon among kings, can take no part in it?

HUNCHBACK: But then the festival, which would have delighted all the people's eyes, was, against the express wishes of the king himself, canceled by that accursed Cāṇakya. This was the situation when Stanakalaśa chanted his incendiary song.

RĀKṢASA: How did it go?

HUNCHBACK *repeats the song*: "Sire, kings of your mettle . . ."

RĀKṢASA (*with joy*): Excellent, Stanakalaśa, my friend, excellent! The seeds of discord sown at the right season are sure to yield a good harvest. Not even a common man will suffer a spoilsport, let alone a king of superior powers.

MALAYAKETU: Indeed!

RĀKṢASA: Go on.

HUNCHBACK: Candragupta was so exasperated by this cancellation of his orders that he praised your Excellency's merits and dismissed Cāṇakya from his post.

MALAYAKETU: By his praise of Rākṣasa's merits, Bhāgurāyaṇa, King Candragupta showed his partiality for my minister!

BHĀGURĀYAṆA: Perhaps less by praising Rākṣasa than by humbling Cāṇakya!

RĀKṢASA: Was the cancellation of the Full Moon Festival the only reason for Candragupta's anger with Cāṇakya, or was there more to it?

MALAYAKETU: What results does he expect from this study of Candragupta's motivations?

BHĀGURĀYAṆA: Your Highness, a man of Cāṇakya's intelligence would never risk Candragupta's fury over such a trifle. Nor would Candragupta himself, who is not an ungrateful king, deny Cāṇakya his proper respect because of a trifle. Only a really big thing would make

Candragupta's breach with Cāṇakya final. That is what Rākṣasa has in mind.

HUNCHBACK: Yes, Candragupta had another grievance: that Cāṇakya had allowed Prince Malayaketu and your Excellency to escape.
RĀKṢASA (*to his secretary Śakaṭadāsa*): Now I have got Candragupta in my power, Śakaṭadāsa! Candanadāsa will be freed from his prison and you will rejoin your wife and sons.

MALAYAKETU: What does he mean by "Now I have Candragupta in my power?"
BHĀGURĀYAṆA: This, of course, that he no longer need eliminate Candragupta now that the king has broken with Cāṇakya.

RĀKṢASA: Where is the fellow now, since he has lost his post?
HUNCHBACK: Still in Pāṭaliputra.
RĀKṢASA (*disturbed*): Still in Pāṭaliputra? He has not retired to a hermitage? Or started swearing another vow?
HUNCHBACK: They say that he will retire to a hermitage.
RĀKṢASA: Śakaṭadāsa, that is out of character!

Would ever the man who refused to forgive
From an Indra on earth, from a Nanda, the shame
Of dismissal from office and honor,
Now condone the same outrage unhurt in his pride
From the son of a slave girl he raised to the throne,
His own creature and puppet, the Maurya?

MALAYAKETU: Friend, why does his own success seem to depend on whether Cāṇakya has retired to a hermitage, or sworn a new oath?
BHĀGURĀYAṆA: It is not difficult to grasp. His success depends on how far Cāṇakya has broken with Candragupta.

ŚAKAṬADĀSA: Your Excellency, don't be too suspicious. It is really in character.

Would a king like the Maurya, whose foot has been set
On the radiantly diademed hairlocks of kings,
Be prepared to forgive any man of his own
Who would dare to infringe his commandment?
And Kauṭilya, enraged as he is, will recall
All the sorrow the vow he accomplished begot,

And if chance helped him once, he will hesitate now
Lest it strike him before its fulfilment.

RĀKṢASA: You are right, Śakaṭadāsa. Go and see that the Hunchback is rested.

ŚAKAṬADĀSA: As you command, your Excellency. (*Exit with the Hunchback.*)

RĀKṢASA: Now I want to see the prince.

MALAYAKETU (*drawing near*): And I, my lord, have come to see you.

RĀKṢASA (*looking up*): Ah, his Highness! (*He rises from his seat.*) Here is a seat, your Highness. Pray be seated.

MALAYAKETU: Your prince is seated. Please sit down, my lord. (*Both sit down according to rank.*)[29]

MALAYAKETU: My lord, is your headache better?

RĀKṢASA: Will my headache grow better before my prince has exchanged his title for that of emperor?

MALAYAKETU: Since you have promised it, my lord, this will not be difficult to attain. But how long shall we have to stand aside with the forces we have gathered and wait for a crisis in the enemy camp?

RĀKṢASA: There is no more reason to delay. March out to victory, your Highness!

MALAYAKETU: Have you then heard something to show that there is a crisis, my lord?

RĀKṢASA: Indeed I have.

MALAYAKETU: What?

RĀKṢASA: A crisis about ministers. Candragupta has broken with Cāṇakya.

MALAYAKETU: A crisis about a minister, my lord, is no crisis.

RĀKṢASA: Not perhaps with other kings. But for Candragupta it is.

MALAYAKETU: On the contrary, my lord. Cāṇakya's faults did much to cause disaffection among Candragupta's subjects. Now that he has been dismissed, the people who were loyal to Candragupta will grow even more loyal.

RĀKṢASA: No. The subjects can be divided into two classes: those who rebelled with Candragupta, and those who remained loyal to the Nandas. Cāṇakya's faults might cause disaffection among the first group, but not among the latter. For when they recall how the Maurya had the house of Nanda exterminated—the house to which he himself belonged—they can only be moved by hostility and indignation; and if they follow Candragupta, it is only because they have no leader of their own. But when they find an invader of your mettle, your Highness, in whose power to overthrow the enemy they can believe, they will desert him at once and come flocking to you. We ourselves are a case in point.

MALAYAKETU: My lord, is this particular crisis in the enemy camp your only reason to order the attack, or are there other reasons?

RĀKṢASA: Should we need more, your Highness? This is the most important one.

MALAYAKETU: Why is it the most important one? Could Candragupta not transfer Cāṇakya's responsibilities either to another minister or to himself, and himself take counter-measures?

RĀKṢASA: In fact, he could not. Only those kings can take counter-measures who are autocrats or, at least, share equal power with their ministers. But Candragupta, the fool, has always completely depended on his minister, and he is as little able to take measures on his own as a blind man who has always lived in the dark can know the ways of the world.

The Fortune of kings stands firm, with her feet planted on both councilor and prince. But if one grows too tall, being only a woman she cannot support her weight and therefore deserts one or the other.

A king dependent on his minister
Who breaks with him is like a baby
That's separated from its mother's breast:
His brain is too confused about a world
He never saw and would not for an hour
Have any sense of acting on its own.

MALAYAKETU (*to himself*): Fortunately my success does not depend on my minister! (*Aloud.*) This may be so, still, if there were more reasons to order the attack, an invader would be surer of complete success against an enemy handicapped by the loss of his minister.

RĀKṢASA: Complete success is assured, your Highness!

For with yourself as king of splendid armies,
The capital still loyal to the Nandas,
Cāṇakya both unseated and revengeful,
The Maurya still too new to royalty,
Myself at your disposal (*he gestures modestly*) as a guide
Merely to point the way to you, of course,

Only your orders will open up the way
Of realizing, Prince, the goals you seek!

MALAYAKETU: Then, if your lordship judges that the time is right to attack, we must wait no longer!

My hundreds of elephants,
War-streaked with red,
Streaming with rut,
Dark looming masses
Of deafening noise,
Which jab at the foes
With powerful tusks,
Will dwindle the might
Of the red river Śoṇā,
Flooding its lowland
Of dark wooded country
With the thundering waves
That broke through its banks!

Let my elephant lines,
Roaring like thunder,
Spouting sprays of water
That is mixed with their ichor,
Lay siege to the city
As dark masses of clouds
Scattering raindrops
Beleaguer the Vindhyas!

(*Exeunt Malayaketu and Bhāgurāyaṇa.*)
RĀKṢASA: Who stands guard at the door?

Enter a Servant.
SERVANT: At your orders, your Excellency.
RĀKṢASA: Ah, Priyaṃvadaka. Which one of the astrologers is waiting at the gate?
SERVANT: The mendicant . . .
RĀKṢASA (*wincing at the bad omen*): What! A mendicant stands first!
SERVANT: . . . Jīvasiddhi.
RĀKṢASA: Have him come in, but see that he is properly dressed.[30]
SERVANT: As you wish, your Excellency. (*Exit.*)

Enter the Mendicant.

MENDICANT:

Embrace the Teaching of the Sages!
They treat you for the Malady
Of Error, like physicians;
Their treatment may seem bitter first,
But in the end you will be cured!

(*He approaches.*) Disciple, increase in the Law!

RĀKṢASA: Reverend, will you consider which day is favorable to launch an attack?

MENDICANT (*after some reflection*): I have considered, disciple. On Full Moon day, from the hour of noon onward, the day is extremely favorable. The lunar house will be southerly and favor you on your march south. Moreover, at the moment of starting, Gemini should be in the ascendant, presided over by Mercury, while the sun is about to set, the moon rises full, and Ketu sets rapidly after its rise over the horizon.[31]

RĀKṢASA: Reverend, the day is unsuitable.

MENDICANT: Disciple, it is a rule of astrologers that the day has one virtue, the lunar house four virtues, but the moon sixty-four. The ascendant in Gemini will give you ascendancy, but avoid an ascendant with Ketu. You will have a long life, if you march with the moon.

RĀKṢASA: Reverend, discuss it first with the other astrologers.

MENDICANT: You may discuss it, disciple. I myself am leaving.

RĀKṢASA: Leaving? Are you angry?

MENDICANT: I am not angry with you.

RĀKṢASA: Who has reason to be?

MENDICANT (*aside*): The Lord of Destiny, since you refuse to serve your own interest and take some other man's interest as your guide. (*Exit.*)

RĀKṢASA: Priyaṃvadaka! What is the hour now?

Enter the Servant.

SERVANT: The sun is about to set, your Excellency.

RĀKṢASA (*rises from his seat and watches the sky*): Yes, the majestic sun is about to set.

The trees which in the morning, when the sun
Dawned high on Sunrise Peak, reflected love
And, as he mounted, rushed to skirt their shades

To keep him closer, now turn back from him,
As he lies wounded on the Sunset Peak—
Like followers who always leave the lord
They served as soon as he declines.

(*Exeunt omnes.*)

ENTR'ACTE

Enter Siddhārthaka. He carries a sealed letter and a jewel-box.

SIDDHĀRTHAKA: O miracle! Like a creeper, Cāṇakya's strategy, sprinkled with cascades of wit bottled by Time and Space, is going to show its luxurious fruits! That is why I am carrying this letter, the same letter Cāṇakya wrote before under Rākṣasa's seal, and also this jewel-box which is sealed with the same ring. I am supposed to go to Pāṭaliputra. Well, here I go! (*He walks around and sees somebody.*) Why, there is a holy man coming. I'll wait for him.

Enter a Jain Mendicant.

MENDICANT: We bow to the Masters who in their inscrutable Wisdom find the Goal in this world by Supernatural Means!

SIDDHĀRTHAKA: Greetings, reverend.

MENDICANT: Disciple, increase in the Law. (*He looks closely at the other.*) Disciple, I see that you have set your mind on an untimely journey.

SIDDHĀRTHAKA: How did you discover that, reverend?

MENDICANT: There is nothing about that to discover, disciple. The letter you have stuck behind your ear betrays you.

SIDDHĀRTHAKA: All right, reverend, you have found me out. Yes, I am going abroad. Tell me, reverend, what kind of day is it today, good or bad?

MENDICANT (*smiling*): Disciple, you first had your head shaved[32] and then you ask about the stars?

SIDDHĀRTHAKA: So it is late, what does it matter? Tell me anyway. If it is a good day, I start, if it is a bad day, I stay.

MENDICANT: It is too late now, disciple, to start from Malayaketu's camp, even if it is is a good day.

SIDDHĀRTHAKA: What is going on now!

MENDICANT: Disciple, I shall instruct you. Before, everybody had free access to the camp and was free to leave it. But now that we are coming close to Pāṭaliputra, nobody is allowed in or out without a stamp. If you are duly stamped with Bhāgurāyaṇa's seal, you can go without trouble. If not, you had better keep quiet and stay, if you do not want to be tied hand and foot and marched off to jail by the camp police.

SIDDHĀRTHAKA: But don't you know that I am Siddhārthaka, reverend, the personal servant of Minister Rākṣasa himself? So who has the power to stop me even if I leave without a pass?

MENDICANT: Disciple, whether you are Rākṣasa's servant, or the servant of any other ogre or hobgoblin, you have no chance of leaving the camp without the stamp.

SIDDHĀRTHAKA: Don't get mad at me, reverend. Just wish me luck.

MENDICANT: Go, my son, I wish you luck. I myself will request a stamp from Bhāgurāyaṇa.

(*Exeunt.*)

ACT FIVE

Enter Bhāgurāyaṇa followed by a Servant.

BHĀGURĀYAṆA (*to himself*): It is wonderful to behold the complexities of Cāṇakya's tactics! All depending on the objective, the manoeuverings of an expert politician are sometimes quite conspicuous at the start, sometimes completely impervious to conjecture, now full-bodied, then extremely attenuated, now stillborn, then profusely productive, like the complicated workings of fate itself! (*Aloud.*) Bhāsvaraka! The prince wants me to stay close to his person. Therefore bring me a seat here in the audience tent.

SERVANT: Here is a seat, sir. Please sit down.

BHĀGURĀYAṆA (*sitting down*): Show in everyone who wants a pass.

SERVANT: As you wish, sir. (*Exit.*)

BHĀGURĀYAṆA (*to himself*): Really a pity. . . . It is not an easy thing to have to deceive someone who has grown as fond of you as Prince Malayaketu. Still,

> If you have sold your soul to a rich man,
> And traded family and decency
> And reputation, and your self-respect,
> For a too quickly disappearing sum,
> The question does not rise whether the job
> You have been ordered to is good or bad;
> You are beyond that stage; the only thing
> Remaining for you is to wonder *what*.

Enter Malayaketu followed by a female Bodyguard.

MALAYAKETU (*to himself*): What a puzzle! There are so many different sides to the question that I cannot make up my mind about Rākṣasa. Will he make common cause with the Maurya now that the king has broken with Cāṇakya, and transfer his personal loyalties, strengthened by his love for the House of Nanda, to this last member of the dynasty?

Or will he let the strength of his loyalty count for more and keep his word to me? My mind keeps turning round, as though it were sitting on a potter's wheel! (*Aloud.*) Vijayā, where is Bhāgurāyaṇa?
GUARD: He is issuing passes to people who want to leave the camp.
MALAYAKETU: Walk on tiptoe, Vijayā. I want to surprise him and put my hands over his eyes while he is not looking.
GUARD: As you command, your Highness.

Enter the Servant.
SERVANT: Here is that holy man, sir. He wants to see you about a pass.
BHĀGURĀYAṆA: Show him in.
SERVANT: At your orders, sir. (*Exit.*)
Enter the Mendicant.
MENDICANT: Disciple, increase in the Law!
BHĀGURĀYAṆA (*looking up to him, to himself*): Ah, that is Rākṣasa's friend, Jīvasiddhi. (*Aloud.*) Reverend! You aren't traveling on an errand of Rākṣasa's, are you?
MENDICANT (*stopping his ears*): Heaven forbid! The only place I want to travel is where I won't hear Rākṣasa's name spoken.
BHĀGURĀYAṆA: Good friends always quarrel badly! What has Rākṣasa done to you, reverend?
MENDICANT: Rākṣasa hasn't done anything to me, disciple. I have done something to myself, wretch that I am!
BHĀGURĀYAṆA: You whet my curiosity, reverend!

MALAYAKETU (*to himself*): And mine!

BHĀGURĀYAṆA: I want to hear about it.

MALAYAKETU (*to himself*): And so do I!

MENDICANT: Why should you listen to something that is unspeakable!
BHĀGURĀYAṆA: Unspeakable? If it is a secret, let it rest.
MENDICANT: It is not a secret! It is an outrage!
BHĀGURĀYAṆA: Well, if it is no secret, tell me.
MENDICANT: And still I cannot tell you, disciple.
BHĀGURĀYAṆA: And I cannot give you a pass.
MENDICANT (*to himself in Sanskrit*): This is the moment to tell him, since he asks for it. (*Aloud.*) What can I do? Listen, disciple. I first became friends with Rākṣasa—and a bad day it was!—when I lived in Pāṭaliputra. And it was about the same time that Rākṣasa had King Parvataka killed by a poison-girl.

MALAYAKETU (*weeping, to himself*): What! Rākṣasa had my father killed, Cāṇakya wasn't the assassin!

BHĀGURĀYAṆA: Go on, reverend.

MENDICANT: Shortly thereafter the accursed Cāṇakya drove me in disgrace out of the city, because of my friendship with Rākṣasa. And now Rākṣasa, this expert in royal affairs, is arranging a situation that will drive me out the world of the living!

BHĀGURĀYAṆA: Reverend, according to our information Cāṇakya was behind that affair, because he did not want to give up half of the kingdom to Parvataka as promised; Rākṣasa had nothing to do with it.

MENDICANT (*stopping his ears*): Heaven forbid! Cāṇakya did not even know that poison-girl!

BHĀGURĀYAṆA: Here is your pass, reverend. Go and tell the prince himself.

MALAYAKETU:

I heard, friend, the ear-rending news
A friend gave of an enemy,
Which doubled after all this time
The crime of father's shameful death!

MENDICANT (*to himself*): Ha, Malayaketu has heard. Well, Kauṭilya, you have succeeded. (*Exit.*)

MALAYAKETU (*staring before him as though at someone present*): Rākṣasa, that is right! You are a monster, Rākṣasa, in all the meanings of your name! My father was happy in the thought that you were his friend; he trusted you so far that he left everything in your charge. And with the tears of his kinsmen, you had him *fall*!

BHĀGURĀYAṆA (*to himself*): Cāṇakya told me to be sure to save Rākṣasa's life. This is the way. (*Aloud.*) Your Highness, please calm down! Pray sit down, I have something to tell you.

MALAYAKETU (*sits down*): What do you want to tell me, my friend?

BHĀGURĀYAṆA: Your Highness, in this world of politics it all depends on the immediate objective whether a diplomat is a friend, an enemy or neither—not on sentiment, as with ordinary beings. There was a time when Rākṣasa wanted to make Sarvārthasiddhi king, because he was stronger even than Candragupta; but his Majesty Parvataka, whose name be honored, was the great enemy who stood in the way of this

objective. Given the objective, I cannot see how Rākṣasa is to blame for what he did. Look, your Highness, politics, which makes friends of enemies and enemies of friends, brings on a man's reincarnation even while he is alive, a reincarnation with all old memories wiped out. You must not challenge Rākṣasa over this affair. Keep him happy until you have the kingdom of the Nandas. After that you yourself can decide whether to keep him on or to get rid of him.
MALAYAKETU: Your grasp of the situation is correct, my friend. Otherwise, if I were to kill him, I might set off a popular uprising, and jeopardize our chances of victory.

Enter the Servant.
SERVANT: Victory, your Highness! (*To Bhāgurāyaṇa.*) One of the camp police, Dīrghacakṣus, wants to inform you that he has arrested a man with a letter, who tried to leave the camp without a permit. He asks you to investigate.
BHĀGURĀYAṆA: Have him come in, my man.
SERVANT: At your orders, sir. (*Exit.*)

Enter Siddhārthaka in fetters, followed by the Servant.
SIDDHĀRTHAKA (*to himself*):

O Servants' Loyalty, fond mother of our kind,
That balances virtue and crime, I bow to you.

SERVANT (*approaching*): This is the fellow, sir.
BHĀGURĀYAṆA (*looking up at him*): A newcomer, or somebody's man here in the camp?
SIDDHĀRTHAKA: I am on Rākṣasa's staff, sir.
BHĀGURĀYAṆA: Then why did you try to leave the camp without a pass?
SIDDHĀRTHAKA: My business was so urgent I had to hurry, sir.
BHĀGURĀYAṆA: How can any business be so urgent that you should infringe a royal decree?
MALAYAKETU: Friend, take the letter from him.
BHĀGURĀYAṆA (*taking the letter away from Siddhārthaka*): Here it is, your Highness. (*He sees the seal.*) The seal has Rākṣasa's name on it.
MALAYAKETU: Unfold the letter and show it to me, but keep the seal.
Bhāgurāyaṇa does so and shows the letter to the prince.
MALAYAKETU (*taking the letter and reading aloud*):

"Hail!

"Someone somewhere begs to inform a certain high authority as follows:

"By discarding our adversary, the truthful one has proved that he is true to his word. Now he may also condescend to be further true to his word and satisfy those who have already allied themselves to him by fulfilling the promised terms on which they contracted. For if they are well treated they will reciprocate to their benefactor by destroying their present one. Among them there are those who covet the enemy's treasure and arms, as well as those who covet territory. Receipt of three ornaments which the truthful one has sent is hereby acknowledged. Lest this letter be empty, I too have sent something, receipt of which should be acknowledged. A verbal message may be had from Siddhārthaka, who is completely reliable."

Bhāgurāyaṇa, what does all this mean?

BHĀGURĀYAṆA: Siddhārthaka, for whom is this letter meant?

SIDDHĀRTHAKA: I do not know, sir.

BHĀGURĀYAṆA: Don't be too clever! You carry a letter and you don't know for whom it is meant? But let it rest for the moment. Who was to hear your verbal message?

SIDDHĀRTHAKA (*stammering*): You . . .

BHĀGURĀYAṆA: I?

SIDDHĀRTHAKA: You have caught me and I don't know what I'm saying!

BHĀGURĀYAṆA (*angrily*): You will find out! Bhāsvaraka, my man, take him outside and whip him till he talks.

SERVANT: At your orders, sir. (*Exit with Siddhārthaka.*)

Re-enter Servant.

SERVANT: Sir, when I was whipping him, this sealed casket fell from his armpit where he had hidden it.

BHĀGURĀYAṆA (*looking at it*): Highness, this is also sealed with Rākṣasa's ring!

MALAYAKETU: This will be the gift to go with the letter. Open it and show it to me, but save this seal too.

Bhāgurāyaṇa does so and shows it to the prince.

MALAYAKETU (*looking at it*): Ah! Those are the jewels which I took from my own person and sent to Rākṣasa! The letter is obviously meant for Candragupta!

BHĀGURĀYAṆA: We shall make sure of that. Bhāsvaraka, whip him some more.

SERVANT: At your orders, sir. (*Exit and re-enter.*) Sir, when I whipped him he said that he would tell the prince.

MALAYAKETU: Let him come in.

SERVANT: As your Highness commands. (*Exit and re-enter with Siddhārthaka.*)

SIDDHĀRTHAKA (*throwing himself at the prince's feet*): Mercy, your Highness! Save my life!

MALAYAKETU: There, there, fellow. Servants are always safe. Tell me all.

SIDDHĀRTHAKA: Please listen, your Highness. I got this letter from Minister Rākṣasa to carry it to Candragupta.

MALAYAKETU: I want to hear the verbal message.

SIDDHĀRTHAKA: His Excellency gave me this verbal message, your Highness: "The following five kings, who are friends of mine, have promised you their alliance: Citravarman, king of Kulūṭa; Siṃhanāda, king of Malaya; Puṣkara, king of Kashmir; Sindhuṣena, king of Sindh; Meghākṣa, emperor of Persia. The first three want Malayaketu's land, the other two his elephant forces. Even as your Majesty has satisfied me by discarding Cāṇakya, so you may also fulfil these terms as they have been agreed upon." End of message.

MALAYAKETU (*to himself*): What! Could Citravarman and the others threaten me with defection? Still, they have the greatest friendship for Rākṣasa. (*Aloud.*) Vijayā! I want to see Rākṣasa!

GUARD: As your Highness commands. (*Exit.*)

Enter Rākṣasa. He is sitting down, care-worn. A servant is with him.

RĀKṢASA (*to himself*): War is like a syllogism: both lead to the proper conclusion if the proving factor—the ground, or the army—is affirmative, supported by positive, and devoid of negative, evidence. However, if the proving factor itself becomes the conclusion, or proves two different issues at once, or flatly contradicts what it set out to prove, king and philosopher rely on it to their peril. . . . Our forces have been increased by deserters from Candragupta's forces. In fact, I am not at all easy in my mind about it. . . . Still, I need not have any doubts about it. For those who have swollen our ranks have deserted for known reasons, or have been won over by persuasion. (*Aloud.*) Priyaṃvadaka! Go and tell the kings who are following Prince

Malayaketu in my name that we are now closing in on Pāṭaliputra. They must continue the march in closed formation from now on. In the vanguard the armies of Khasa and Magadha will march in battle order immediately following myself. The main body will be formed by the Greek chieftains of Gāndhāra. The rear will be held by the Scythian chiefs along with the Cedis and Huns. The nobility of Kulūṭa and the other kingdoms will be in reserve; they will ride with the prince.

SERVANT: At your orders, your Excellency.

Enter the Guard.

GUARD: Victory, your Excellency. His Highness wants to see you.

RĀKṢASA: Wait a moment, girl. Hallo! Who is on guard?

Enter a second Servant.

SERVANT: At your orders, your Excellency.

RĀKṢASA: Tell Śakaṭadāsa that I have been summoned by the prince. The other day he decked me with jewels, so it would be a discourtesy if I now visited the prince without jewelry. Therefore let me have one of the three jewels we bought that same day.

SERVANT: At your orders, your Excellency. (*Exit and re-enter.*) Here is the piece, sir.

RĀKṢASA (*looking at it, putting it on, and rising*): Show me the way to the royal tent, Vijayā.

GUARD: Follow me, your Excellency.

RĀKṢASA (*to himself*): Responsibility always means anxiety, even if one is innocent of any shortcomings. . . . Any subordinate person must always live in fear of his master, then there lurks danger from the side of the reigning favorite, and finally anyone in a position of authority invites the envy of the wicked. One can count on falling as far as one has climbed. . . .

GUARD (*walking around*): The prince is staying here, your Excellency. Please draw near.

RĀKṢASA (*looking at the prince*): There is his Highness.

> His eyes gaze staring at his toes
> But, vacantly, take nothing in;
> The head rests on his hands as though
> The weight of cares had bent it down.

(*He approaches the prince.*) Victory be yours, your Highness!

MALAYAKETU: I greet you, my lord. Here is a seat. Sit down.

RĀKṢASA (*sitting down*): Your Highness, why have you summoned me?

MALAYAKETU: We were disturbed, not having seen you for some time.

RĀKṢASA: Your Highness, the time-consuming preparations for the march have earned me your reprimand!

MALAYAKETU: How have you arranged the marching order? I wish to hear it.

RĀKṢASA: I have passed the following orders to the kings who follow you. (*He repeats*: "In the vanguard . . . ride with the prince.")

MALAYAKETU (*to himself*): What? The very people who are prepared to sacrifice me to Candragupta are to ride with me! (*Aloud.*) Your Excellency, has anybody gone to Pāṭaliputra, or come from there?

RĀKṢASA: All need for the coming and going of spies has ceased to exist, your Highness. Shall we not be there ourselves in five days?

MALAYAKETU (*to himself*): Yes, we know how. . . . (*Aloud.*) Your Excellency, if that is the case why have you dispatched this courier with a letter to Pāṭaliputra?

RĀKṢASA (*noticing Siddhārthaka*): Ah, Siddhārthaka! What is the matter, my man?

SIDDHĀRTHAKA (*weeping and feigning embarrassment*): Mercy, your Excellency, mercy! I couldn't keep your secret when they began beating me!

RĀKṢASA: What secret, man? I don't understand you.

SIDDHĀRTHAKA: I am telling you, I couldn't keep your secret when they began beating me!

MALAYAKETU: Bhāgurāyaṇa, the fellow is too much frightened and ashamed to tell it before his master. You tell it to his Excellency.

BHĀGURĀYAṆA: As you please, your Highness. Your Excellency, this fellow declares that you ordered him to carry a letter and a verbal message to Candragupta.

RĀKṢASA: Siddhārthaka, is that true?

SIDDHĀRTHAKA (*feigning embarrassment*): I told them the secret when they began beating me!

RĀKṢASA: It is a lie. A man who is beaten will tell anything!

MALAYAKETU: Bhāgurāyaṇa, show him the letter. His man will repeat the verbal message.

BHĀGURĀYAṆA: This is the letter, your Excellency. (*He hands him the letter.*)

RĀKṢASA (*reads it*): Your Highness, this is a manoeuvre of the enemy!

MALAYAKETU: Your lordship sent this jewelry along with it as a present. Is that also a manoeuvre of the enemy?

RĀKṢASA (*examines the jewels*): I did not send them, your Highness. You yourself gave them to me, and I gave them to Siddhārthaka as a reward for highly gratifying service.

BHĀGURĀYAṆA: Your Excellency, these are priceless jewels, your own prince took them from his own person and honored you with them as a very special gesture, and yet you threw them away on this fellow?

MALAYAKETU: The letter ends: "A verbal message may be had from Siddhārthaka, who is extremely reliable."

RĀKṢASA: What does the verbal message matter, your Highness! The letter itself is not even mine!

MALAYAKETU: Whose seal is this then?

RĀKṢASA: Your Highness, there are crooks who are quite capable of counterfeiting seals!

BHĀGURĀYAṆA: Your Highness, Rākṣasa is right. You, Siddhārthaka, speak up! Who wrote this letter?

Siddhārthaka looks at Rākṣasa's face, drops his head, and remains silent.

BHĀGURĀYAṆA: Better make sure you aren't beaten any more, fellow! Speak up!

SIDDHĀRTHAKA: Śakaṭadāsa, sir.

RĀKṢASA: Your Highness, if Śakaṭadāsa wrote that letter I myself have written it!

MALAYAKETU: Vijayā! I want to see Śakaṭadāsa.

GUARD: As you command, your Highness. (*She starts to leave.*)

BHĀGURĀYAṆA (*to himself*): "Cāṇakya's agents shall never propose anything before they are sure of the consequences." (*Aloud.*) Your Highness, Śakaṭadāsa will never confess in front of his Excellency Rākṣasa that he has written it. It is better to get another sample of his handwriting. If the writing is the same this will prove it just as effectively.

MALAYAKETU: Vijayā, do as he says.

GUARD: Your Highness, do I also demand the ring?

MALAYAKETU: Bring both.

GUARD: As your Highness commands. (*Exit and re-enter.*) Your Highness, here is a sheet Master Śakaṭadāsa has written with his own hand, and here is the ring.

MALAYAKETU (*studies both*): My lord, the letter is written in the same hand.

RĀKṢASA (*to himself*): In the same hand! But it cannot be! Śakaṭadāsa is my friend. Could Śakaṭadāsa have forgotten his loyalties, because he remembered his wife and children, or wanted fast money instead of slow fame? How can I doubt it? The signet ring was always on his finger; Siddhārthaka was his friend; and the other sheet with his handwriting proves that the fabricated letter comes from his hand. It is plain. He has made common cause with the others, who are so clever at alienating people, and committed this treachery, to save his life by sacrificing his devotion for his master.

MALAYAKETU: My lord, the letter has it that "receipt of three ornaments which the favorite of fortune has sent is hereby acknowledged." Is this one of the three? (*He studies Rākṣasa's jewelry closely; to himself.*) What! This is the ornament father used to wear! (*Aloud.*) My lord, where is this ornament from?

RĀKṢASA: I bought it from some merchant.

MALAYAKETU: Vijayā, do you recognize it?

GUARD (*looking at it, weeping*): Your Highness, how could I fail to know it! His Majesty Parvataka used to wear it, honor to his name!

MALAYAKETU (*with a tear*): Ah, father,

> They were your favorites, favorite of right,
> These fitting jewels, O jewel of your race,
> Irradiating you, of moonlike radiant face,
> Like asterisms of the autumn night.

RĀKṢASA: Have they been worn by Parvataka? It is clear now! The merchant who sold them was a creature of Cāṇakya.

MALAYAKETU: My lord, it cannot be true that you bought these priceless jewels, for if they were my father's, they must have fallen in Candragupta's hands. But it *can* be true! Candragupta was the seller, but he asked for a greater return; and you, assassin, fixed the price, my life!

RĀKṢASA (*to himself*): Aho! This manoeuvre with the jewels is perfectly constructed! I cannot answer that the letter is not mine, for the seal is. And will anybody believe that Śakaṭadāsa has betrayed his friendship? Who would credit that the Maurya, a reigning king, had been selling his jewels? A confession of guilt is a more elegant reply than any of these churlish reactions!

MALAYAKETU: I am asking you, my lord.

RĀKṢASA: Then ask one who is a lord. I have become ignoble.

MALAYAKETU:

The Maurya is your former master's son—
I am your ally's son and dance attendance.
He gives you largesse—I am at your heels
And have to live on what you're pleased to give me.
To be his minister is slavery
Adorned with honors—here you are the master.
What greater things then can you covet still
That they should make you an ignoble serf?

RĀKṢASA: Your Highness has himself passed the verdict by the way he framed the accusation!

The Maurya is my former master's son—
You are my ally's son and dance attendance.
He gives me largesse—you are at my heels
And have to live on what I'm pleased to give you.
To be his minister is slavery
Adorned with honors—here I am the master.
What greater things then can I covet still
That they should make me an ignoble serf!

MALAYAKETU (*pointing at the letter and jewelry*): But this?
RĀKṢASA (*with a tear*): That is destiny's game, not Cāṇakya's.

It is the game of destiny,
Disposing of what man proposes,
To slay with malice those great kings
Who justly tried and judged their men
And in their gratitude esteemed
Our likes as high as their own sons:
Great kings indeed who dare to love
Those whom they may contemn as serfs!

MALAYAKETU (*angrily*): Are you denying guilt? It is only a game of destiny, not of greed! Serf! You first killed my father, ingrate, who had come to rely upon you always, by rearing a girl denatured by a diet of poison. And now you place such weight upon a minister's post with the enemy that you have begun to trade me as a piece of raw meat!
RĀKṢASA (*to himself*): That is what is called a boil on top of a tumor! (*Aloud, stopping his ears.*) Heaven forbid! I am innocent of Parvataka's death!

MALAYAKETU: Then who assassinated father?
RĀKṢASA: God knows!
MALAYAKETU: But not the mendicant Jīvasiddhi?
RĀKṢASA (*to himself*): What? Jīvasiddhi too a creature of Cāṇakya's? Ah, the enemy has taken my very heart!
MALAYAKETU (*angrily*): Bhāsvaraka! Carry my orders to Commander Śikharasena. Five kings have allied themselves with Rākṣasa and intend to sacrifice my life to Candragupta's cause. The names are Citravarman of Kulūṭa, Siṃhanāda of Malaya, Puṣkarākṣa of Kashmir, Sindhuṣena of Sindh, and Meghākṣa of Persia. The first three wanted my land: throw them in a deep pit and bury them alive with my land! The other two wanted my elephants: have them killed by the elephant!
SERVANT: As your Highness commands. (*Exit.*)
MALAYAKETU: Rākṣasa, *I* am not a monster of ingratitude. I am Malayaketu! Go then and throw yourself at Candragupta with all your soul. But even if Viṣṇugupta and Candragupta are reinforced by you, I shall extirpate the three of you as bad faith extirpates faith, hope, and charity!

Enough time wasted. Let our armies march at once on Pāṭaliputra and surround it.

Let the columns of dust
That rise from the hoofs
Of my thundering horses
And are cut from their base
By the flowing rut
Of my elephant forces
Rain down on my foes
Till their women's rouged cheeks
Are withered and shaded,
And the bumblebee blackness
Of their beautiful curls
Is coarsened and faded!

(*Exit with his retinue.*)
RĀKṢASA (*sorrowfully*): Alas! Citravarman and the other hapless kings executed. . . . Must Rākṣasa then always work for the destruction of his friends instead of the destruction of his enemies? What must I do in my misfortune? Withdraw to a hermitage? No austerities will pacify my revengeful thoughts. Follow my king in death? But as long

as the enemy lives? The manner of women! Should I throw myself upon the enemy, with my sword as my only companion? No, even this would be wrong. My heart has been urging me to set Candanadāsa free, and my gratitude demands it.
(*Exit.*)

ENTR'ACTE

Enter Siddhārthaka. He is gorgeously dressed, wearing jewelry, and very happy.

SIDDHĀRTHAKA:

> Glory to Kṛṣṇa who, dark as a cloud, has defeated the Devil!
> Glory to Candra our Moon blessing all good people's eyes!
> Glory befall Cāṇakya's manoeuvres that rendered our army
> Ready for triumph and struck, crushing the enemy's cause!

For quite a while now I have been looking for my friend Samṛddhārthaka. . . . (*He walks about and looks up.*) Ah! There is Samṛddhārthaka just coming now! I am going to meet him.

Enter Samṛddhārthaka.

SAMṚDDHĀRTHAKA:

> Friendly our friends may be when we dine and wine them at parties,
> When they desert us and leave, enemies could not be worse!

I heard that my good friend Siddhārthaka has returned from Malayaketu's camp. And that is why I am looking for him. (*He walks about and looks up.*) There is Siddhārthaka! (*He runs to meet him.*) Friend, how are you!

SIDDHĀRTHAKA (*looking at him*): Samṛddhārthaka! (*He runs to meet him.*) Samṛddhārthaka, my friend, how have you been doing? (*They embrace.*)

SAMṚDDHĀRTHAKA: How do you think I have been doing when you don't come to my house the instant you are back from your long stay abroad?

SIDDHĀRTHAKA: Peace, peace, my friend! No sooner did Cāṇakya see me than he told me to go and report the happy news to his Gracious

Majesty Candragupta! So I went to report, and look how royally I was treated! But then I went immediately to your house to see you, my friend.

SAMṚDDHĀRTHAKA: Tell me the happy news, friend, if you are at liberty to tell. What did you have to report to his Gracious Majesty that he was so pleased?

SIDDHĀRTHAKA: Is there anything I would keep from your ears? Listen. That accursed Malayaketu was so completely fooled by Cāṇakya's manoeuvres that he dismissed Rākṣasa and killed his five principal allies, Citravarman and the other princes. When the remaining chieftains saw that their leader was a blunderer who acted without proper inquiries, they deserted him *en masse*, with all the greater alacrity since their troops and retinue were in a panic because they had to move in completely unfamiliar terrain. They all withdrew to their own countries. Then Bhadrabhaṭa, Puruṣadatta, Hiṅgurāta, Balagupta, Rājasena, Bhāgurāyaṇa, Rohitākṣa, Vijayavarman, and some others arrested Malayaketu, just like that!

SAMṚDDHĀRTHAKA: But, friend, people here were saying that Bhadrabhaṭa and the others had joined Malayaketu because they were disaffected from his Majesty our King! Why did they put such an improbable end to their first acts, like a playwright who does not know his job?

SIDDHĀRTHAKA: Friend, Cāṇakya's policy is like the course of the Ganges in heaven.[33] There is no way of charting it.

SAMṚDDHĀRTHAKA: Then what happened?

SIDDHĀRTHAKA: Then Lord Cāṇakya made a sortie with a numerous and vigorous army and captured the prince and his own forces.

SAMṚDDHĀRTHAKA: Where are they now?

SIDDHĀRTHAKA: Where are they?

> Where the elephants thunder like clouds that are bursting
> And frenziedly roam with a surfeit of rut,
> Where the horses are rearing, and prance to the whiplash,
> And dance to the drone of the victory drums!

SAMṚDDHĀRTHAKA: All right, all right. But quite a while ago Lord Cāṇakya publicly resigned his office. Has he now again taken charge of his post?

SIDDHĀRTHAKA: Aren't you too naïve! You hope to understand Cāṇakya's mind which even a Rākṣasa failed to grasp?

SAMṚDDHĀRTHAKA: Where is Rākṣasa now?

SIDDHĀRTHAKA: According to Cāṇakya's information, he fled from Malayaketu's camp when the troops mutinied. A shadow, a fellow called Undura, followed him to Pāṭaliputra.

SAMṚDDHĀRTHAKA: But when he left the city he promised to restore the Nandas. Has he returned a failure? Why?

SIDDHĀRTHAKA: I think it is on account of his friendship for Candanadāsa.

SAMṚDDHĀRTHAKA: Did you see Candanadāsa released?

SIDDHĀRTHAKA: Released? Poor fellow! His Honor just passed orders that you and I are to go to the execution field and finish him off.

SAMṚDDHĀRTHAKA (*angrily*): What! Has Cāṇakya run out of headsmen that we must do the dirty work?

SIDDHĀRTHAKA: Friend, no one who likes to live resists his Honor's orders. Come on. We'll disguise ourselves as pariahs and take Candanadāsa to the execution field.

(*Exeunt.*)

ACT SIX

Enter a Man with a rope in his hand.

MAN: Glory to my rope which is like Cāṇakya's statecraft, firmly corded with six twines and looped with the four tactics—ever ready to subdue the enemy. Ah, there is the spot where Undura told Cāṇakya Rākṣasa would be found, and that's where Cāṇakya told me to find him. (*He looks about him.*) Hey! There he is coming, the minister himself, with a cloth pulled over his head. I'll hide behind the trees of that dilapidated garden and see where he is going to sit down. (*He circles the stage and remains standing.*)

Enter Rākṣasa as described; he carries a sword.

RĀKṢASA (*weeping*):

Luck, like a whore, has panicked and deserted
Her ruined protector for a better house;
The people, always running after, ran,
Forsook their loyalties, and followed her.
For even trusted followers will shed
The yoke when courage seems to yield no fruit.
Why should they not? No limb will long survive
After the head is severed from its trunk.

A bastard woman, she forsook her man,
A nobleman, king of a world, a god,
To rush and cuddle with his bastard son. . . .
She found her station with him! Should we now,
However steadily, go on to try
What destiny is certain to defeat?

For when my king had died—and no king's death
Was meted out to him—I did go on

And served a king of mountain folk; he died,
Murdered. And after him his son; I failed.
For Destiny more than that Brahmin
Is Nanda's enemy. . . . Oh, the foolishness
Of that barbarian! I, Rākṣasa,
Who listened still to masters long since dead,
Should turn an interloper and join up,
Hearty and hale, with their old enemies?
This the barbarian of simple mind,
Devoid of all sound judgment, never grasped.
No blame to him: the man whom Destiny
Has doomed has no mind left to grasp. . . .

And now Rākṣasa may fall captive to his foes and perish—he shall not make peace with Candragupta! Or wouldn't he? The greater shame is not to be bested by an enemy's wiles, but to break one's faith. . . . (*He looks about him, with tears in his eyes.*) These grounds beyond the city walls, they have been hallowed by my king's wandering footsteps. Here, on this spot, his Majesty once shot at moving targets on horseback, and the horse started galloping when the king let go of the reins to stretch the bow! And in this grove he paused and chatted with the princes. . . . To revisit the city grounds without him makes me sadder still. . . . Where should I go, chased by misfortune? (*He looks around.*) Good. An old garden. Let me go there and ask someone for news about Candanadāsa. (*He walks around.*) Alas, who can foresee what luck or ill luck fate will deal a man? There was a time when the townspeople pointed me out like the waxing moon, when I slowly rode out of the city, surrounded by a thousand kings! And now, in this same city, this same man is at one with the hunted and condemned and has to sneak furtively like a robber into a little old garden. . . . No matter. For he to whom I owed my pomp is gone. (*He enters the garden and looks about him.*) Oh, the ugliness of a ruined garden!

The white pavilion, carefully laid out,
Has like a clan of noble deeds collapsed.
The pond is dry, dry as a good man's heart
Whose friends have one by one been lost to death.
The trees bear no more fruit than policies
That were frustrated by a bitter fate.

And like the mind of a misguided sage
The ground is covered with some futile straws.

And, breathing sighs of pity for the friends
That came to grief, the hooded cobras seem
To bandage with the shreds of cast-off skin
The open wounds which whetted axes cut
In these tired branches that with the long plaint
Of nestling pigeons moan in agony.

And croaking that their heart has dried, the trees,
In desperate ailment of worm-eaten canker,
Their skin, unsoothed by shadow, withering,
Hope in their plight for mercy from the fire.

I shall sit down here for a moment, on this broken stone bench, a seat too easy to come by when luck has changed for the worse. . . . (*He sits down and listens.*) Ah, what is this sudden noise? Is this the sound of jubilation with horns blowing and drums beating?

Crushing the ears, its weight is deafening,
Too big to be drunk up by the great houses,
This shouting, swollen with trumpet and drum,
Runs curious to see how wide the world.

(*Thinking.*) Ah, certainly. I see! The shouting proclaims the pleasure of the king's men—(*he interrupts himself*) a curse!—the *Maurya's* men in Malayaketu's taming. . . . (*With a tear.*) Disaster follows disaster! Not only was I made to hear how well the enemy is faring, I also had to be brought here to be a witness of it. And now, I am sure, chance will try to make me feel it!

MAN: He is sitting down. Now I can do as Lord Cāṇakya told me. (*He pretends not to see Rākṣasa, and in the other's full vision ties his rope around his neck.*)

RĀKṢASA (*looking up*): What is that? He is hanging himself! The wretch must be as miserable as I am. Let me ask him. (*He approaches the other.*) My good fellow, what are you doing?
MAN (*weeping*): The only thing a man like me can do when he is mourning the death of his friend.
RĀKṢASA (*to himself*): I was right, the wretch is as miserable as I am!

Let me ask him. (*Aloud.*) You fellow student of misery, if it is not a secret, or too painful, I wish to hear why you want to kill yourself.

MAN: It is no secret, nor even too painful to tell. But I have no time to waste before dying, I am in such agonies about my friend!

RĀKṢASA (*sighing, to himself*): Ah! This man accuses me that I stand unmoved by a friend's plight like any stranger! (*Aloud.*) My good man, if it is no secret and not too painful to tell me, I do wish to hear it.

MAN: Why don't you leave me in peace! What can I do? I'll tell you. There is man in the city called Jiṣṇudāsa, the provost of the jewelers' guild.

RĀKṢASA (*to himself*): Yes, there is a Jiṣṇudāsa. He is a good friend of Candanadāsa's.

MAN: He is my best friend.

RĀKṢASA (*with joy, to himself*): His best friend, he says! So he is very near to Candanadāsa and should have news of him.

MAN (*with a tear*): Today he has given his whole fortune away to the Brahmins and left the city to die in the fire. And I came to this old garden to kill myself before I should have to hear the terrible tidings of his death.

RĀKṢASA: But why should your friend want to die in the fire, my man? Has he been stricken by a deadly disease no drug can cure?

MAN: Oh no, my lord.

RĀKṢASA: Is he doomed by the anger of the king of the land, which is as deadly as fire or poison?

MAN: Surely not, my lord. Candragupta is not cruel to his people.

RĀKṢASA: Or does he love a beautiful woman he may not have?

MAN (*stopping his ears*): My lord! Heaven forbid! That would fit no provost, and certainly not Jiṣṇudāsa!

RĀKṢASA: Then must a friend of his die helplessly, as yours is doing now?

MAN: Indeed, my lord.

RĀKṢASA (*disturbed, to himself*): Candanadāsa is a good friend of his, and he is ready to die in the fire because a good friend of *his* has died. . . . In truth, I am disturbed by a heart so devoted to a friend. (*Aloud.*) My man, this noble deed of your friend is most edifying for the depth of friendship it reveals; I should like to hear more about it.

MAN: Sir, I cannot permit any more delay in my dying!

RĀKṢASA: Do tell your tale, my good man, which is so worth hearing.

MAN: What can I do? I'll tell you. Listen, my lord.

RĀKṢASA: I am all attention, my man.

MAN: On the Flower Square here in the city lives a provost of the jewelers' guild, Candanadāsa.

RĀKṢASA (*dismayed, to himself*): Here destiny opens the door to my consecration for death! Heart, be calm! Worse things you must hear. (*Aloud.*) They say that he is a good man and a stanch friend. What of him?

MAN: He is Jiṣṇudāsa's best friend.

RĀKṢASA (*to himself*): The lightning of grief that will strike my heart is close now.

MAN: So today Jiṣṇudāsa presented a petition to Candragupta, dictated by his friendship.

RĀKṢASA: What did it say?

MAN: "Your Majesty, my wealth suffices to feed my family. Take it as ransom for Candanadāsa and set him free!"

RĀKṢASA (*to himself*): Bravo, Jiṣṇudāsa, bravo! You have shown what real friendship is.

For fathers kill their sons like strangers, sons their fathers,
And friends are ready to sell out the friendship of their friends,
For just the price you set upon a friend in need:
Tradesmen know price, you know what value is!

(*Aloud.*) And what did the Maurya reply to your friend's request?

MAN: Sir, Candragupta gave him the following answer: "Provost Jiṣṇudāsa, the provost has not been imprisoned by us for ransom, but because he has refused to surrender the family of Minister Rākṣasa in spite of our repeated demands. He shall be set free as soon as he delivers Minister Rākṣasa's family into our hands. If he refuses, only his death shall placate our displeasure." No sooner had he replied than he ordered Candanadāsa to be executed. And Provost Jiṣṇudāsa departed from the city, saying that he would enter the fire before the terrible tidings of his friends death could reach him. And I have come to this old garden before I could hear the terrible tidings of my friend's death.

RĀKṢASA: Then Candanadāsa has not been executed yet?

MAN: No, not yet, my lord. They are still interrogating him, asking him again and again to give up Rākṣasa's family. He won't, he loves his friend too much. This has delayed his execution.

RĀKṢASA (*joyfully, to himself*): Bravo, my friend! Bravo, Candanadāsa! The fame that Śibi won because he protected his supplicant, you have now won because of me, your friend! (*Aloud.*) Go, my man. Stop Jiṣṇudāsa immediately from entering the fire. I shall save Candanadāsa from death.

MAN: But how will you save Candanadāsa's life?

RĀKṢASA (*drawing his sword*): With this sword, faithful companion in my hour of need.

This sword as blue as the blue autumn sky,
Friend to my fist erect in love of war,
Whose character my foes saw proved in battle,
Drives me, like friendship, helplessly to fight.

MAN: My lord, the news that Provost Candanadāsa's life was in danger threw me into such a confusion that even now I cannot say for sure whether you are really the worshipful minister Rākṣasa, whose name be honored. Pray favor me, my lord, and settle my doubts!

RĀKṢASA: Yes, my man, I am he who is rightly called a Rākṣasa, I who saw my master's house destroyed and became the cause of my friend's destruction, dishonored and of dishonorable name!

MAN (*with joy, throwing himself at his feet*): Oh, miracle, thank God I have succeeded!

RĀKṢASA: Stand up, good man, stand up. There is no more time to waste now. Tell Jiṣṇudāsa that Rākṣasa will free Candanadāsa from death. (*Draws his sword and repeats the verse*: "This sword . . . to fight." *He sets off.*)

MAN (*throwing himself at his feet*): Pray pardon me, your worshipful Excellency! At the time the accursed Candragupta ordered Master Śakaṭadāsa to be executed too. But somebody managed to abduct him from the execution field and carry him beyond the borders. Candragupta—a curse on his name!—inquired who was to blame for negligence, and extinguished the fire of his fury, which had been lighted by Master Śakaṭadāsa's escape from death, with the blood of the headsmen. Since then the executioners, whenever they see somebody they don't know with a sword in his hand, there and then kill off the criminal they are conducting, before they have even reached the execution field, to make sure of saving their own lives. Therefore if your Excellency goes about with your sword drawn, you will only hasten Provost Candanadāsa's execution! (*Exit.*)

RĀKṢASA (*to himself*): The ways of Cāṇakya's policy are inscrutable. If it was one of his own henchmen who brought Śakaṭadāsa to me, then

why did he in a rage kill off his would-be executioners? And if it was not one of his men, then how could he produce that counterfeit letter? Between these alternatives I see no solution. (*He reflects.*) This is not the time for a sword, if the executioners have already been put to death for failure. Every policy takes time to show results, and there is no time to try one now. But when my friend has to face a ghastly death because of me, it would be a crime to remain inactive. . . . I know now. I shall offer my own life in return for his.
(*Exit.*)

ACT SEVEN

Enter the First Headsman.

HEADSMAN: Out of the way, sirs, out of the way. Make room, folks, make room!

> Men, do you want to keep your health and wealth?
> Your wife and family?
> Then shun the poison! Better stay away
> From all that displeases the king!
>
> A man who eats what does not agree with him
> Will ail and die alone,
> If he does what does not agree with his king,
> His family dies with him!

Don't you believe me? Look for yourself. There is Provost Candanadāsa coming. He did something that did not agree with the king, and now he is being brought to the execution field, and his wife and son with him. (*He listens to imaginary persons.*) What do you say, sirs? Is there any way for him to be freed? Why should the wretch have his freedom? He might at that, if he gave up Minister Rākṣasa's family. (*Again listening.*) What are you saying now? He would never commit such a crime just to save his own life, he loves his friends too much? Well, sirs, if that's how it is, you can be sure that he will die a martyr's death! Nothing you can do for him now!

Enter Candanadāsa, in the red shroud and wreath of the condemned, carrying on his shoulder the pole on which he is to be impaled. A second headsman accompanies him, and he is followed by his wife and son.

CANDANADĀSA: Woe! Woe! Because I always was fearful lest I violate any law, I must now die a robber's death! I bow to fate! The cruel never distinguish between the innocent and the others. Else why should hunters insist on murdering the innocent deer, which shuns meat and eats grass so as to save the other creatures from the fear of death? (*He looks around him.*) Oh my good friend Jiṣṇudāsa! Why don't you answer me? But then, scarce are the men who dare to stay in sight at a time like this. (*With a tear.*) Our best friends help us only with a tearful face. Their bodies are already running home, only their woebegone faces are still turned to us and they follow us with their lachrymose eyes. . . .

HEADSMEN (*having walked around*): Master Candanadāsa, you have gotten to the execution field. Tell your family to go.

CANDANADĀSA: My lady, mistress of my house, turn back now with our son. It is not right to follow me any further.

WIFE (*weeping*): My lord, you are leaving for another *world,* not for another country! It would not be right for a well-bred wife not to follow you!

CANDANADĀSA: Oh, no! What have you decided to do?

WIFE: To bless myself by following my master's course.

CANDANADĀSA: You are wrong, woman. It is our son who needs your blessing. He does not yet know the ways of the world.

WIFE: Our family gods will graciously bless him! Son, for the last time, bow at your father's feet.

SON (*throwing himself at Candanadāsa's feet*): Father, what must I do when you have left me?

CANDANADĀSA: Live in a country, my son, which is safe from Cāṇakya.

HEADSMAN: Master Candanadāsa, the pole is set up. Prepare yourself.

WIFE: Save us, people, save us.

CANDANADĀSA: Are you so fond of life that you must cry out? The only one who would have pity on a man in need, our king Nanda, has gone to heaven.

FIRST HEADSMAN: Come on, Billavatta, get Candanadāsa.

SECOND HEADSMAN: All right Vajjaloma, here I go.

CANDANADĀSA: Please, my good fellow, wait till I have kissed my son good-bye. (*He kisses his son on the head.*) Death is inescapable, my son, and therefore, when you must die, die for a friend!

SON: Why need you tell me, father? That is our family law! (*He falls at his father's feet.*)

HEADSMAN: Get him now. His people will leave by themselves.

WIFE: Save him, people, save him!

Enter Rākṣasa brusquely through the back curtain.
RĀKṢASA: There is nothing to fear, nothing to fear! Hullo, commander! This good man does not have to die!

On me, who contemplated the destruction
Of my king's family as of a foe's,
On me who undisturbed participated
In my friend's ruin as in a festival,
On me who loved a self that had become
The stage of ignominious deceptions,
On me should hang the wreath of the condemned
And it shall lead me down the road of death!

CANDANADĀSA (*looking at him through his tears*): Minister, what is this?
RĀKṢASA: But the imitation of a part of your noble example!
CANDANADĀSA: Minister, you do not act like a friend if you make all my efforts fruitless!
RĀKṢASA: Candanadāsa, my friend, all living beings serve their own interests. Don't blame me. (*To the headsman.*) Man, go and tell your evil master Cāṇakya. . . .
HEADSMAN: What?
RĀKṢASA: Candanadāsa,—

In this vile age, joy of the evil,
He saved a man with his own life
And won such fame as has reduced
King Śibi's name to nothingness,
So pure his soul that his great deeds
Even outshine the Buddha's works:
And he for whom this man of honor
Did turn your enemy am *I*.

FIRST HEADSMAN: Hey, Billavatta, hold on to Provost Candanadāsa and wait a while with him in the shade of that tree over there on the burning grounds, while I tell Lord Cāṇakya that Minister Rākṣasa has been captured.
SECOND HEADSMAN: All right, Vajjaloma.
Exit First Headsman with Candanadāsa and his Wife and Son.
SECOND HEADSMAN (*walking about with Rākṣasa*): Hey, who is standing guard at the gates? Report to Lord Cāṇakya, thunderbolt that shattered

the rock piles of the Nanda's House, founder of the House of the Maurya, treasury of civic virtue. . . .

RĀKṢASA (*to himself*): And even this I, Rākṣasa, must hear!

FIRST HEADSMAN: Minister Rākṣasa has been captured and the self-will of his genius has been tamed by his Honor's cunning!

Enter Cāṇakya; only his face is visible, the rest of his person being hidden by the rear curtain.

CĀṆAKYA: Tell me, my man, tell me,

> Who tucked the Golden Fire of Lofty Flamecrest
> In the hem of his garment?
> Who caught the Running Wind of Restless Motion
> In the maze of his net?
> Who locked the Lion of Elephant-Reeking Mane
> In the jail of his cage?
> Who held the dread Ocean of Dragons and Sharks
> In the grasp of his arms?

HEADSMAN: Who but your Honor whose genius is expert in policy?

CĀṆAKYA: No my man, no. I say it was Fate which hated the Nandas. (*He sees Rākṣasa.*) Ah, there is Minister Rākṣasa, the noble hero,

> Who long has driven Maurya's army and my wits
> To troublous measures, fruit of many sleepless nights.

(*Pushing away the curtain, he approaches.*) Minister Rākṣasa, Viṣṇugupta greets you!

RĀKṢASA (*looking up, to himself*): The title of Minister puts me to shame. (*He glances at Cāṇakya.*) Yes, there is the evil genius, or must I now say *holy* genius? Kauṭilya!

> Mine of all science, as of pearls the sea,
> Whose talents we ignore because we grudge them . . .

(*Aloud.*) Viṣṇugupta! Pray do not touch me, for I have been defiled by pariahs.

CĀṆAKYA: He is not a pariah, Minister Rākṣasa. He is the king's servant, Siddhārthaka, whom you have seen before. He was the one who at my orders had the poor Śakaṭadāsa innocently copy that counterfeit letter after he had struck up a friendship with the scribe. The other headsman is also a king's man, Samṛddhārthaka.

RĀKṢASA (*to himself*): Thank God my suspicions of Śakaṭadāsa are removed!

CĀṆAKYA: Why waste many words? In a word, Bhadrabhaṭa and the others, the counterfeit letter, Siddhārthaka, the three ornaments, the Jain monk who was your false friend, the miserable fellow you encountered in the garden, and the plight of the provost were all in my very own (*he interrupts himself and gestures modestly*) design to make *you*, incorruptible friend, meet with the Maurya. There is the Maurya coming to meet you. Look at him!

RĀKṢASA (*to himself*): What can I do? I must look at him.

Enter the King and his retinue in state.

KING (*to himself*): Indeed, I am ashamed that the well-nigh invincible army of the enemy has been vanquished by my minister without bloodshed. My aimless arrows, mortified that victory could be won without their aid, have bent their heads and lie in their quiver as though they had entered upon a hermit's vow. Yet, even without cording the bow a king may be able to vanquish all that is vincible on earth while sleeping as I did, if his guide, wakeful in all matters, watches over his affairs. (*He approaches Cāṇakya.*) My lord, Candragupta bows to you!

CĀṆAKYA: Maurya, all the things you have wished for are now achieved. Salute his Excellency Minister Rākṣasa, who stands before you. He is the chief minister bequeathed to you by your father.

RĀKṢASA (*to himself*): So an old connection is confirmed by him.

KING (*approaching Rākṣasa*): My lord, Candragupta greets you.

RĀKṢASA (*studying the king, to himself*): This is Candragupta.

> People predicted of the child his future rise,
> And like the elephant he rose, to sway his herd.

(*Aloud.*) Majesty, victory be thine.

KING: My lord, what victory could *not* be mine in the world, one wonders, if your lordship were my guide and watched over my affairs and government?

RĀKṢASA (*to himself*): True pupil of Kauṭilya, he refers to me as though he were my keeper! But no. Candragupta is merely courteous, and only my jealous mind turns the compliment to insult. Indeed, Cāṇakya well deserves his fame. Even a fool will be able to maintain himself in a position of fame, if he has chosen as his master a man of substance who yearns for victory. But a minister, however discerning his policies, must fall when his support collapses, if he has chosen a man without substance—fall as the tree falls that grows on a river bank.

CĀṆAKYA: Minister Rākṣasa, do you wish Candanadāsa to live?

RĀKṢASA: Can there be doubt, Viṣṇugupta?

CĀṆAKYA: Doubt there can be, since the Maurya will not be graciously disposed as long as you do not accept his sword of state! If you truly wish Candanadāsa to live, then accept this sword.

RĀKṢASA: Don't offer it to me, Viṣṇugupta! We are unfit to carry a sword that was so illustriously wielded by yourself!

CĀṆAKYA: Fit or unfit, what does it matter? Look!

> Beside our horses, so long kept in harness
> And saddled that their bodies have grown thin,
> Our elephants are waiting with their backs
> Still sorely swollen from the loads they bore—
> They had to go deprived of food and bath
> And play and rest and drink—they were athirst—
> Solely because of your magnificence
> In humbling, man of genius, our pride!

But what does it matter? Unless you accept the sword, Candanadāsa shall not live.

RĀKṢASA: I bow, Viṣṇugupta, to the demands of friendship which forces me to accept any task. . . . What can I do? I stand prepared.

CĀṆAKYA (*handing Rākṣasa the sword with joy*): Maurya! Minister Rākṣasa has favored you by accepting the responsibility. May you increase in blessings!

KING: Candragupta is aware of his lordship's favor.

Enter a Servant.

SERVANT: Victory, your Honor! Your Honor, Bhadrabhaṭa, Bhāgurāyaṇa, and others have just brought Malayaketu to the gates with his feet in chains. Your Honor may dispose of him.

CĀṆAKYA: Report to Minister Rākṣasa. *He* now minds things.

RĀKṢASA (*to himself*): Ah! First he brings me under his control, and now he compels me to pronounce judgment, Kauṭilya! What can I do? (*Aloud.*) Your Majesty, you know that for some time we have lived with Malayaketu. Therefore now spare his life.

King looks at Cāṇakya.

CĀṆAKYA: Maurya, this is the first token of your favor that Minister Rākṣasa asks of you, and you must grant it. (*He glances at the Servant.*)

My man, tell Bhadrabhaṭa and the others in my name that at Minister Rākṣasa's request, his Majesty Candragupta returns to Malayaketu his paternal territories; they should remain at his side and not return until Malayaketu is restored.

SERVANT: As your Honor commands. (*Exit.*)

CĀṆAKYA: Wait! Further tell Vijayapāla, the captain of the citadel, that his Majesty Candragupta, out of affection for Minister Rākṣasa, orders the captain to raise Candanadāsa to the rank of provost in all the cities of the empire. Also, let all be set free, save the horses and the elephants. But no! Now that Minister Rākṣasa is chancellor, what use are our horses and elephants? Let all that are kept in fetters be given their freedom, even the draught oxen! But one thing will now be tied, my hairlock, for I have fulfilled my vow! (*He ties up his hairlock.*)

SERVANT: As your Honor commands. (*Exit.*)

KING:

> Rākṣasa is our friend, and we are king,
> And all the Nandas are exterminated:
> What then is left that you could do to please me?

RĀKṢASA (*to himself*):

> Now I must cut the trees that I have reared,
> And, ruthless, use the sword on my old friends.
> The drops of the old love I bore the Nandas
> Still touch my heart, but now I serve their foes:
> The course of man's affairs escapes man's mind,
> And is a mystery to destiny.

CĀṆAKYA: But still this wish may be fulfilled:

> The Self-begotten God did once assume
> The fitting body of a mighty Boar[30]
> And on his snout did save the troubled Earth,
> Nurse of all beings, when she was deluged:
> Now, terrified by the barbarian hordes,
> She has sought shelter in our king's strong arms:
> May Candragupta, our most gracious King,
> Whose people prosper and whose kinsmen thrive,
> For long continue to protect the land!

(*Exeunt omnes.*)

THE END

NOTES

INTRODUCTION

1. This Introduction is in part based on a chapter I contributed to *An Introduction to Indian Literature* which is being sponsored by the Asian Literature Program of the Asia Society.
2. The mythical author of the *Mahābhārata*.
3. So, for instance, Bharata, in the *Nāṭyaśāstra*.
4. They are generally portrayed in a more realistic fashion.
5. Āryan is a technical term for the Indo-Iranian language family; Indo-Āryan thus is the Indic branch of that group.
6. Harvard Oriental Series (Cambridge, Mass., 1965).
7. *The Daśarūpa of Dhanaṃjaya*, a treatise on Hindu dramaturgy, translated by George C. O. Haas (Columbia University Press, New York, 1912); I have adopted some of Haas's terminology.
8. *The Nāṭyaśāstra of Bharata Muni*, a treatise on Hindu dramaturgy and histrionics, translated by Manomohan Ghosh, Bibliotheca Indica series (Calcutta, 1950).

THE LITTLE CLAY CART

1. Śiva the Dancer is patron of the stage. Here he is pictured in the yogic "palanquin position," intertwining the snakes that garland him.
2. Once more Śiva, whose throat was darkened by the poison which he drank to save the world; Gaurī is one of his consort's names.
3. The cakora bird is supposed to feed on moon beams.
4. Actors were notoriously low-class.
5. Not in a business venture, but because of his liberality.
6. To ward off evil. "The Mothers" is a collective name for quasi goddesses—counterparts of the "Fathers," or deceased ancestors—who are patronesses of evils, such as cholera or pox. In South India

these crossroad offerings are still made, to equally anonymous deities.

7. Saṃsthānaka or Śakāra is portrayed as a cowardly but cunning upstart vulgarian whose language is coarse and synonymous, and whose ignorance of mythology is appalling. I have not identified the many mythological errors because they are too erudite in reverse; they are in a class with "O Helen who from Paris fled / And Herakles found thee in Ares' bed."
8. The Libertine is forever precious and studied in his language.
9. Thunder was supposed to impregnate cranes.
10. The meanings of the servants' names.
11. Euphemism for the brothel quarter.
12. This incident is never explained; it may derive from an earlier episode in the Cārudatta cycle.
13. The implication is that she could not love anyone of a lower station.
14. Marco Polo recounts a similar incident of a debtor trapped in a drawn circle from South India, in Book 3, chapter 20.
15. This is my interpretation of the difficult passage; it is the old bag trick: "Will you put up half if another party does the same?" It is essential that neither party knows what deal has been made with the other; this is not clearly indicated in the text, but the interpretation seems obvious.
16. Dardura speaks polished Sanskrit and seems to have been one of the educated hangers-on of Cārudatta when he was rich.
17. A favorite exercise in mortification is to stand on one foot all day long; here it is the arrested motion of a debtor in flight.
18. One of the great events in the Buddha's career, often pictured in sculpture, was his taming a mad elephant in a city street with one glance from his steadfast eye. Here the friar-to-be resolves to equal the feat.
19. The "braggart."
20. A mountain range in central India.
21. The man is of course illiterate.
22. For a Brahmin cleanliness *is* godliness.
23. An infamous episode in the Sauptika book of the *Mahābhārata.*
24. From urine.
25. The god Kārttikeya is the patron of thieves.
26. A dummy head which thieves would insert through the hole to

catch the blows in case the householder was waiting with a stick.

27. Magic or illusion.
28. The thief is a gentleman and ought not to look at a married woman's face.
29. The prostitutes of the household were apparently indentured to the family head, which in this matriarchic establishment was the mother of Vasantasenā.
30. Śiva wears the crescent moon on his head.
31. She enacts the despair of the bride who is taken by her groom from her family and village.
32. Gopāla was Pālaka's elder brother, and Āryaka is next in succession.
33. This is the subject of Bhāsa's play *Yaugandharāyaṇa and the Promise*.
34. As far as one can gather, the "bastards" were the illegitimate sons of the prostitutes, kept perhaps as male prostitutes.
35. The god Indra's elephant.
36. In character, Maitreya, as servitor of a *grand seigneur*, tries not to be impressed.
37. White rice was so uncommon that the birds did not even recognize it.
38. Indra's paradise.
39. Possibly a reference to the icon of the famous Mahākāla temple of Ujjayinī, which was shaped like a gigantic phallus.
40. To best the poor Prakrit-speaking Brahmin?
41. At the beginning of the rainy season peacocks dance about excitedly, while swans set out for Lake Mānasa in the Himālayas.
42. In his Dwarf Incarnation Viṣṇu covered heaven with one foot.
43. A bird that always flies up with its mate.
44. Heroes from the *Mahābhārata*. Dhṛtarāṣṭra was the king of the losing side, Duryodhana his arrogant general. Yudhiṣṭhira, king of the winning party, lost a game at dice, and the sons of Pāṇḍu, although victorious, died, one by one.
45. Technical term for a woman on her way to a love tryst.
46. Smiles and laughter are described as white in poetry.
47. The god of rain, who once seduced Gautama's wife Ahalyā.
48. The word for cloud is masculine, that for lightning, feminine, in Sanskrit.
49. Vasantasenā's personal maid probably.
50. The moon is masculine, the moonlight, feminine, in Sanskrit.

51. A region in South India.
52. The barber is low-caste.
53. The mother of one family in the *Mahābhārata.*
54. A celestial musician.
55. This must be the body of the woman that the Libertine earlier saw felled by a tree.
56. An ancient lawgiver; Brahmins were not subject to the punishment of death.
57. An Indian version of the maypole, erected and emblazoned to secure the prompt breaking of the monsoon.
58. Śiva, whose banner shows his bull Nandī, was not invited to a sacrifice offered by Dakṣa, whom he thereupon destroyed. His son Kārttikeya is credited with breaching Krauñca pass in the Himālayas. Mount Kailāsa is Śiva's abode in the Himālayas.

THE MINISTER'S SEAL

1. Śiva is conventionally represented as sitting with his consort Pārvatī, Daughter of the Mountain, on the Kailāsa plateau in the Himālaya. On his head is pictured the Ganges, in the form of a goddess, because of the legend that the Ganges, which originally flowed only in heaven, was brought down to the earth by a sage. In order to break her fall, which would have shattered earth, Śiva consented to catch Gaṅgā in his hair. A second woman lives on his head, the crescent moon. It is a convention of kāvya poets to picture Pārvatī's jealousy of either goddess. Vijayā is Pārvatī's handmaiden. The point of the poem is to introduce the play in an appropriately ambiguous dialogue form.
2. Inspired by the myth of the dancing Śiva. The verse is introduced for similar reasons of propriety: Śiva's dance, too, was a theatrical performance. Śiva has a third eye in his forehead with which he burns evildoers to ashes.
3. Nāṭaka, highest genre of theatre. Its subject matter must be legendary, its heroes kings or Brahmins. See Introduction.
4. Traditionally, eclipses are supposed to be caused by cometlike celestial bodies which "devour" the sun or moon. There is a play on Ketu (comet) and Malayaketu, and moon/Candragupta.
5. Kauṭilya is a family name, but it may also be translated as "cunning."
6. He untied it when he vowed to exterminate the Nandas.

7. Cāṇakya is consistently characterized as a typical Brahmin; the student is a *brahmacārin* who lives with his teacher and is frequently used as a whipping boy.
8. *Mleccha*, usually applied to non-hinduized aliens.
9. The lotus, symbol of beauty, is identified with the Goddess of Beauty who is also the patroness of Wealth and Chance.
10. The poison-girl has become a stock figure of folklore, but there is no reason to deny her reality; she was made immune to certain poisons and so could slip the king a poison after she had tasted his dish or drink. It is also said that her touch poisoned, so that one may think of her as a carrier of specific diseases.
11. Both spell bad luck.
12. An institution started, it seems, by the Indo-Greek kings. The reason was that a woman *had* to be more faithful since she herself could not benefit from disloyalty.
13. A northern Indian region, home of the barbarians mentioned before.
14. Jewelers and goldsmiths were frequently moneylenders.
15. A king, prototype of generosity. He saved the God of Fire, who had assumed the form of a pigeon, from his pursuer, Indra, who had taken the form of a vulture, by offering Indra an equal weight of flesh from his own body.
16. Otherwise, the magistrates just named would have to indict him. Cāṇakya does not want Candanadāsa indicted.
17. In the *Mahābhārata* battle the tribe of the Vṛṣṇis, whose chieftain was Kṛṣṇa, chose the side of the Kauravas. Kṛṣṇa himself, because of personal ties to Arjuna, chief warrior of the other party, the Pāṇḍavas, acted as nonbelligerent charioteer to Arjuna; his advice decided the war in the Pāṇḍavas' favor. Later the Vṛṣṇis wiped each other out at a drinking bout.
18. Sugāṅga is the resident palace of Pāṭaliputra.
19. The sudden twitching of the left eye spells trouble.
20. Rākṣasa here commits a mistake; not instantly remembering the identity of the spy, he mentions his name; he covers up by remarking on his beard.
21. The cosmic Serpent on whom all the world rests.
22. Kaumudī is the name of the Full Moon Festival of the month Kārttika after the rainy season.
23. The river Ganges personified as a goddess. See note 1.

24. Cāṇakya sitting higher.

25. A white flower very much in evidence in autumn. Śiva (below) is white with rubbed-on ashes, on his dark hair shines the crescent moon (see note 1), and he carries a skull.

26. Viṣṇu sleeps on his serpent Śeṣa/Ananta in the periods between creation.

27. A play on Rākṣasa's name.

28. Śiva once used earth as his stage to dance the Dance of Destruction, in the Mood of Terror, one of the moods recognized by the theatre of which he is the patron.

29. Malayaketu sitting higher.

30. One sect of Jain mendicants went naked.

31. A complicated pun: Mercury = Budha (a planet) = the Wise One = Cāṇakya. The moon = Candragupta. Ketu (a comet) = Malayaketu.

32. One shaves before an extended journey.

33. See above, note 1.

34. One of Viṣṇu's incarnations was the Boar; when the earth was deluged, the boar dug it up and carried it to safety on its snout; the incarnation was worshiped by the Guptas.